AFRICA

In this edition the Report of the Committee on Africa, the War, and Peace Aims on THE ATLANTIC CHARTER AND AFRICA FROM AN AMERICAN STANDPOINT is followed by the Supplement entitled EVENTS IN AFRICAN HISTORY.

This represents a Second Printing of both publications, with a few minor additions and corrections.

MANUFACTURED IN THE UNITED STATES OF AMERICA
BY THE HADDON CRAFTSMEN, INC., CAMDEN, N. J.

THE
ATLANTIC CHARTER AND AFRICA
FROM AN AMERICAN STANDPOINT

A Study by

THE COMMITTEE ON AFRICA, THE WAR, AND PEACE AIMS

*The application of the "Eight Points" of the Charter
to the Problems of Africa, and especially those related to the Welfare of the African People living
South of the Sahara, with related material on African
Conditions and Needs*

NEW YORK CITY

1942

"The effective genetic improvement of mankind is dependent upon major changes in social conditions, and correlative changes in human attitudes," and "there can be no valid basis for estimating and comparing the intrinsic worth of different individuals without economic and social conditions which provide approximately equal opportunities for all members of society instead of stratifying them from birth into classes with widely different privileges." The manifesto calls for the "removal of race prejudices and the unscientific doctrine that bad or good genes are the monopoly of particular peoples or of persons with features of a given kind."—The "Geneticists Manifesto" adopted by the Genetics Congress in Edinburgh in 1939.

"The modern confusion of culture and race has grown out of the belief that culture is a product of biological heredity and that Anglo-European culture is superior because it has sprung from superior human strains. We believe that all racial groups have contributed outstanding cultural gifts to civilization and that the exchange of such gifts has enriched all mankind. A just and durable peace should provide and insist upon a framework that allows more opportunity for creative expression of all groups and for greater exchange of such cultural creations in the field of music, art, medicine and literature. Assimilation of culture does not mean amalgamation of racial stocks."—Delaware Conference of Commission on a Just and Durable Peace called by the Federal Council of Churches of Christ in America, 1942.

"The Government desires a better life for the people, and when we say 'the people' we mean the whole people, not just the European section but all sections of the people. It is of course much easier to put forward attractive plans for the post-war world if you think only in terms of the Europeans . . . but there can be no social justice in South Africa when the aim is merely to hold a just balance between Europeans."—The Honorable J. H. Hofmeyr, Minister of Finance and Minister of Education of the Union of South Africa, at a meeting in Pretoria, September 1941.

Table of Contents

Prefatory Note

The Committee on Africa, the War, and Peace Aims had its origin in correspondence in August, 1941, between officers of the Phelps-Stokes Fund—probably the only American foundation which refers to work in Africa in its Act of Incorporation, and one which has shown its active interest in African problems for over a quarter of a century. This correspondence had to do with a possible conference of representative white and Negro citizens especially interested in Africa and interracial relations, to discuss what might be done by an American group to help develop an intelligent public opinion in this country regarding present conditions in this vast continent so little understood in this country, and how they might be improved. A few friends with long experience in Africa or in dealing with African problems were consulted. As a result, it was decided to call together about a dozen persons especially qualified to consider Africa's present and future, to discuss what, if anything, Americans might wisely do to help carry out the proposal. If this small group thought it worth while a larger committee would be organized—independent of the Phelps-Stokes Fund—and a suitable memorandum or report prepared.

The conference approved the plan, being unanimous that America had a contribution which it might make toward the solution of African questions. It was felt that as the United States had no territorial interests in Africa—aside from its historic concern for the integrity of Liberia and its welfare—and no political axes to grind there, it might perhaps approach its problems with some degree of detachment. It also felt a natural concern about Africa at present because of war conditions involving the United Nations. This is because of the serious threat of Axis activity in the French territory of Senegal (especially Dakar) and other parts of West Africa, and because the trans-Atlantic air service is making large use of various places both in British and French territory in connection with the vitally important transport of planes, men, and war materials to the various battle fronts in Africa and the Far East. Yet it is true that the United States has nothing which can be called a direct territorial interest in Africa. Its financial and commercial interests are doubtless considerable and have been increasing in recent years, but, in general, relationships between the United States and Africa are such that it can approach its problems with more detachment, if with less first-hand knowledge and experience, than can European powers directly concerned with its government.

vii

The larger committee met September 8, 1941. Those present, almost all of whose names are signed to this Report, represented four groups:

(1) Missionaries and others who have spent considerable time in Africa.

(2) Educators, sociologists, anthropologists, and other students who have visited Africa for the express purpose of studying political, social, economic, or interracial conditions.

(3) Other persons who have long made a special study of Africa and its needs.

(4) Officers of committees and foundations giving special attention to international problems.

At this meeting a plan was presented for a "Report on Africa and Peace Aims," embodying in outline the main features developed in this Report.

The most important decisions reached at the first meeting, and all reached unanimously, were the following:

(1) That it is desirable to form an independent Committee to formulate Peace Aims for Africa in the hope of influencing public opinion along wise lines.

(2) That its major objectives should be the focussing of public attention on the wise, just, and adequate treatment of Africa and Africans by the Peace Conference and the Colonial Powers.

(3) That the Committee's statement should deal with fundamental principles and their major applications, and that it should deal with all the major economic and social problems of Africa—especially those in relation to the native population in the area south of the Sahara, as these differ greatly from those of the Mediterranean Littoral.

(4) That those who called the meeting were right in including only American citizens, with the understanding that non-Americans, including representative native Africans, might be consulted.

(5) That the application of the Roosevelt-Churchill "Eight Points" to African welfare be considered the heart of the Report, and that each of these should be dealt with.

The scope suggested under clauses (1) and (2) was later somewhat broadened as the Committee felt increasingly, as it proceeded with preparing the Report, that its findings as to existing conditions might be of some service in connection with the war, and that some of its recommendations could wisely be put into effect prior to its close. With these considerations in mind the name of the Committee was changed to "Committee on Africa, the War, and Peace Aims."

An Organizing Committee was provided for to serve as an Execu-

tive Committee, with power to add to its number. Its members'
names are marked with an asterisk in the list of the General Committee printed before the Index.

The Chairman was also authorized to name an Editorial Committee. He named Professor Ralph Bunche, Professor Charles S.
Johnson, Dr. Thomas Jesse Jones, Dr. Emory Ross and Dr. Channing H. Tobias, to serve with him on the Committee. This Editorial
Committee had two full-day sessions on December 29, 1941, and
January 15, 1942. The Committee submitted its preliminary draft
to the Executive Committee at meetings on February 7 and 21. At
the latter meeting the following persons were present by invitation
to present their points of view as representative Africans in this
country: Mr. Walter F. Walker, Liberian Consul General in New
York; Mr. Ako Adjei, of the Gold Coast, a student at Hampton
Institute; Mr. Ross Lohr, of Sierra Leone, M.A., of Columbia
University, now doing advanced work at Teachers College; Mr.
Francis Nkrumah, of the Gold Coast, first graduate of Achimota
College, now studying at Lincoln University and the University
of Pennsylvania; Mr. Ibanga Udo Akpabio, of Southern Nigeria,
studying at Columbia University, treasurer of the African Students'
Association. They were all invited to prepare memoranda prior
to the meeting. The "Eight Points" in the preliminary draft, which
were read in full, were the main matters of discussion. The conference was in every way a constructive and helpful one. Other
African students living at a distance from New York and representing other parts of Africa were also invited to submit memoranda, some of which have proved most helpful.

By action of the Executive Committee, copies of the preliminary
draft of the Report, as revised at the meeting on February 21, were
then sent to the following authorities on Africa for their criticisms
as Consultants: Dr. Edwin W. Smith, former President of the Royal
Anthropological Institute of Great Britain, author of *The Ila-speaking Peoples of Northern Rhodesia, The Golden Stool, Aggrey of
Africa*, etc.; Dr. W. B. Mumford, head of the Colonial Department
of the London Institute of Education, and formerly Superintendent of Education in Tanganyika, author of *Africans Learn to Be
French*; and Mr. Julian S. Huxley, author of *Africa View* and one
of the authors of the *Report on Tropical Countries and Colonies*
by "Political and Economic Planning"—the British Board that is
devoting itself to problems of post-war reconstruction. Their comments and other suggestions were considered at a meeting of the
Executive Committee on March 28. The revised draft was then
again submitted for comment to these gentlemen—except for Mr.
Huxley, who had returned to England—and also to the late Professor

Malinowski of Yale University, the eminent authority on African anthropology. On April 25 the Executive Committee, all of whose members had been supplied a week in advance with mimeographed copies of the proposed Report, held an all-day meeting to which members of the General Committee were invited. At the conclusion of the session—at which all the letters from the Consultants and other advisers were read—the Report was approved in principle and ordered printed in galley form for submission to the General Committee. This met on May 23 and after due consideration and some minor modifications adopted the Report and ordered it published. All the sessions of the various committees have been marked by deep interest and great frankness, and by virtual unanimity.

The Committee is under great obligations to the members of its Executive and Editorial Committees, its Consultants, the representative Africans who gave most helpful advice, and to certain authorities on race relations, such as Mr. Basil Mathews, for helpful suggestions and criticisms.

The Committee also owes a debt of thanks for constructive suggestions to various European correspondents, including especially Senator Rheinallt Jones of the Union of South Africa, one of the four elected representatives of the native African population in the Union Parliament, and the highly competent, courageous, and respected Adviser of the South African Commission on Race Relations; Professor R. F. Alfred Hoernlé, the Chairman of that Commission; Dr. J. H. Oldham of the International Missionary Council, a member of the Advisory Committee on Education in Tropical Countries of the British Colonial Office; Sir Hanns Vischer, for many years Secretary of that Committee and Secretary General of the International Institute of African Languages and Cultures; Miss Margery Perham, Director of the Nuffield College Colonial Research, Oxford, an authority on Africa; Miss Margaret Wrong, Secretary of the International Committee on Christian Literature for Africa; and many others. The Free French Delegation in New York City, and the Embassies in Washington, have also provided important information regarding recent developments in relation to African colonies.

The naming of certain persons should not in any way involve them in responsibility for the Report. They have not seen the final document, although most of their suggestions have been included in it.

The reader of this Report should constantly bear in mind the early decision that "The Committee's statement should deal with fundamental principles and their major applications. . . ." This decision was reached after two alternatives were discussed, namely, that the Report should deal only with "general principles"; and that it should take up in turn the special problems of each colony. In other words, the Committee felt that all it could wisely try to do, in facing the extremely diverse and complicated problems of Africa under its various types of administration, was to consider the more important facts and problems—especially those dealing with the welfare of Africans—and to treat them in a concrete and realistic way.

It is hoped that this study may stimulate many readers to go further into the various present-day questions related to Africa. With this purpose in mind a "Selected African Bibliography" has been provided. For those who wish a single book of reference on the parts of Africa with which this Report deals, no work is so inclusive or up to date in its information as that by Lord Hailey, *An African Survey* (1938), prepared with the aid of the Carnegie Corporation. It can be highly recommended, although it does not entirely take the place of a somewhat similar survey made a decade earlier by Dr. Raymond Leslie Buell, *The Native Problem in Africa*, which is still a source book of information and documents of much value for reference purposes. For a general introduction to the history, spirit, and problems of Africa and the Africans, no better work can be suggested than that of Dr. Edwin W. Smith, *The Golden Stool*.

It was originally planned to include a "Table of African Dates," but it was found that there was not sufficient space for the comprehensive study prepared by Dr. Edwin W. Smith. This compilation has consequently been published as a supplement with the title *Events in African History*, uniform in format and typography with this Report. It will fill a long-felt want for those interested in the study of African history and present conditions.

Introduction—The Approach

A few words of general introduction will show the point of view of the Committee in approaching the problems of Africa at this time.

1. The New World Situation and Africa

The emergence into political consciousness of the non-white peoples of the world is a recent phenomenon of great significance. It is full of promise and full of possibility of danger— promise, if the nations now in authority in Africa are wise in helping to fit its people in the different colonies for self-government in a modern state, and if the latter respond adequately; dangerous, either if the objective is withheld, or if complete self-government is provided before the people are qualified through education and experience to make use of it wisely and effectively. To assure effective self-government will prove a difficult but highly important task. Its accomplishment will challenge all that is best in the governments responsible and in their representatives, in the Europeans, Americans, and other non-Africans living in Africa or with financial interests there, and in the native people and their leaders, so that the desired result may be attained as soon as practicable. This will require great imagination, faith, patience, and earnest effort by both major groups concerned.

Recent events in Asia, following especially upon the fall of Singapore and Rangoon under Japanese attack, the closer cooperation of India and China in the Far East, and the assurance that India will have self-governing Dominion status if its various political and religious groups can unite on a mutually satisfactory plan, are highly significant. So is Chiang-Kai-shek's recent visit to Nehru, representing as it does the new spirit of cooperation between two great non-European nations with about one half of the population of the world. His allegiance to the Atlantic Charter; his emphatic appeal "that our ally Great Britain, without waiting for any demands on the part of the people of India, will as speedily as possible give them real political power so that they may be in a position further to develop their spiritual and material strength . . ."; his urging that the people of India and China "should exert themselves to the utmost in the cause of Freedom for all mankind . . . ," and that they "should ally themselves with the anti-aggression front" and so participate "in the struggle for the survival of a free world" —are all important. So also is the Chinese leader's oft-repeated statement of the need of Christian faith and Christian social idealism for the solution of problems of human relationship.

Wise men in Europe and America fully realize the significance of the recent historic events in Asia. An editorial in *The Times* of London of February 28, is highly suggestive and encouraging on this point. Referring to the fall of Singapore, it says:

In the perspective of history the fall of Singapore may appear as the greatest blow which has befallen the British Empire since the loss of the American colonies. In one sense it is equally irretrievable: British dominion in the Far East can never be restored—nor will there be any desire to see it restored—in its former guise. But in another sense defeats must serve, just as defeat in the American war of independence served, as the starting-point of a fresh advance in which, adapting herself to changed needs, Great Britain may once more become the pioneer of new policies and a new outlook. No alternative is open to her if she wishes to remain a Great Power. In the future scheme of things there is no place for the Britain of the past. She must and she can offer to the world of the twentieth century something which that world needs.

Any nation whose leading organ of public opinion can take so open-minded, objective, and constructive an attitude in a time of national crisis and of deep sorrow over the loss of treasured territorial dependencies, is one which should command the respect of all thoughtful people. It means that white people as represented in Great Britain should give up any thought of trying to control the world in the way often characteristic in the past, even though this policy has been marked at its best by "benevolent imperialism."

It must be realized that these lessons apply to Africa as well, for, although the people of Africa are awaking later than the people of the East, and have a considerably longer road to follow before they can take their full place in the family of nations, that place is sure to be won sometime if they are given the right opportunities under sympathetic auspices. Furthermore, experience has shown that where the ruling Power identifies itself most actively with the interests of the native people without thought of exploitation, and does the most to fit them for self-government, their loyalty to Government is strongest, and dangers from within and without are the least serious. Uganda and the Philippines are good examples. Americans may look with pride to the fine spirit of coöperation shown between the American and Filipino troops. Perhaps—as some British leaders of public opinion have themselves stated—if Holland and Great Britain had been earlier in modifying some of their policies in the Far East, recent war losses might have been less serious. They have perhaps been right in thinking that it has been a case of "too little and too late" in modifying colonial policies in the interest of the people of the territories concerned.

In terms of the African Continent this should clearly imply such changes as that there should be more emphasis on education for native leadership; that European officials should gradually give way to a trained native African Civil Service; that duly elected Africans should play a larger part in the legislative councils of the colonies; and that investments should be further controlled in the interest of better wages for native workmen, and better working and living conditions. It is believed that if such things are done the African peoples, and the nations in which they will form the large majority, will be happier, and will ultimately have an important contribution to make to the civilization of the world.

This general thought was brought out clearly in a debate on the labor laws of Kenya in the House of Commons on March 26, of this year, when Mr. Creech Jones said:

There have been criticisms and complaints of our failure to associate the Colonial peoples with the war effort and to secure their free co-operation, to make them feel that we, with them, have a common cause, and that for them, too, this is a war of liberation. . . . We talk of liberation. Let us secure the cooperation of the Colonial peoples identifying themselves freely with us because they are conscious that this war is not only a war of liberation for the great outer world, but also a war of liberation from the Imperialism we have in the past obliged them to experience.

In the same debate another speaker said:

. . . We have lately witnessed an appalling series of disasters in our Colonies. We have seen Malaya and a great part of Burma go, and I think that perhaps one of the most distressing features of these disasters was summed up by a correspondent of "The Times" recently when he said, writing from Batavia:

"The Government had no roots in the life of the country. With the exception of certain sections of the Chinese community, some inspired by the Free Chinese struggle for survival and others by Soviet precept and example, the bulk of the Asiatic population remained spectators from start to finish."

Will the same be true of the African population? Will they also remain spectators if Japan should reach the shores of Africa one day? If we pursue the sort of policy in Kenya which has been suggested today [in the matter of conscription of native labor to improve farm production to meet war needs], we shall undoubtedly find that the inhabitants of Kenya will not only be spectators but will not help us and may, even, help the enemy.

The changed world situation constitutes an inspiring challenge to the white peoples to give up all that remains of imperialistic ambition, and to fit themselves not only for the more democratic political and economic life of their own free nations but for helping other nations and peoples to attain to the same freedom. This has been increasingly characteristic of official utterances and of governmental actions in recent years in most African colonies. But this encouraging general attitude needs more effective implementation.

The main purpose of the Report is to promote an intelligent understanding of Africa and its problems as a help to their wise treatment during the war and at the Peace Conference which will follow. European and American statesmen have repeatedly stated that if the peace treaty is to be a constructive and wise one, it will be so only as a result of a large amount of study in which many people unite. Such study is being given in large measure by important groups to the problems of Europe, the Americas, and the Far East. It seems equally important that it should be given to Africa, especially by a nation which owes to it one tenth of its population—the most influential Negro group in the world—and which during the past half century has acquired considerable experience in dealing with other races, not only within its own borders, but in the Pacific, the Far East, and the West Indies.

2. MAIN BASIS AND PURPOSES OF THE REPORT

The Report assumes that a victory of the United Nations in the present war is both highly important from the standpoint of the future of civilization, and is to be ultimately expected. If such a victory does not take place, no part of the world will suffer more than Africa. An Axis victory would give no possibility that the constructive program outlined in this document could be carried out. But if there is a victory of the United Nations, especially in view of the liberal spirit regarding colonies prevailing in Great Britain and among the Free French today, and the provisions of the Atlantic Charter as agreed to by all the anti-Axis Powers, there is every reason to hope that some such program as that outlined may be adopted.

It will be noted that the main basis of the report is the application of the "Eight Points" of the Charter to African problems. The Committee has felt that, as this pronouncement not only represents the point of view of this country and of Great Britain but has been endorsed by the Governments in exile and by all the other nations fighting the Axis, it is a fitting basis for study with a view to pointing out its implications for Africa in general and for its native population in particular. The fact that this Charter is made the basis of our study does not, however, indicate that the members of the Committee think it in every respect a satisfactory and adequate statement. It needs, for instance, supplementation in the matter of religious and other freedoms—partly covered by the endorsing statement of the Twenty-Six Nations Agreement—and also very particularly in the field of international organization to bring about effective coöperation, the development of various needed international agencies and services, and collective security. It is quite clear that the high ideals which dominate the Charter will never be adequately implemented unless there is some form of international organization in which our nation unites with other nations to see that the principles and ideals of the "Eight Points" are carried into effect.

In preparing the Report the Committee has had in mind two major objectives:

(1) That it help to focus public opinion on the constructive treatment of Africa's problems at the Peace Conference, as well as before and after it.

(2) That it form a basis for study in college, high school, church, and other groups, especially those which concern themselves with international and interracial affairs.

With these objectives in mind it has endeavoured in preparing the Report to emphasize accuracy of facts, fairness of interpretation, and a realistic attitude in making constructive suggestions.

The Committee is of the opinon that the wise settlement of Africa's problems will not only prove a fair test of the peace negotiations, but that without such a settlement there can be no enduring basis for world peace. Furthermore, it is of importance to America, in view of its large and increasingly influential Negro population, which is naturally concerned about the welfare of its distant African kin. Indeed, few things will do more to convince the Negro population of this country, and those interested in their welfare, that the United Nations are true to their principle of overcoming the extremes of Nazi racialism, than the way in which they approach the whole problem of Africa and its people. On its solution will depend to a large extent the whole future of interracial coöperation both here and in Africa.

In dealing with the complicated interracial questions of Africa, the Committee has concentrated its attention mainly on European-African relationships. It is well aware that there are other serious racial problems in connection with the presence of a large number of Asiatics or persons of Asiatic origin in Africa, and that in East and South Africa the difficulties resulting, especially because of the acute tension between the more ambitious native Africans and the East Indians in matters of trade, are serious. These Asiatic elements in the population are duly referred to in Appendix I. The "Cape Coloured" population in South Africa, made up mainly of an admixture of European, Malay, and African (especially Hottentot), constitute another interracial problem that must not be overlooked, but it is virtually confined to the Cape Colony (and the neighboring Southern Rhodesia), where this population group has a fairly clearly defined status between the European and the

Bantu. The Union has also the difficult task—in which General Smuts has accomplished so much—of welding together the Europeans of Dutch and British traditions, and of effectively integrating into national life about two hundred thousand "poor whites." When we think of these divergent elements we may well sympathize with our friends in South Africa and admire the courage of those outstanding leaders of liberal public opinion—centering especially around the South African Institute of Race Relations—who are trying to deal fairly and constructively with the complicated and very serious issues involved.*

3. BASIC CONSIDERATIONS IN APPROACH TO AFRICAN PROBLEMS

Two fundamental matters must be borne in mind in all discussions of African policy.

(1) Differences in European Governmental Policies

The *first* is the fact that Africa south of the Sahara—which is the part in which this Report is especially concerned—is, apart from the independent States of Ethiopia, Liberia, and the Union of South Africa, under the control of various European powers. These are, in order of the extent of their territory in this area, Great Britain, France, Belgium, the Free French, Portugal, and Spain—the colonies of the last-named being backward and so small as not to require special attention here. The points of view of the home governments named differ greatly. For instance, Great Britain is definitely committed to emphasis on native cultures, traditions, languages, and ideals. It recognizes that tribal customs and practices will inevitably be modified, but it wishes to see the new branches grafted on the old trees rather than to have the old trees disregarded or cut down. Similarly, it favors the rule of native chiefs—so-called "indirect rule"—wherever the conditions are favorable.

France stands for a more centralized type of colonial government with less emphasis on native chiefs but more on the French educated *élite*. It wishes to have the native Africans educated in the French language and culture and to consider themselves part of the French state. It makes, however, a line of distinction

* See *infra*, Appendix I, 5 (2).

between the small group of *élite*, to which it gives a position of more importance than is given native Africans in any other part of Africa, and the mass of the African people—the *indigènes*. The education of the former, that is, the so-called "assimilated" Africans, is based on the educational system of France and is intended to assimilate those who receive it into the French cultural tradition. The educational policy regarding the second group is that of "association," which represents a stage considerably less advanced than assimilation but is considered a preparation for it. Even the elementary schools are frequently referred to as "schools of initiation"—that is, they exist largely to initiate the African into French civilization.

The Free French Government in Equatorial Africa has recently shown a tendency to adopt a position midway between that of France and that of England.*

Furthermore, it must be realized that the colonies under Great Britain are so varied in character and in the relative advancement of their inhabitants as to yield with difficulty to any single type of government, although certain common elements, as we have indicated, generally prevail in them. This is why the British, in contrast to the French, definitely oppose standardization. Their theory, as recently stated by Lord Lugard, is an "intentional avoidance of standardization and uniformity, on the principle that every community is entitled to follow its own way of life, provided that it does not thereby injure its neighbors and that it obey the law."

Belgium has made great strides forward in its African policy in the past thirty years, thanks largely to deeply interested groups at home, and its attitude is somewhat between that of Great Britain and France, but it is still doing very little in education above the elementary and lower secondary levels. Portugal, which was long open to a great deal of criticism for the neglect of native interests, and especially for the exploitation of native labor, has in recent years, since the *Report on Native Labor in Portuguese Africa* by Professor Edward Ross in 1925, changes in the Home Government, and the passing of the Colonial Act in 1935, improved its administration. But it is still far from satisfactory. The last comment also applies to the Spanish colonies.

* See *infra* IV, 1, (3), (d).

The Mandate System adopted to care for German colonies after the last war has been an important factor in the improvement of conditions of native life and welfare. It is being administered in different areas by Great Britain, France, Belgium, and the Union of South Africa. It will be discussed at length later,* but it is well to refer here to the fact that most impartial observers are of the opinion that this form of government, if supplemented by the practice of international reports on conditions found and international inspection, as well as by the right of presenting statements of alleged grievances, should prove a highly important factor in protecting native interests.

(2) Differences in Areas with and without Large European Population

The *second* matter always to be borne in mind is the difference between areas of large white permanent settlement and those where there is no such group. The former include, outside of the Mediterranean Littoral, only the Union of South Africa, Southern Rhodesia, and territories to the East and West adjoining the Union—that is, Angola and Mozambique (both Portuguese) and Southwest Africa (a Union mandate), and, to some extent, Kenya. The first named is a self-governing Dominion and the British Government consequently cannot control its policy any more than could the Congress of the United States. The second named has semi-dominion status. It is self-governing, but the acts of its Parliament are subject to revision by the British Parliament, which has in several instances declined to approve measures which seemed unfair to the native Africans. The last (Kenya) is a Crown Colony for which the British Government is entirely responsible, but where there is a large group of British settlers, some of whom feel that their interests should be given the major consideration. The problem here is still acute. In all parts of Central and West Africa conditions are definitely tropical, and there is only a handful of Europeans—mostly government officials, traders, missionaries—and there is no acute race problem.†

In the parts of the continent with small white settlements, that is, in most of Tropical Africa except for the Kenya region

* See *infra*, II, 5, (5).
† These matters are discussed in Appendix I, 3-6.

mentioned, it is much easier for the European Governments concerned to devote their major attention, without complicating issues, to the welfare and advancement of the indigenous population. It is, consequently, in this region that the African has been enabled to make his greatest advances, and this with relatively little friction. Nigeria, the Gold Coast, and Uganda are conspicuous examples of the best conditions. In general, it is in the West Coast—both in French and British colonies—that there is the largest group of educated Africans, and that consequently the native people have attained to the largest participation in colonial government.

4. SUGGESTED PROCEDURES AT THE PEACE CONFERENCE AND AFTER

To accomplish the plans outlined in this Report, it would seem highly desirable that there should be at the Peace Conference some persons specially qualified to give information not only about African conditions, as would be inevitable, but also about the native African, interracial problems, and the opinions of thoughtful Africans and of the Negro people generally. The Committee would therefore suggest that among those chosen by our Government to give testimony at the Peace Conference and to prepare for its work, should be some representative Negro Americans specially qualified to deal with African problems, and some other American citizens who have given the questions of Africa and of interracial adjustment in this country and in Africa much study and thought.

It is also to be hoped that the European nations and the Union of South Africa may bear the same idea in mind. There are, for example, in British East Africa and in some French and British colonies of the West Coast native Africans who by training and experience are qualified to speak with wisdom and authority on native questions. There are also in the Union of South Africa Europeans of outstanding position elected by the native people to be their representatives in Parliament, as well as a few highly educated Africans of a broad and fair point of view. If the principle were adopted of recognizing some of these spokesmen not merely as representing unofficial delegations but as men on the regular staffs of the Peace Commission, it would be an important step forward and would be specially appreciated by thoughtful Negro Americans and native Africans.

It seems clear that the Conference should not repeat the error of Versailles in trying to cover exhaustively the details of international problems which have arisen or which may arise as a result of the war. The most that can be effectively accomplished is to have the major issues settled, and then to leave to expert international commissions the working out of plans for detailed adjustments to be submitted later for the approval of whatever international organization is decided upon. In this way only can we expect the complicated problems of Africa to receive anything approaching fair and adequate attention.

As a help in dealing with the permanent problems of Africa from day to day in the years to come and in putting the continent "on the map" in American public opinion, it is suggested that a division dealing with Africa be established in the State Department.* As the Latin-American Republics, the Far East, and the Near East have divisions, so there should be one for Africa, which in the past has been relegated either to the care of the European or the Near Eastern Division.

The solution of Africa's problems is an extremely complicated one. Neither the Government, nor the missionary, nor the man of commerce or of industry, nor the scientific expert, nor the educated African, can supply the whole solution. It will only come as all coöperate. More social vision, better agriculture and animal husbandry, better roads, better transportation, more research and its application to African problems, less erosion, better health conditions, more constructive methods of government, more effective controls to prevent all forms of native exploitation, larger participation of natives in public affairs, better education, a deeper and more sympathetic understanding of the native African culture and point of view, the spread of a spiritual and ethical faith, and many other things, must all play their part. In other words, there must be a constructive attack on the problem of African poverty and backwardness of development all along the line, with the definite goal of fitting the African in the colonial possessions for ultimate self-government.

* It is possible that Egypt and the various other areas on the Mediterranean Littoral should be left in their present divisions.

If the constructive program outlined in these pages is to be carried out it will require broad and courageous statesmanship, the application of modern scientific knowledge and method, a deep and unselfish interest in the welfare of the African people, sympathy with their ambition for an increasingly large share in determining their own destiny, and loyalty to the faith and ideals of the Christian religion. If any one of these factors is lacking the program cannot be effective. With them there is large hope of success.

ANSON PHELPS STOKES

Chairman

101 Park Avenue
New York City
June 15, 1942

While this Report was passing through the press, the Under-Secretary of State of the United States, Honorable Sumner Welles, delivered a highly significant Memorial Day address at the Tomb of the Unknown Soldier in Washington. In it he said "The principles of the Atlantic Charter must be guaranteed to the world as a whole—in all oceans and in all continents." . . . The official position of the speaker and the occasion of the utterance at the nation's capital add weight to the statement quoted. This substantiates one of the underlying theses of this Report, namely, that the principles of the Atlantic Charter must be applied to Africa—a thesis which will be developed on page 30.

CHAPTER I

Africa and the United States

1. CONTACTS OF AFRICA WITH THE OUTSIDE WORLD

The significance of Africa in all plans for world peace is of paramount importance. This is true of all Africa, although in this Report the Committee is primarily concerned with that part of the continent south of the Sahara, sometimes spoken of as "Negro Africa," because of its being the historic home of the Negro people. Through the centuries Africa, largely because of its extensive undeveloped resources, has often been the object of the selfish competition of other continents, and especially, in recent times, of European nations. If the Union of South Africa, although now an independent nation, is included, these control, directly or indirectly, all but one sixteenth of the area and all but one sixth of the population.

(1) Reasons for European Penetration of Africa

The reasons for the modern acquisition of territory in Africa have been manifold. They had their foundations in many cases in past centuries when Europe was interested in Africa partly for legitimate trade and missionary effort, but partly also for commercial exploitation and the promotion of the slave trade—a tragic blot on the history of Portugal, England, the United States, and many other nations for about four centuries, and especially in the two centuries after the introduction of slaves into Virginia in 1619. The enormous slave trade of the past is, of course, a major cause of the African's relative poverty and backwardness today. Fortunately, this cruel and inhuman trade in human beings with Europe and America has long been a thing of the past, although Arab slave traders have been occasionally reported in the North-East in recent years. Commercial exploitation still exists, however, although many of its most serious evils have been mitigated.

The extension of European trade was an important factor in the extension of territory in the nineteenth century. This was largely due to the desire to acquire influence in areas which produce raw materials and to find markets for manufactured goods. Professor Malinowski calls attention to the fact "that it was not accidental that the scramble for Africa followed the Industrial Revolution of the last Century." Peoples of Europe —with the constantly increasing assistance of American mining and other financial and commercial interests—have gained control over a large part of the rich resources and the "cheap labor" of the continent of Africa. This has been largely because of their desire for profitable investments, and, as is well known, the non-resident owner or controller of property is not generally the most considerate of local labor conditions. There are honorable exceptions to this rule, but serious dangers are inherent in the situation.

Other selfish motives also played their part in the acquisition of territory, showing that there is some truth in the cynic's remark that Europe was not in Africa mainly for the latter's "health." For instance, in the case of the former German colonies and to some extent in those of France, territorial expansion in Africa was largely due to political considerations and to ideals of national prestige—which also played some part in later British and Belgian policy, although the latter developed out of a personal commercial exploitation project of King Leopold II.

But the reasons for the acquisition of territory in Africa have not been always due to selfish, materialistic, or political motives. In the case of some of the West Coast colonies it was directly related to the attempt to put down the slave trade, which the conscience of France and England would no longer countenance. In connection with the site of Freetown—out of which the Colony of Sierra Leone developed—it was because the group of British philanthropists who had acquired the territory as a home for freed slaves found themselves unable to support the venture alone, and persuaded the British Government to take it over. In the case of Uganda it was mainly to promote the cause of missions. In the case of the taking over of Basutoland by the British it was the request of the Africans themselves. Negotiations with chiefs for purchase were employed in many areas, while in some sections such as the Union of South Africa the dominant motive in the extension of territory has been European settlement.

Lord Lothian once described the division of Africa by the European powers as an operation which had excited at various times heroism, greed, pity, political passion, and a scramble for control. There is some truth in this analysis which at least shows some of the motives which have played a large part. Perhaps it would be fairer to say that the old-time imperialism which in one way or another has been so largely responsible for European influences in Africa, has in the last four hundred years involved the following varied major motives: barter and trade for profit; investment for profit, often involving exploitation; acquisition by force or negotiation, or political control, to protect investments and secure a satisfactory labor supply; national defense and prestige; protection of nationals and their interests; protection of native welfare, especially through the abolishment of the slave trade and slavery—at times practised by native tribes as well as by foreigners; the saving of people from cruel and despotic chiefs; the advancement of white colonization; and the desire to advance Christian missions. In some cases two or more of these motives have all been combined. It will be noted that the motives mentioned are referred to as dominant ones in the past hundred years, that is, since the abolition of the slave trade, in which the nations of Europe and the United States played such a highly discreditable part in the earlier period.

(2) Balance Sheet of Results

Fortunately, many individuals and groups in Europe, America, and in Africa itself have been deeply concerned with advancing the interest of the native population. Although we cannot refrain on the one hand from condemning selfish exploiters, we should also on the other hand remember missionaries such as the White Fathers (founded by Cardinal Lavigerie), the Anglicans of Uganda, the Scotch Presbyterians, representatives of the Dutch Reformed Church of South Africa in Nyasaland, and many other equally honored groups. We should not forget the explorers, such as David Livingstone (also a great missionary) and Henry M. Stanley; and administrators such as Theophilus Shepstone in South Africa, Lord Lugard in Nigeria and elsewhere, Sir Gordon Guggisberg (founder of Achimota College), Sir Donald Cameron, Minister of the Colonies Franck of Belgium, who was deeply interested in the welfare of the Belgian Congo, Marshal Lyautey in Morocco and Algeria, and their many assistants in the Civil Service. We are glad to record the names of such men with deep gratitude, without necessarily approving all their acts. Similarly, the great emancipators of over a century ago—Zachary Macaulay, Granville Sharpe, William Wilberforce, Thomas Clarkson, Thomas Buxton, and their associates and successors—rendered Africa a service for which we cannot be too thankful, for it was their influence on the British Parliament which abolished the iniquities of the slave trade and later eliminated slavery itself from British territory. Such men and scores of others like them in various professions and occupations are among the heroes of Africa whom Africans themselves love to honor.

The development of European governmental control in Africa has been a long process, with a balance sheet showing both assets and liabilities as far as native life is concerned. The major assets are clear. Speaking generally, there have come the formal abolition of the slave trade; public order; more personal and social security; the opening of roads; new means of transportation resulting in decreasing the burdens and evils of hand porterage, for whose commercial development Europeans had earlier been largely responsible; the cessation of tribal wars and of many cruel customs; increase in markets for native products; larger opportunities for productive labor; improved education and agriculture; higher standards of justice; the control of many pests; the manufacture or importation of many useful objects and products; better health conditions; release from the ill-effects of certain fears and superstitions; and the spiritual, educational, and social benefits of the Christian religion when interpreted and applied in the spirit of Christ.

The liabilities are equally clear. They include—in addition to the early development of the slave trade—the break-up in many cases, although often unwittingly, of tribal solidarity and family life, without providing adequate new safeguards; the weakening of some old taboos which had an ethical significance; the loss of extensive areas for farming, ranging cattle, and hunting; the evils of urbanization and industrialization in European centers, especially through the disturbances brought about by the introduction of the modern system of industry with wages

on a low level and poor working conditions; the greater consciousness of racial differences; the introduction in some sections
of gin and other intoxicating liquors, in spite of mandate regulations and the 1919 Convention relating to the Liquor Traffic
in Africa; the spread of certain diseases not known before; and
the dragging of Africa into the maelstrom of European military
events which have resulted in the death of hundreds of thousands of African soldiers and members of labor battalions
accompanying them.

Dr. Edwin Smith, writing in *The Golden Stool* (1926), thus
sums up his chapter on what he calls the "debit and credit
account" of the European penetration of Africa: "If only we
Europeans do our duty in a Christian way, the Africans will be
the ultimate gainers from this invasion. But as regards our
interim balance sheet, it must be confessed that were anyone
to say that the account is against Europe it would be difficult to
contradict his statement."

Dr. Smith has, however, authorized the Committee to state
that: "in view of the enhanced sense of trusteeship among some
of the European powers, the author of *The Golden Stool*, if he
were now re-writing his interim balance-sheet, would be rather
more optimistic in his estimate of European influence in
Africa."

2. REASONS FOR AMERICA'S SPECIAL INTEREST IN AFRICA

The fundamental elements of concern of the United States in
the welfare of the African peoples seem so important, both for
the United States and for Africa, as to require definite formulation. The reasons are mainly nine in number:

(1) That thoughtful Americans are increasingly convinced
that the sincere application of the principles underlying the
"Eight Points" of the Atlantic Charter to Africa is an acid test
of democratic ideals in any new World Order to be achieved
after the present war. This does not imply that the Charter is
a complete and altogether satisfactory basis for the establishment of permanent justice and peace, but that it points the
way to wise solutions of the most pressing world problems.

(2) That the thirteen million Negro Americans constitute
one tenth of all Americans in the United States and that they
are the equivalent of about one tenth of all African people.

Such numbers and numerical proportions are of significance in the long-time adjustments of people of African stock to world affairs. Far beyond the implications of these impressive numerical proportions are those of the historic and racial relationships of Negro Americans to the African peoples, however far separated may be their present condition and their geographic position. More and more groups are becoming mutually conscious, seeking to exchange their heritage and their experiences, especially in the perplexing fields of elemental rights, interracial relationships, and opportunities to achieve the fullness of life.

(3) That the people of the United States have for many years maintained philanthropic, educational, and religious activities in many parts of Africa. Their interest in missionary work in Africa was in the early days due in part to the doctrine of "recompense." Many Americans realized that through their active participation in, and encouragement of, the slave trade and the trade in rum they had done much to demoralize Africa, and wished to make a suitable return. The idea has not been, and should not be, entirely forgotten, but a definitely Christian missionary spirit of service has generally characterized the efforts. Americans are more and more concerned that the people of the continent of Africa shall receive full recognition as members of the world community and be given every opportunity to achieve as rapidly as possible standards that will entitle them to the privileges and responsibilities of self-government. The Republic of Liberia both historically and contemporaneously is of special interest to the United States.

(4) That many Americans are, for good or ill, largely interested in Africa's commercial development, and have consequently a heavy responsibility for insuring fair labor conditions.

(5) That Americans are also increasingly conscious of the fact that modern industrialism, with the frequently selfish exploitation by non-African peoples of the resources of Africa, has been among the influences responsible for cruel wars, of which the latest, and it is hoped the last, now engulfs the Americas and indeed the whole world. They should, therefore, be willing to unite with other nations in adopting "controls" which will prevent the abuses of the past without interfering with the de-

velopment of Africa's resources in the interest of Africans and of the world.

(6) That the development of transportation and communication, and especially of aviation, has so reduced distance as to make conditions not only on the West Coast but also in other parts of Africa of increased significance to the United States.

(7) That the United States has had in the past forty years considerable experience in dealing, outside of its own borders, with people of different races including some on various stages of civilization differing greatly from our own. In some places, such as Hawaii and the Philippines, it has had considerable success in securing coöperation and good feeling between the different racial groups. This experience should be of some value in Africa.

(8) That the United States has certain legal rights and responsibilities in Africa under treaties and conventions to which it is a signatory. These are explained in a subsequent section (I, 5).

(9) That direct American penetration in Africa has grown by leaps and bounds during the past year, and especially since Pearl Harbor. This activity has been commercial, diplomatic, and semi-military, if not military. New consulates are being opened, such as the recent one established at Brazzaville. Pan American Airways has developed an extensive service covering West and Central Africa. American bases are being built, and a significant number of American survey expeditions has been sent out. The number of Americans in Africa today is many times greater than the number of Americans present on that continent at any time during the past, and this number is rapidly increasing. West and Central Africa have become a beehive of American activity.

It is highly important that everything possible be done to assure that the new contacts being thus made between Americans and Africans should be on the basis of mutual understanding and respect.

3. HELPFUL APPROACHES TO AFRICA'S PROBLEMS

Before presenting definite proposals for the future Africa, there are three statements which should be made in fairness to the European powers which have borne for so many years both the advantages and the burdens of their African colonies and other possessions:

(1) Recognition of America's Own Shortcomings, with Evidences of Recent Improvements

The *first* is that in making suggestions which imply, or seem to imply, criticisms of past conditions and some of those which still exist, the Committee is fully aware of the shortcomings of this country as far as the treatment of Negroes, and also of American Indians, is concerned. We continued slavery a generation after it was practically abolished by the leading European nations in their African colonies. America has no right to point criticisms at others except as it asserts a full realization that it has also been guilty of much race prejudice and of failure to give under-privileged or retarded people their due, and that we are still far from being above criticism in dealing with important groups in our population. Although the Negro American has made impressive progress since emancipation, due to many factors of which his own innate desire to help himself has been one of the most important, there are still many serious social injustices, such as lynchings (fortunately now reduced to a very few a year); "Jim Crow" legislation; poor housing, health, and industrial conditions; inadequate political rights, educational privileges, and opportunities for government service; and other unfortunate factors.

The feeling of the Christian Churches of the United States on the subject of racial discrimination has been emphatically and authoritatively stated in the reports adopted at the National Study Conference at Delaware, Ohio, in March of this year, under the auspices of the Commission on a Just and Durable Peace of the Federal Council of Churches of Christ in America. In discussing the social basis of a durable peace, as approved in substance by the Conference, there was a statement on Race Relations and Cultures of which the three paragraphs following have large general significance:

Among the primary factors in the maintenance of a just and durable peace will be equitable treatment of all racial groups that make up the world's population. Therefore the securing of justice now for racial groups is essential if America is to make its full contribution in securing a just and durable peace.

We acknowledge with profound contrition the sin of racial discrimination in American life and our own share, though we are Christians, in the common guilt. So long as our attitudes and policies deny peoples of other races in our own or other lands the essential position of brothers in the common family of mankind we cannot safely be trusted with the making of a just and durable peace.

In our own country millions of people, especially American Negroes, are subjected to discrimination and unequal treatment in educational opportunities, in employment, wages and conditions of work, in access to professional and business opportunities, in housing, in transportation, in the administration of justice and even in the right to vote. We condemn all such inequalities and call upon our fellow Christians and fellow citizens to initiate and support measures to establish equality of status and treatment of members of minority racial and cultural groups.

Fortunately, however, most of the tendencies in this country are now definitely forward and upward, and there are increasingly influential interracial, Negro, and white groups in both North and South determined that the Negro American shall receive full justice. The recent decisions of the United States Supreme Court protecting Negro rights under the Civil War amendments to the Constitution; the growing practice of having Negroes on juries, both North and South, when Negroes themselves are accused of high crimes; the movement for the equalization of pay of Negro teachers in public schools when they have the same training and experience as white teachers; the increasingly effective Southern campaigns against lynching and certain other abuses; the growing integration of Negroes into municipal, political, and civic life in various cities such as New York; the increased employment of educated Negroes in some Government departments in Washington, and of Negro mechanics in more industries; the decision of the Government, although inadequate in its scope and unfortunate in the manner of its announcement, to let down some of the bars against Negroes in the Navy and Marine Corps, where tradition has in the past opened to them only the positions of cooks, stewards, and messmen; the attempt by the Federal Government to prevent discriminations against Negroes in Defense industries—these are examples of many trends which point toward a better day as far as Negro rights and economic progress in this country are concerned. They are mentioned primarily because of their significance for Africa. It has been the experience of those who have discussed racial matters publicly and privately in many African communities that the educated African is aware of the discriminations against Negroes which have existed in our democracy as well as of certain other unfavorable conditions, such as municipal and other forms of political corruption, financial scandals, labor disputes involving at times violence, sensational journalism and movies, and similar matters. If such abuses can be corrected here it will greatly strengthen American influence in Africa and stimulate those working for better African conditions.

It must also be remembered, as already indicated, that Americans have profited from the exploitation of Africa, so that in criticizing others we must also criticize ourselves. Furthermore, to the regret of most members of the Committee, the United States was unwilling to enter the League of Nations, and consequently did not as a nation make any direct contribution to the development of the Mandates System in Africa, on which so much depends directly and indirectly, although Woodrow Wilson's advocacy of it did much to secure its adoption.

(2) Recognition of Recent Progress in Africa

The *second* is that if any of the Committee's comments would seem to imply an over-critical attitude, this does not involve any lack of appreciation of the progressive steps forward which have been taken in recent decades by various Colonial Powers —such as the creation of protectorates with provisions to protect and improve the status of the native peoples; the high type of most Governors and other civil servants in Africa; the Government medical service in the Anglo-Egyptian Sudan, the Belgian Congo, French West Africa, and other colonies, with African assistants; the repeated declarations of the British Government that its objective is colonial self-government with due participation by the native people; the large measure of local self-government in the Native Transkei Territory of the Union of South Africa; the "indirect rule" under native Kings and Chiefs in such colonies and mandates as Nigeria, Uganda, and Tanganyika—whose advantages in most cases seem to more than balance its disadvantages; the training of engineers and mechanics by railroad and mining companies in some of the French colonies and the Congo; the agricultural, social welfare, and native education departments in many colonies; the growing appreciation of the danger of large "concessions," and the development of strictly limited rather than more or less indefinite franchises in many of the colonies; the building up of native colleges under Government auspices or with Government support, such as Achimota in the Gold Coast, Fort Hare in South Africa, Makerere in Uganda, the William Ponty and Faidherbe School in Dakar, Senegal, and Gordon College in Khartoum; the granting of considerable powers to native councils, and the inclusion of some native African members in some Legislative Councils; the education and recognition of the native *élite* in some French colonies; the recent decision of the British Government—in spite of war conditions—to make grants of five million pounds a year for ten years to be used primarily for "the improvement of the economic conditions of the Colonies, including protectorates and mandates"; the wise action of the Free French National Committee in London in naming M. Eboué, a Martiniquan Negro with long experience in the French African colonial administration, as Governor General of French Equatorial Africa; the recent decision of this French colony to modify its policy by laying more emphasis on native chiefs, their training, and their traditional powers, and on developing a native Civil Service rather than importing so many "functionaries" from abroad; and the appointment in a few British colonies of native Africans to high courts and to such a post as the Residency at Lagos. These are encouraging signs and many others might be named.

What is true of encouraging government accomplishments is also true of much of the work done by volunteer agencies such as the International Institute of African Languages and Cultures, the South African Institute of Race Relations in Johannesburg, various Protestant and Catholic missionary societies, and the foundations—European, South African, and American—which have interested themselves in African welfare. It is on such beginnings and achievements that the governments can and must work in securing further progress.

(3) Recognition of Danger to Africa of Totalitarian Victory

The *third* is that the Committee realizes that any victory for the Totalitarian Powers would result in far worse conditions for the native people than those which now exist, especially because of their destructive racial views and their detailed plans for the virtual enslavement of the African population. This idea is brought out in an address recently given at Talladega College by one of the leading Negro Americans, Dr. William Pickens:

The Negro, if the world were lost to democracy, would lose all schools and colleges like this; and he would lose the right to engage in the professions. . . . The difference between fascism and democracy might be thus stated: In democracy there is a reasonable fighting chance for a minority; while in fascism there is absolutely no chance for a minority. Most of the written rules of democracy are made expressly to protect minorities; in a democracy a negligible minority, or even an individual, may win a decisive victory over the great majority,—in the courts of last resort. This is impossible in a dictatorship,—for the dictatorial power also dominates the judiciary. . . . Negroes sometimes get so vexed at white people, who can sometimes be so very vexing, that the Negro momentarily forgets that his interests ride at least in the very same boat with the interests of the whites. This is our war. We want the continued legal right to strive, even if it is difficult to attain: the right to strive is inspiring, and there is always Hope while there is the right to contend.

If this is true of Negroes in the United States, it is doubly true of Negroes in Africa, as they are nearer the centers of the Totalitarian controls. It must also be remembered that the leader of Nazi Germany has stated in no uncertain terms his view of their status and destiny as the racially inferior slaves of the race of "supermen."

Educated Africans understand this situation. Those who have kept in touch with the native press in Africa in the last two years have informed the Committee that African editors are frequently calling attention to the importance of a victory of the United Nations, even though frankly acknowledging that existing conditions in their colonies need much improvement from the standpoint of native representation and native rights. A characteristic statement of this kind is found in a Gold Coast paper quoted by Dr. Mumford in his article in *Time and Tide* for February 10, 1940, on "The Future of the Colonies."

This is our war even more than it is that of the Poles or the Czechs: Hitlerism symbolizes the glorification of a master-race which is to govern and control in its privileged interests all smaller or weaker races. Hitler has shown us how he treats the weaker races of Europe, he has dubbed us "semi-apes" and implied how he would treat us. We believe that Britain intends that we shall ultimately win self-government and independent status. Let us, then, for the present forget our minor grievances and join with Britain against a common tyranny.

4. WAYS IN WHICH THE UNITED STATES SHOULD HELP

It is believed that in the solution of Africa's problems the United States has a contribution to make from its experience as a "melting pot" of many cultures, religions, and racial groups, including the large population of African descent, and that the successes, limitations, and failures of our experiment in democracy, and their causes, should throw light on African problems, even though it is frankly recognized that the conditions in the two continents are very different.

In view of the fact that the United States is in a position to give experience of value, Americans should also be willing to help make possible and to carry out some of the proposals made in this Report. For example, they should coöperate in every possible way to advance the economic and social-welfare interests of the native population. This will involve substantial expenditures for education, health, housing, irrigation, etc. The promised grants (see p. 50) by Great Britain to its colonies for development and research purposes are encouraging, but they are only beginnings. If the advance of the native population is to be accelerated there will be need during the next decade of more help from outside than the colonies or their European sponsors can alone supply. As a definite demonstration of a worth-while service which should be repeated and extended, reference may be made to the public health work of the Rockefeller Foundation, the surveys of native education by the Phelps-Stokes Fund, and the surveys and other undertakings made possible by the Carnegie Corporation. Lord Hailey's monumental *African Survey* (prepared with its co-

operation) lays special emphasis on the need for further research into African problems, and the British Government has
recently decided to establish a Colonial Research Advisory
Committee to which a maximum of £500,000 a year is to be
allocated for colonial research. Much of this will be spent in
Africa. There are many ways, especially in such fields as scientific agriculture, forestry, and public health, in which American
experience could be of vital help. There is also great need for
the financing of more adequate statistical work so that there will
be more reliable data regarding such facts as births, deaths,
sicknesses, population, urban trends, etc. All this means that
our American foundations, missions, and other agencies should
stand ready to make larger expenditures in behalf of work in
Africa. It is possible also that the United States Government,
through some such plan as that of the Lend-Lease Act, could
aid to a limited extent in encouraging the development of
public works, education, and health and social-welfare services,
not only in a country like Ethiopia, which has suffered so ter-
ribly from the war, but also in other regions of Africa. The
money could be expended by the Governments concerned, or
by some international agency in ways approved by our Government or its duly appointed representatives.

The people of the United States should also favor the participation of their nation not only in developing some representative international organization with the good features,
and without the limitations, of the League of Nations, including in particular its Mandates Section, but also in helping to
make it effective through active membership. They should also
support the International Labor Organization in its efforts to
secure fair labor conditions and wages in Africa, and take pride
in trying to see that African mining and other corporations in
which they are financially interested are conducted with due
regard to the welfare of African workmen.

There are many other ways in which America can help, such
as by showing a sympathetic attitude toward the small but important group of native African students studying in this country; continuing to aid visits here of African leaders—white,
Negro, "Cape Coloured," and others—for study of specific
activities; and taking a special interest in the Republic of
Liberia founded about a century ago as a home for freed

American Negroes. If the Republic—which deserves credit for surviving over such a long period—should decide to invite this country to aid it in the development of its social-welfare activities, especially public health, it would be a field in which our Government and foundations could render notable service. Liberia, as the only independent African republic, has a great responsibility and opportunity. Other African peoples and the outside world are watching her successes and failures with intense interest. This country should consider it a privilege— without in any way interfering with Liberian independence— to aid the Republic in such ways as are acceptable to her Government, to make steady advances in the interest of her own people.

5. Legal Rights and Responsibilities of the United States in Africa

A member of the Committee, Mr. Huntington Gilchrist, formerly Assistant Director Mandates Section, International Secretariat, League of Nations, has prepared the following statement regarding treaties and conventions involving Africa, to which the United States is a signatory.

The Government of the United States has long shown a general interest in the welfare of the people in Africa, concluded treaties with Great Britain in 1862 and 1870 for the suppression of the slave trade, participated in the general international conferences on African affairs at Berlin in 1885 and at Brussels in 1890, and became a party to the Brussels Conventions of 1890 on the slave trade, and of 1899 and 1906 in regard to the liquor traffic in Africa.

It was largely due to the insistence and influence of President Wilson at the Paris Peace Conference in 1919 that the Mandates System was applied to Africa and became effective in practice by reason of the existence of the international machinery of the League of Nations.

At the Paris Peace Conference there were also negotiated with American participation general international conventions replacing the older treaties in regard to the liquor traffic and the Act of Berlin, which provided, among other things, for freedom of trade and navigation, and for freedom of religious, scientific and charitable institutions and missions in the "Congo Basin."

On account of the domestic political controversy concerning the Treaty of Versailles and the entrance of the United States into the

League of Nations, the Government of the United States did not at the time adhere to these conventions of 1919 or take part as a member of the League in the development of the Mandates System.

During the 1920's, however, the Government of the United States negotiated a series of treaties with the African Mandatory Powers (Great Britain, France, and Belgium, but not the Union of South Africa) which recited the text of the Mandates and provided that copies of the annual reports by the Mandatories should be communicated to the United States. These treaties also provided that the United States and its nationals should have all of the rights under the Mandates of a State member of the League of Nations and its nationals, and that these rights could not be taken away by modification of the Mandates without the consent of the United States.

During this same period, the United States adhered to the St. Germain Liquor Traffic Convention of 1919, the Geneva Slavery Convention of 1926 and even (in 1934) the Convention of 1919 which revised the General Act of Berlin of 1885. This Convention among other things provided that "the signatory powers exercising sovereign rights or authority in African territories will continue to see to the preservation of the native population and the improvement of their moral and material condition," and American adherence to this Convention signified the interest of the United States in the fulfillment of these provisions.

More recently American Government representatives, as well as representatives of American employers and employees participated in the Conferences of the International Labor Organization at Geneva at which the following Conventions were adopted: in 1936 on the Recruiting of Indigenous Workers, and in 1939, with the affirmative vote of the American delegates, on Contracts of Employment (Indigenous Workers) and Penal Sanctions (Indigenous Workers). These Conventions were, of course, very largely directed at labor problems in Africa.

The Government of the United States has thus accepted legal rights and corresponding responsibilities in general treaties in regard to parts of Africa (and also in certain special treaties, for instance, with Liberia) and is, therefore, very definitely concerned, for instance, with any plan for a change in the Mandates System as set up by the Covenant of the League of Nations or for new arrangements in regard to the administration of that large belt of Central Africa known as the Congo Basin.

In brief the Government of the United States has for years had increasing legal and political responsibilities for the future of Africa. The American share in the victory in the present war will give the Government of this country added power and responsibility for bringing about a just settlement in all parts of the world, including Africa, insofar as political adjustments or new arrangements may appear advisable.

CHAPTER II

The "Roosevelt-Churchill Eight Points" and Africa's Future

INTRODUCTION—THE ATLANTIC CHARTER AND ITS APPLICABILITY TO AFRICA

Fundamentally, the "Eight Points" as set forth by the President and Prime Minister Churchill in their historic Atlantic meeting of August 14, 1941, are all applicable in varying forms to Africa and Africans. They are now especially significant in view of the fact that they have been accepted by the representatives of all the nations engaged in resisting Nazi aggression. This so-called "Twenty-Six Nation Agreement," proclaimed January 2, 1942, not only "subscribed to a common program of purposes and principles embodied in the joint declaration of the President of the United States of America and the Prime Minister of the United Kingdom of Great Britain and Northern Ireland dated August 14, 1941, known as the Atlantic Charter," but also stated that they were "convinced that complete victory over their enemies is essential to defend life, liberty, independence, and religious freedom, and to preserve human rights and justice in their own lands as well as other lands." This is important as implying a guarantee of religious freedom* and of the conservation of human rights and justice in more specific terms than in the original agreement. Furthermore, the President of the United States in his broadcast to the world February 23, 1942, showed his conviction that the broad policies of the Charter were universally applicable. He said, "The Atlantic Charter applies not only to the parts of the world that border the Atlantic, but to the whole world; disarmament of aggressors, self-determination of nations and peoples, and the four freedoms—freedom of speech, freedom of religion, freedom from want, and freedom from fear." This declaration is particularly

* The Berlin Conference of 1884-85 specially guaranteed "liberty of conscience and religious toleration" in the European colonies of Africa.

important as it supplements, and in a measure supplants, the statement by the Prime Minister in the House of Commons early in September to the effect that

At the Atlantic meeting we had in mind primarily the extension of the sovereignty, self-government and national life of the states and nations of Europe now under the Nazi yoke and the principles which should govern any alterations in the territorial boundaries of countries which may have to be made. That is quite a separate problem from the progressive evolution of self-governing institutions in regions whose peoples owe allegiance to the British crown. We have made declarations on these matters which are complete in themselves, free from ambiguity and related to the conditions and circumstances of the territories and peoples affected. They will be found to be entirely in harmony with the conception of freedom and justice which inspired the joint declaration.

Although the Atlantic Charter—even with the broader implications in the form of its approval in the "Twenty-Six Nation Agreement"—needs supplementing, it is the most authoritative present-day statement of policies to be applied in the international field that has yet been adopted. It is to be hoped that it will become the basis of a covenant among all the nations of the world.

The principal lack in the Charter, in addition to a clear-cut statement about the freedoms of religion, press, and speech, to which attention has already been called, is the fact that it contains no statement as to the international body which must be developed on the basis of the old League of Nations, or independent of it, to promote collective security and to see that the provisions of the new Charter are carried out. Without such a body the Charter will be of relatively little avail. In this connection attention should be called to the conviction of the Committee that it would be both impossible and undesirable for the Peace Conference which follows this war to try to deal with the problems of Africa in detail. This must be left for the formulation of various international commissions of qualified experts which the Conference should itself arrange for, and which should report their recommendations from time to time to the international body determined upon.

It now seems desirable to give the "Eight Points," and to outline some of their more immediate and vital implications for the protection of African rights and for the full development of the native African peoples.

The President of the United States of America and the Prime Minister, Mr. Churchill, representing His Majesty's Government in the United Kingdom, being met together, deem it right to make known certain common principles in the national policies of their respective countries on which they base their hopes for a better future for the world.

1. *"First Point"*—NO AGGRANDIZEMENT

"Their countries seek no aggrandizement, territorial or other."

This assurance is important and must, of course, be applied to Africa in letter and spirit. The policy is revolutionary in world affairs and especially for Africa, which for centuries has so often been the object of various kinds of selfish exploitation, whose results must as far as possible be redressed. The application of the policy in future negotiations will be most difficult.

Recent years have given evidence, under the lead of the Totalitarian Powers, of increasing differences between the European "haves" and "have nots" in Africa, with too little regard for the basic fact that most of the native Africans are themselves the real "have nots." Such differences involve endless possibilities of disputes with accompanying bitterness and strife. On the long view, justification of territorial or other possessions in Africa requires primary regard—in harmony with the mandate principle—for the present and future welfare of the native peoples. Certainly the United States, although it has large commercial interests in Africa, has no desire to annex any African territory. Yet coöperation for and with Liberia has been the long-time American policy and should be continued and increased. Similar coöperation for the full development of the Ethiopian people would also be a worthy policy.

The principle of this first point involves not only the actual abandonment of the policy of territorial aggrandizement wherever it may have existed, but also of any form of commercial aggrandizement at the expense of the native peoples.

The fact that Africans unaided were not in a position to develop their own resources for their own benefit and for that

of the world may have justified in the past some measure of
outside intervention, but it cannot justify in the future any
form of exploitation. Africa must now be developed primarily
in the interest of its own people. The principle of "He must
increase but I must decrease" should be adopted by every outside power in its relation to the African.

2. *"Second Point"*—NEED OF CONSULTING PEOPLE
   CONCERNED BEFORE TERRITORIAL CHANGES

> *"They desire to see no territorial changes that do
> not accord with the freely expressed wishes of the
> peoples concerned."*

In varying and very real forms this peace aim applies to
African areas and populations. Obviously, there are great difficulties in some parts of Africa in the proposal to secure the
"freely expressed wishes" of the native peoples. However, much
can and must be done, for many more or less arbitrary changes
of government controls from outside in the past have had most
unfortunate results, and their repetition must be avoided in the
future. A better way to define and establish territorial boundaries of lands and peoples can be achieved through the "collaboration of nations," including, of course, the collaboration
of the African peoples. Through such means as native councils,
assemblies of chiefs, representatives of native people in Government, Native Affairs Commissions, international and interracial committees, and outstanding missionaries and Africans,
the most intelligent native public opinion has opportunity for
expression. This should be increasingly provided for and obtained in the future.

The application of the essential principle of the "Second
Point" further involves that there shall be no exchanges of territories, as well as no acquisitions of new territories, without
first ascertaining the wishes of the people concerned. There
have been proposals in recent years of forms of union of con-
tiguous colonies which involve very serious problems. For example, it is clear that the British Government could not yield
to the desire of the Union of South Africa to have Southern
Rhodesia incorporated within the Union without adequate
means of assuring the protection of native rights in the Rhodesian territory, as otherwise it would inevitably mean that

the extreme "segregation" policy of the Union of South Africa, and the theory that its development should be primarily concerned with the best interests of Europeans, would be further extended northward. Southern Rhodesia has itself, by referendum vote, turned down the proposal, but it is likely to be made again in modified form. The same is true of the Union's desire to acquire Bechuanaland, Basutoland, and Swaziland, which the British Government has retained under a High Commissioner so as to continue to protect native rights in a way that it fears they might not be protected under the Union Government. Similarly, there have been plans for the union of Kenya, Uganda, and Tanganyika which might result in less satisfactory conditions than now exist for the native population in Uganda and Tanganyika. These are typical of several proposals which have been made in recent years. It is clear that the implications of the "Second Point" should prevent the plans being carried out unless there are more clearly defined guarantees than have yet been proposed as to the protection of native rights.

In this whole matter it must be remembered that the Union of South Africa is anxious to play a dominant part in the future development of African policy south of the Sahara. Although it faces extremely difficult problems in adjusting and protecting the rights of European, Asiatic, Cape Coloured, and native peoples, and has latterly combined some progress with some unsatisfactory steps in matters of adjustment between these groups, it would seem most unfortunate to have its present racial segregation policy extended north. We must realize that it is most difficult for any country which has a very large and dominant settler population to be entirely fair to the needs and rights of a primitive native population. Our historic American experience with the Indian—about which we cannot be proud—has shown this clearly. The peace settlement, as far as the Union of South Africa is concerned, will constitute a specially serious problem because under the leadership of its Prime Minister, Field Marshal Right Honorable Jan Christiaan Smuts, it has played and is playing such a courageous and important part in preventing the victory of the Axis Powers in Africa. Fortunately some recent utterances of this statesman and thinker, and of his outstanding colleague in the Government, the Honorable Jan Hofmeyr, the Minister of Finance and Education, give some promise for a more liberal attitude.*

The Peace Conference will raise many other difficult territorial questions in Africa. For instance, what should be done with Eritrea and such parts of Libya as may remain in Allied hands at the close of the war? It is extremely difficult to be dogmatic on such questions as these, further than to say that all responsible groups in the populations of these territories should be consulted and that major consideration should be given to protecting their interests. It is clear that Ethiopia should have some access to the sea as it had in the past. Such territories as Libya and Eritrea—formerly under Italy—should undoubtedly be placed under some form of mandate control. The mandate question will be discussed in a later section.†

3. *"Third Point"*—FORM OF GOVERNMENT TO MEET WITH POPULAR APPROVAL

> *"They respect the right of all peoples to choose the form of government under which they will live; and they wish to see sovereign rights and self-government restored to those who have been forcibly deprived of them."*

(1) Historical Background

The Africans have, in the last century, had less adequate opportunities for what is called "self-determination" than the inhabitants of any other continent—due in part to complications connected with new forms of governmental and economic control. During the early centuries of European and Asiatic history, geographic barriers excluded the exploiters of those continents from much of the interior of the so-called Dark Continent. Most parts of Africa then experienced the advantages and the disadvantages of the independent control of their own resources and of living their own lives apart from foreign intrusion. Thus Africa continued the simple values and the limitations of its traditional forms of social organization.

Drastic changes in African affairs began about five hundred years ago, although they did not reach their most acute stage

* See *infra*, II, 5, (5). The large increase in appropriations by the Union Parliament for native education since the beginning of this year is most heartening.

† See *infra*, II, 5, (5).

until much later. During the early centuries of this period selfish commercial adventurers from Asia and Europe engaged in vigorous competition for the rich resources and the cheap, although relatively limited, labor supply of Africa south of the Sahara Desert. The historic records of the last century reveal the increasing domination of Africa and Africans by Europeans. Recent events have cruelly demonstrated in the case of Ethiopia how quickly sovereignty can be ruthlessly destroyed by an aggressor nation. Today only the Republic of Liberia, and to varying extents Egypt and Ethiopia, claim governments independent of European control or connection, although the Union of South Africa is an independent nation as a Dominion within the British Commonwealth of Nations.

Recognition must also be given to the movements that have made their healthful and helpful influences felt on the continent in recent decades. Since the beginning of this century colonial Powers have more and more realized their responsibilities for the development of the native peoples. The early period of exploitation is being gradually superseded by the adoption of the principle and the method of trusteeship, or guardianship, for the lives, property, and cultural heritage of Africans. Still more recently there are definite and encouraging evidences, especially in some of the British crown colonies, protectorates, and mandated areas, and in the Free French possessions in Equatorial Africa, of the official recognition of the right of the native peoples to participate in their own traditional forms of government, with only such modifications as modern conditions may demand.

These developments need to be encouraged that there may be a progressive and more effective participation of the African peoples in the various processes of government, including a larger opportunity for their duly chosen representatives to take part in the discussions and actions of Legislative and other councils.* This point is brought out in a memorandum from an African student in this country, who lays a stress, which all of his colleagues would approve, on the need of integrating African public opinion more completely into that of the governing group. He says:

* See development *infra*, IV, 1, (3).

On behalf of 'Africa and the Africans, we appeal strongly to this Committee on Africa and Peace Aims to use its good offices to see to it that due recognition is given to African opinion and African interests in the various reconstruction programs after this war is over. When the need arises, native Africans will be found in many walks of life who are capable, ready and willing to cooperate or participate in formulating educational programs, economic policies, or in social planning for the future, in so far as these plans and policies affect the welfare of Africans.

(2) Stages in Securing Self-government

Although conscious of the long and depressing past of selfish control in many parts of Africa, but encouraged by the hopeful trends toward a larger measure of self-determination in recent years, many thoughtful observers take renewed hope from the demand of President Roosevelt and Prime Minister Churchill that we "respect the right of all peoples to choose the form of government under which they will live." Here is an ideal seemingly as foreign to Africa as the statement in the Declaration of Independence that "all men are created equal" still seems to be in human affairs, and more difficult of realization because of the hundreds of native African tribes—often with inherited animosities and conflicting interests, and in a relatively backward condition. But despite the seeming futility of Jefferson's statement, Americans have been inspired by its ideals of equality and freedom. More and more they are determined that equality of opportunity and of all civic rights before the law shall be won for all men. So also Africans and those interested in their future welfare must be inspired by the democratic ideals of self-realization, self-expression, and ultimate self-determination. Already there are authentic records of significant trends away from complete control and toward trusteeship or guardianship *for* Africans, and for increasing participation *by* Africans in the sovereignty and in the government of their countries.

A fundamental matter to be borne in mind at all times is the ultimate purpose of European governments in those African territories which they control. The British Government is right in its "Statement of Policy on Colonial Development and Welfare," issued in 1940, in which it said: ". . . The primary aim of Colonial policy is to protect and advance the interests of the inhabitants of the Colonies (in which term are included for the purpose of this statement Protectorates and Mandated Territories). . . ."

But this is a general statement which will require much interpretation and implementation. Lord Hailey is more specific. He says that "The political future which British policy has assigned to the African Colonies must be understood to be that of self-government based on representative institutions." The Committee would go somewhat further, and, accepting the view that the purpose in every African colony should be to aid its people with sincere effort to have a steadily increasing share in the determining of governmental policy, would try to indicate the major steps in the process which should be aimed at in most areas. These, as it seems to the Committee trying to take a long look ahead, involve, in addition to the further development of "indirect rule" discussed later, four general stages, at least in the colonies with the most advanced native populations—all necessitating an intensive educational campaign, without which the trained leaders needed cannot be provided.

(a) The increasing representation of native Africans in the Government Civil Service so that they may themselves have training in the methods of governmental administration, and the provision for some African members in every Legislative Council. The immediate steps to be taken will be discussed in a later section.*

(b) The gradual extension of this principle of native participation in Colonial Government to the second stage, in which Africans—aided and guided by competent and sympathetic advisers—might well have a comparable status with Europeans in their own Government, as far as the Legislative Council (or corresponding body) and the administration under the Governor is concerned.

(c) The stage where the native members of the Legislative Council and administrators, under the Governor, will be in the majority, and a beginning made of native membership in the Executive Council where such exists.

(d) The stage† where each colony with its varied important

---

* See *infra*, IV, 1, (3).

† This account of the various "stages" through which most African Colonies may reasonably be expected to pass was prepared before the Editorial Committee had its attention called to Dr. W. B. Mumford's important article on "The Future of the Colonies" in *Time and Tide*, February 10, 1940. In this article he

population groups—all coöperating as far as possible and given adequate representation—will control its own destiny.

When native representation is referred to above it is understood that this will generally involve representation of three types: members nominated by the Government, who should form a relatively decreasing minority; members elected by the duly constituted native electorates, which will vary in composition in different places; and members who hold their positions ex-officio, such as chiefs and various native "notables," who will be specially helpful in integrating the colonial administration and local indirect rule.

These stages are not applicable in just the way indicated to the four self-governing nations of Africa, as conditions in them differ from those in the "colonies." The nearest approach to similar conditions is in Liberia, where, if "Americo-Liberians" are substituted for "Europeans," the conditions are somewhat comparable, for up to the present the native population of the hinterland has not been encouraged to play any considerable part in the public affairs of the Liberian Government. In the other cases conditions differ greatly. Egypt is already governed by the Egyptians, Ethiopia by the Ethiopians, although in each case Great Britain is in a position to exert special influence. Even in these cases there is doubtless need of extending the privileges and duties of self-government to a larger extent to the indigenous local rural groups. In the Union of South Africa (and Southern Rhodesia), with its large population of European descent and its specially complex race problems, conditions, as will be shown in another section,* are radically different, and yet even here the ideals indicated should be borne in mind, and the native Africans, especially in areas where Europeans form only a small minority of the population, given an increasingly large share in administration and legislation.

It is impossible to state how long each of these stages will continue. That will depend very largely on the response of the African people as increased responsibilities are placed upon

said that "There must be publicly laid down in the near future a definite 20-40-60 year plan, leading ultimately, even in the more backward areas, to Dominion status." The two proposals have much in common.
* Appendix I, 5, (2).

them. This will involve highly trained and unselfish native leadership and a large supporting group of people who have had the foundations of a sound modern education. The length of the different periods will also differ largely in different parts of Africa. West Africa, for example, has colonies with many advanced native peoples, and there are to be found there the beginnings of the feeling of nationalism for which the European Power in control should itself be thankful and should try to guide into wise channels. The whole process must be encouraged with great earnestness, although it is evident that in dealing with a people of very different cultural background and without any inherited written literature, and no long experience in the European type of representative government, there should not be undue discouragement if it takes some decades for realization.

What form the governments in Africa should ultimately take cannot be determined in advance. That they must have the representative element is, however, clear. It is also essential that they be able to maintain order and financial solvency, dispense justice, develop wisely social-welfare activities, protect minorities, and observe such agreements as they may enter into with the parent state or the mandate authority.

These suggestions and recommendations regarding representation in government are based on the belief that there are groups of Africans in every African colony of much potentiality, and capable of a larger share in government than they now have; that the capacities of the ordinary African are normal considering his past and present opportunities; and that his development may be largely increased by education, proper health conditions, and experience. This matter will be discussed at greater length in Appendix I, 3, (2). Here it will be sufficient to quote the opinion of one experienced British administrator, the late Lieutenant Governor C. L. Temple of Northern Nigeria:

If we content ourselves with securing for the native peace and plenty, and nothing more, that is much, but it is not all; it is not enough to avert from us, in the long run, the effects of a growing desire for freedom on the part of the conquered on the one hand, and the throes of an unquiet conscience amongst ourselves on the other hand. We must, I submit, do more than that. We must give scope to the higher yearnings of human nature. We must open up channels and opportunities for the exercises of what I have described as the social ambitious instinct. We must permit, within certain limits—and the more they can be gradually extended the better—the native communities to manage their own affairs; we must impede as little as possible the circulation in the body politic and allow the native leader endowed with a legitimate and useful ambition to enjoy to a reasonable extent opportunities for the exertion of his talents.*

If some such ideal or purpose as that outlined for progressive native participation in government is adopted, the question will answer itself as to what type of civilization should ultimately prevail in Africa. This will depend mainly on the native leaders themselves. It will doubtless be close to history and to the soil, retaining much that is best in native tradition and life, but it will also include important features which have been brought to it by European governments and by missionaries.

The accomplishment of this purpose is largely a matter of personnel. Experience shows that the happiness, prosperity, and participation in public affairs of the native population is to a considerable extent dependent on the character of colonial officials—high and low. The former, as mainly responsible for the policies adopted, the latter for their execution, are both in positions of large influence. This is specially true of representatives in the back country, where they come close to the native people and, as "Gods of the Bush," have great influence. Civil servants are generally men of integrity and ability, but they are not always men of much imagination or as sympathetic with native aspirations for advancement as is desirable. Everything possible should be done—in accordance with the best recent practice of the most enlightened European Powers—to secure officials who are known not only for character and ability but for their imagination and broad human sympathies, who are willing to look forward to "career" service. The policy already initiated by Great Britain, France, Belgium, and Portugal, of giving them intensive training in African studies prior to being sent out, is to be recommended and should be further developed.

* Mbadiwe, K. O., *British and Axis Aims in Africa* (1942), p. 68.

4. *"Fourth Point"*—EQUAL ACCESS TO RAW MATERIALS

"They will endeavor, with due respect for their existing obligations, to further the enjoyment of all States, great or small, victor or vanquished, of access, on equal terms, to the trade and to the raw materials of the world which are needed for their economic prosperity."

The competitive desire for the exploitation of the material wealth of Africa has undoubtedly been among the primary causes of unfortunate conditions that have prevailed for centuries within many parts of Africa. Such competition has been partly responsible for impelling foreign nations to bitter strife among themselves. But surely this declaration for the enjoyment by all nations "of access, on equal terms, to the trade and to the raw materials of the world" must be wisely interpreted. Although there is still need for foreign capital for developments under proper State controls, such developments must be subject to the major consideration that the land and its resources belong primarily to the people of Africa and must be administered in the interests of the whole people. This should apply especially to minerals, water power, and forests. Some plan is also worthy of serious consideration by which the profits made by foreign corporations in Africa should be strictly limited, so that more may be available for higher wages and for larger expenditures on social-welfare developments in connection with the housing, education, health, and recreation of native workmen. There is also need in every colony of more effective regulations to prevent all forms of native exploitation.

The declaration of the fourth point should be interpreted to include not only the continued and increased enjoyment by Africans of access to the trade and resources of their own country, but also to a larger measure of free trade between different parts of the continent. In this latter purpose the principles underlying the Congo Basin Treaties might well be extended to include a broader area, and their provisions for freedom of trade further implemented.

With full recognition of the mistakes, injustices, and dangers of economic undertakings in Africa, the elemental truth is that Africa has needed, and still acutely needs, the skills, the experiences, and the financial coöperation of other nations and groups, and especially in the field of modern scientific agriculture. The final test of their value to the African people is the quality of the economic services rendered judged in terms of native welfare. The indiscriminate condemnation of these groups is to be judged on the same basis as thoughtless criticism of economic interests in Europe and America. Their motives and methods are avowedly similar to those of commerce, industry, and agriculture in their home countries, with both good and bad features. It must be recognized, however, that the separation from the corrective influence of public opinion in the more advanced home communities, and the absence of a sense of permanency of abode, have too often stimulated selfish actions. But authentic records reveal illustrations and demonstrations of sound and worthy economic enterprises that have helped to build the better economic foundations so vitally required in Africa. Unfortunately, the number is all too small. Probably David Livingstone, who favored the opening up of Africa—"an open path for commerce and Christianity"—as an aid to the suppression of the slave trade, would, if with us today, while rejoicing in its abolition, realize that such commerce had brought to his Africans much evil as well as much good.

The great responsibility for the immediate and long-time future of Africa requires a more sincere and effective recognition of the rights of African peoples in all economic enterprises, and their full protection. They should be given every opportunity, as their training increases, to develop their own industries and to become proprietors more frequently and on a larger scale than at present. There is also need for experimentation in matters of native economic improvement, such as through the further development of coöperatives—industrial, agricultural, and credit—among the native peoples. Enlightened self-interest is a motive which deserves encouragement. The successes of the Chaga coffee growers in Tanganyika, and of native cocoa producers of the Gold Coast, are encouraging examples of what can be done through native coöperation in labor and industry. Their work should be studied, and their basic principles adopted more generally where conditions permit, especially in the marketing field. Somewhat similar experiments in the

Belgian Congo and French West Africa also deserve study, although these seem to have depended more on government stimulus and less on native initiative.

5. *"Fifth Point"*—ECONOMIC COLLABORATION AND PROTECTION OF LABOR

"They desire to bring about the fullest collaboration between all nations in the economic field with the object of securing for all improved labor standards, economic adjustment and social security."

The implications for Africa of this comprehensive peace declaration should be interpreted to include especially Land Rights, Freedom of Labor, Economic Welfare, Housing, and some form of Trusteeship or mandate protection.

(1) Land Rights

Native peoples in Africa and throughout the world are elementally concerned in their land, the primary source of their economic existence, and one of which they have been all too frequently deprived. The Peace Conference of 1919 defined the vital importance of such rights in the following significant statement: "Sound land policy implies that sufficient ground should be reserved for the present and prospective needs of the people and supervision should be provided to prevent the alienation of the land recklessly to a privileged class of land-owning natives or Europeans." This principle, which has been most inadequately observed in some colonies, needs further strengthening and implementation by adjustments which will assure the native population land of adequate area and satisfactory character, with guarantees against alienation without full mutual consent. Indeed, the alienation of land from native to foreign owners has in some colonies been the cause of serious abuses which have not unnaturally created unrest and at times indignation.

The communal system of land ownership still prevails in most parts of Africa. It is in keeping with native "folkways." It is clear, however, that it must be increasingly supplemented, especially in and near urban centers, by a system of land tenure—within or without communal holdings—which would serve as a stimulus to the thrifty prospective owner and later add to his sense of security. In this connection a system of land holdings on a long lease, or a lease and occupancy basis, might be worked out. In any case it must be more generally recognized both by Europeans and native owners and tenants that land rights carry with them social responsibilities, and that consequently when land is deeded to individuals it is perfectly proper to have a clause outlining safeguards which must not be abused, such as the prevention of over-grazing, careless burning, erosion, etc.

(2) Freedom of Labor

"Improved labor standards, economic adjustment and social security" are vital for the people of Africa. Among their essential rights none is more important than a free choice of employment at a living wage and under decent working conditions. This right is often denied the African, and his lack of economic freedom is aggravated by such practices as organized labor recruiting, contract labor, anti-strike and anti-union laws, etc. Closely related is the right to carry on the trade of his choice, or to cultivate certain crops in competition with the European, or even to maintain a store—rights that are virtually denied him in one or two colonies.

Lack of training for modern industry, the restrictions imposed by the industrial color-bar legislation in certain territories, and the legal obstacles to the development of responsible organizations to protect labor and to conserve its results, are all factors which deserve attention under this Fifth Point. Such policies, for example, as that of excluding Africans from driving trains and doing other skilled work in connection with Northern Rhodesian and other railroads must be modified in keeping with the more liberal policy which prevails in the neighboring Belgian Congo and French Equatorial Africa. In this connection the liberals in South Africa and the Rhodesias are right in trying to abolish those restrictive laws—due in part to white labor unions, which have frequently shown a similar attitude in this country towards the Negro—which virtually aim to confine native labor to the ranks of the unskilled, farm workers, and domestic service.

The Under Secretary of State for the Colonies, Mr. Ball, re-cently made a statement on this subject of the industrial color bar. He said:

It is the accepted policy of His Majesty's Government to give the Africans in Northern Rhodesia, as well as those of all other Dependencies in tropical Africa, opportunities for qualifying for any post or employment for which they are capable, and to supply the requisite educational training. It is important to create condi-tions in which an increasing number of applicants can be trained for large-scale employment—agricultural, medical, educational, technical, legal, clerical, and the like. But we must remember that the pace of this movement depends largely on our ability to pro-vide trained African teachers and give adequate education.

It is to be earnestly hoped that this assurance may eventuate in fairer practices.

It is clear that "forced labor" is never justified except under carefully controlled public auspices for public works, or in the case of some public emergency. There is no objection to the practice, common in rural regions in this country and elsewhere, of requiring a certain amount of local public labor, for instance on roads or irrigation works, in part payment of taxes, subject to the usual form of commutation when desired. But no type of forced labor by any concession or other private corporation should ever be allowed, and such labor, even under public auspices, should be used sparingly and with great caution. Simi-larly, the whole question of the recruitment of labor requires careful study and attention to prevent abuses.

Forced military service on terms other than those applicable to all groups must always be considered a denial of an essential right. Taxation—which for Africans generally means taxes in the form of a flat "hut" or "poll" tax (adult male head tax)— without some form of representation on, or formal right of ap-peal to, the taxing body, also appears to be an infringement of basic civic rights wherever it is practised. Fortunately, in the territories under "indirect" rule, which have been increasing in number, there are generally native councils with more or less large powers, and the tax is frequently collected by the native administration under native treasurers. The question of some closer relation than the existing system of taxation envisages, between taxation and representation, and between taxation, individual income, and social services, is one deserving careful consideration.

The real freedom of the African is mainly involved in land rights, labor freedom, and increasing participation in industry and government. Such rights should be made the constant concern of the International Labor Organization or of some other international organization. In view of the special problems of colonial labor and industry, the I.L.O. would require the further development of its colonial section. It is especially important that in countries where Europeans and East Indians have settled in large numbers the native population should be protected and encouraged in attempts to improve its industrial status. In connection with the whole question of freedom in Africa, it must be remembered that, whereas Westerners have in mind mainly individual freedom, Africans have in mind primarily group freedom. If we are to add the idea of personal freedom it must be incorporated in some way into their pattern of group freedom. This will help to make the transition to new conditions without the likelihood of freedom degenerating into license. The African needs, as much as the American, the constant reminder that freedom involves grave responsibilities.

The problem of compulsion in native labor has recently come to the front in a serious form in East Africa due to war conditions.

In the House of Commons, in the debate on the bill for the conscription of Africans (March 26, 1942) to work on private European farms in Kenya, so as to increase the food supply that might be sent to the United Nations' forces in the East, the proposal was criticized on many grounds, but especially:

That there has been no serious attempt to improve agricultural conditions in the "reserves" with their potentiality for a large increase in crops;

That there would be no difficulty in securing adequate native labor if pay and conditions were suitable;

That there were not adequate guarantees against school boys of 16 being conscripted;

That the adoption of the plan would mean an exodus, including those in war service, up to at least 55% of the population—the legal limit of Africans that can be taken from the reserves;

That there was no provision in the Kenya Legislation for governmental inspection, although the Colonial Office later promised that this would be provided;

That the present wage scale of three and a half pence a day, or twice this amount if various allowances for food, accommodations, etc., are included, was entirely inadequate;

That the bill was adopted without any representatives of the native population sharing in the decision;

That it was contrary to the spirit and of the letter of the terms of the International Forced Labour Convention of 1930, ratified by Great Britain in 1931, which—although allowing for certain modifications in case of war or other emergency—provided among other things that no forced labour was to be used for the benefit of a private person or private company, and that it was not in any case to exceed 60 days in 12 months.

The Under Secretary of State for the Colonies, Mr. Harold Macmillan replying, stated that the Government was entirely opposed to the principle of compulsory native labor under normal conditions, but that in war time compulsory labor had been introduced in England and that it seemed necessary to do the same in Africa so as to provide the Army with the necessary food; that there was no other way of securing the needed additions to the food supply; that the project was not one developed to help the white settlers, but to help the Government; that it had been hedged in with every kind of protective restriction including consultation with native chiefs and other representatives to prevent abuses; that the Government would make sure that the carrying out of the plan would not interfere with school work, and that adequate inspection would be provided; that the Provisional Selection Committee would be composed entirely of Africans; that large responsibilities were placed on the responsible District Commissioners and a carefully selected Exemption Committee; and that every possible effort would be made to improve rations and increase wages. "The sole object of the Colonial Office," said Mr. Macmillan, "is to meet the cry that has come to us from the Middle East and from all parts of the Empire that Africa as everywhere else should play its full role in the immense struggle that lies before us."

(3) Economic Welfare—Agriculture, Industry and "Big Business"

The Committee realizes that the improvement of the economic condition of native Africans is a matter of vital importance, and that it involves much more than land rights and freedom of labor. It will depend largely on the improvement of agricultural conditions, on the development of more effective native industries, on better transportation and other facilities for marketing, and on the adopting of further governmental controls to protect the interests of native workmen in the larger industries.

There is a close relationship between agricultural and industrial development because as a result of modern machinery agriculture tends to employ fewer laborers and industry more, and, although the industrial era is late in coming to Africa, it is on the way. The Government is right in doing everything in its power to improve agriculture. It is in many ways the basic and most healthy form of life. But it must not be indifferent to the needs of industry, both local and on a larger scale. Indeed, if the standard of living of the farm population, which makes up the overwhelming mass of African dwellers, is to be raised, with better tools and some machinery on the farm, there will probably be a surplus of labor, and the slack must be taken up in some way by industry. This has been the history of the past, and there is no other solution. There is, therefore, great need of developing small local industries in the villages of Africa, as in the long run such native industries are essential to the improvement of economic conditions and will do much to counteract the effect of the inevitably disturbing connections with mines or other large industrial enterprises. Small hand mills, coffee dryers, oil presses, and coöperative undertakings of various kinds are all important, but they generally need outside initiative to get them started in wise ways, as well as sympathetic government aid in their development and in the prevention of over-taxation. In this connection a study might well be made by competent persons of the measures adopted in India to develop local industries to see to what extent they are applicable to Africa.

To realize the importance of the economic improvement of Africa we must overcome the prevailing notion that it is an extraordinarily rich continent. Aside from its mines, especially those of gold, copper, and diamonds, this is not true. Over a quarter of it is desert or savannah. It suffers from more pests, such as locusts and tsetse flies, than any similar region in the world. It has tropical diseases of every kind. Its soil, with the exception of relatively few sections, such as the Nile Valley, is not specially rich, and is deteriorating in many places. Its desert area is increasing through the decline of rainfall, due largely to the cutting down of the forests.

Even its greatest financial assets, its Rand Gold Mines, are believed to be very limited in scope, and what will happen to South African economy and to Africans who depend on the mines for cash wages when gold can no longer be produced profitably there, is difficult to say. All this means that much more study, thought, and effort must be given to the problem of improving economic conditions in Africa, which have their basis in the earth, than ever before. As Dr. Shantz in a memorandum to the Committee has stated: Africa has a basis for much development, but "it will need much ingenuity to build up and maintain its productivity." On these accounts the Committee welcomes the "Statement of Policy on Colonial Development and Welfare," presented by the Secretary of State for the Colonies and approved by the British Parliament in February, 1940, in which a fund of £5,000,000 a year for ten years was set apart as a colonial development fund, being five times the amount of previous grants. Attention is called to this clause in the statement:

The first emphasis in this much enlarged policy of Colonial development will be on the improvement of the economic position of the Colonies. That is the primary requirement, upon which advance in other directions is largely consequential. It is by economic development that Colonies will be placed in a position to devote their resources, to the maximum extent possible, to the provision of those Government and other services which the interests of their people demand. . . .

It is only as the economic status of the different colonies can be raised—and this involves in all cases the status of the native population—that the necessary improvements and developments in health, agriculture, and other social-welfare departments can be brought about. This will go back largely to improvement in soil conditions, which in most parts of Africa are not very rich, and are—unless improved by scientific methods—unable to support a large population. There is no way in which the economic condition of most colonies can be more effectively improved than by encouraging the improvement of the soil and sound methods of agriculture. This involves the whole problem of forest protection, re-forestation, the control of grazing, reduction of erosion, water conservation, local irrigation projects, animal husbandry, and the control of pests.

There is no part of the world where there is greater need for the development of the conservation movement than in Africa. This applies to all of its recognized aspects but particularly to forestry and soil conservation, for it is a well-known fact that in large areas of Africa the soil has been greatly decreasing in productivity due to the cutting down of forests, over-grazing, faulty methods of agriculture causing needless erosion, and other factors which have been mentioned. Such tendencies can only be counteracted by a most thorough-going policy of conservation of natural resources. This not only involves a highly trained scientific staff of experts but the winning of the coöperation, through wise extension methods, of tens of thousands of native Africans engaged in agriculture and pastoral life.

Lord Lugard is authority for the statement in a recent article, that the cash earnings of the average peasant in Africa vary from only one to four pounds a year! Until these can be increased no African colony will of itself have sufficient money to develop its social services adequately. The improvement of transportation facilities will also help to develop markets, but in most areas there will be no supply of foods produced, over and above subsistence, to make farms profitable, unless agriculture is improved.

Africa, prior to European intervention, was almost entirely on a subsistence economy—and this should continue to be the basic condition. But owing to only fairly good soil, poor transportation, and poor tools (only the axe and the hoe and a very primitive plow), and poor weapons, support of families on a satisfactory basis was extremely difficult. Such a condition could not continue indefinitely as long as there were undeveloped resources which Africa itself and the world needed, and which the Africans, unaided, were not in a position to make use of. Foreign capital, foreign experts, and foreign methods were all essential, but the difficulty was to make use of these without the serious dangers involved in absorbing native economy, exploiting native labor, and alienating native land. The historic process of securing the needed results in ways entirely fair to Africa and Africans has been a long and arduous one, and is still going on, with the native population not yet receiving an adequate proportion of the proceeds of its toil. This is a matter which deserves the prompt and sympathetic attention of all corporations and governments concerned.

Lord Lugard's theory of the "Dual Mandate"—that a colony should be developed both in the interest of its own people and of the world as a whole—has much to commend it, as long as emphasis is placed on considering the needs and welfare of its people first.

It is necessary to make a much sharper differentiation than has been done in the past between legitimate commerce and trade development on the one hand, and exploitation on the other. In the former category may be included the activities of businesses large and small which provide Africa and Africans with needed supplements to their food supply, implements of labor, books, motor cars, machinery for the building of roads and the development of mines, equipment for hospitals and schools, medicines, and all kinds of supplies for the governments concerned, as well as with needed utilities and public works. These latter, however, will probably be increasingly undertaken by the State. But it must be understood that these enterprises are conducted in conformity with law and under proper controls to safeguard the native population.

Under the category of exploitation those corporations should be included which are in Africa primarily for the purpose of exploiting its resources and native labor in the interest of European and American capitalists. Such corporations may render, incidentally, important services in providing not only employment but large sources of public revenue through taxes, but in spite of improvements in recent years there is still evidence that many of them have a serious debit side to the ledger, as they tend to care less about native welfare than they do about dividends. Their profits are often very large, and yet a relatively small percent goes into an adequate increase in wages, improved housing conditions, and social-welfare activities. Such corporations must be placed under the more definite influence, so far as labor conditions and wages are concerned, of the International Labor Office. Native organizations to protect their own labor must be permitted, and aided rather than discouraged by Government. The fact that the owners of the largest properties are non-residents not only of the country but of the continent makes the danger all the more acute. They are not subject to the same curbs and controls of law and public opinion as they would be in their homeland. Indeed, the whole relationship between European and American capital and Negro labor, involving high profits, low wages, and cheap raw materials, is an extremely complicated one and full of danger. Fortunately the old type of commercial concession, with virtual state powers, is becoming increasingly a thing of the past in Africa. The Portuguese Government has just announced that the franchise of the most influential corporation in Mozambique is not to be renewed, and other large monopolistic concessions have little by little disappeared, but in their place have often come organizations of industry with more restricted franchises but with inadequate public control.

(4) Housing

The housing of the rural African is a problem which will largely take care of itself with the improvement of education, and of general economic and health conditions. This, however, is not true of urban housing, where there is a vital need for public aid in improving conditions. The seriousness of the general situation is shown by the fact that under existing laws native Africans in towns are required to live in "locations" or other special areas set apart for them, except in a few cases such as household employees. Much has been done in recent years in towns like Johannesburg, Elizabethville, and other places with a large native population, but far more remains to be done if the so-called "locations" and other native residential areas are to be not only sanitary but to provide conditions where families may live with a reasonable degree of decency and comfort. In the case of many industrial towns it is not only that there are inadequate homes available but that the wages are too small to permit families to live in most urban areas with due regard to the basic needs of their children. General Smuts in a recent address has called attention to the unsanitary conditions of natives in these centers in South Africa, and has added that "Taking the big town, all the facts went to show that the African could not support a family in most places on the wage he received." Unfortunately also very few of the native Africans who migrate to the mines are able to secure decent housing conditions for a family, so this means the breaking up of homes, with all its attendant demoralization. There are, according to Hailey, only 1,518 native married quarters for the 300,000 native miners on the Rand.

Closely related to housing is, of course, the whole problem of adequate nutrition and health service, especially for children, and the need of adequate recreation facilities for families and for domestic servants, now almost wholly lacking in large urban centers.

(5) Protective Guarantees—Trusteeship and Mandates

Ever since the mandate principle was made a part of the Versailles Peace Treaty and implemented by the League of Nations at the close of the last war, there has been an extension in Africa of the idea of trusteeship or guardianship—that is to say, some one of the more "advanced" nations of the world assumes the responsibility for the native people placed under its protection and leadership, to improve their condition, and fit them for self-government.* This involves, particularly, appropriate education and an increasing experience in governmental participation.

The extent to which this general idea has taken root and grown is shown by a courageous utterance made on January 21 of this year at a public meeting in Cape Town, under the auspices of the South African Institute of Race Relations, by General Smuts, Premier of South Africa, who is himself credited with originally advising the mandate plan. It is heartening to find the recognized leader of South Africa, which has been on the whole so backward in interracial matters, taking as the subject for his address "The Basis of Trusteeship," and saying that the whole question of race relations must be taken "out of the heated atmosphere of politics and controversy." He shows

---

* Mandate conditions are given in Appendix II.

how the battle has gone on in South Africa between those who advocated "equality" as the only proper relation, and those who have taken the ground of the "superior race," but says that as a result of a hundred years of this controversy there has been "little result and little good for the country." He shows the connection between this idea and that of the "master people" theory of Nazism, and says that this latter is "really going back to the old, discarded form of slavery." He frankly acknowledges that the results of the "segregation" theory in South Africa, based largely on the "master race" idea, have been disappointing. He now advocates closer contacts between various sections of the people, on the ground that "Isolation has gone and I am afraid segregation has fallen on evil days too." This latter remark was greeted with special applause!

He feels that the concept of trusteeship, rightly understood, is the way out, but that it should be considered as being definitely "for the benefit of the ward," and not of the trustee, and that "'If the Trustee exploits his ward he breaks his trust and neglects the duty which rests on him." He calls attention to the sacred character of this trust and says that "Hard as it may be, it is the conception we have to make real if ever we are to have success and happiness in this country." He also refers to the failure of the South African people to recognize this obligation to the native population, especially in matters of education, health, housing, and improved economic conditions. He says that to him it is an "outrageous view" that South Africa was looked upon as though it included merely the two million or so white population. This seems to imply that the Africans "did not count," or "were not worth counting." He closed by making a strong appeal for "a spirit of helpful coöperation" between Europeans and Africans. The address was stimulating and highly encouraging.

It is important in connection with realizing its significance to remember the point of view of the old Boer population. This, as embodied in the original Constitution of the Transvaal, was to the effect that "There shall be no equality between black and white, either in church or state." The Boer position has always been that not only should white and black be kept entirely separate, with the blacks segregated "in their place," but that this arrangement was to be considered as permanent, without any real opportunity for the black man, no matter what his character or talents, to rise to any position of political or economic equality with his white neighbors. This is at the opposite extreme from the French position which has set an example by drawing no color line in schools, industry, or the Civil Service.

It is worth while noting that Lord Harlech, High Commissioner for the South African Protectorates, formerly as the Right Honorable William Ormsby-Gore, Under-Secretary of State for the Colonies, in proposing a vote of thanks, added, what was of course the serious omission in General Smuts's statement, "That the true conception of trusteeship was that of a guardian for a *ward who would eventually come of age*"* (italics ours).

"Collaboration of Nations" in a definite form may well imply mandates with some effective type of international inspection and report, and with guarantees to supplement, or possibly in some cases to replace, those now existing. Some friends of Africa have urged such "collaboration" to bring at least the advice of the best international experts to bear on African problems, and to help prevent inequalities and injustices too frequently thwarting the progress of the native peoples.

It is significant that Christian leaders of Britain, including Anglicans, Catholics, and Non-conformists, have recently proclaimed as a peace aim: "That international institutions must be created or recast to insure the loyal and faithful execution of international agreements." Of course the stability and success of any such international organization will require a broad and comprehensive arrangement for the coöperation of a sufficient number of nations, including our own, sincerely and effectively devoted to the principle and method of international federation.

The Committee believes that all colonial areas in Africa should be under some form of international mandate inspection and report, and that all such areas should pass through the stages of guardianship and participation in government, leading to autonomy. Further than this it believes that international administration should be introduced into those colonies

---

* This address is found in the *South African Outlook*, February 2, 1942. It has also been printed as a pamphlet by the South African Institute of Race Relations.

—not including independent states such as Ethiopia—which have changed hands or which may change hands during the war; and that similarly such administration might well be tried in some other area or areas. The Committee believes that conquered territories in Africa should not be considered as spoils of war.

It is self-evident that until and unless the present German Government is overthrown and its successor disclaims Nazi racialism, it will be impossible for Germany to become a Mandatory Power in Africa. The same holds true both of Italy and Japan—the latter a Power which has in recent years gained a strong commercial hold on East Africa. It is the opinion of the Committee that there should be native African representation on any International Mandates Commission which may be established dealing with African territory and problems.

A significant analysis and proposal regarding the type of Colonial Charter needed to safeguard the interests of colonial peoples in keeping with the ideals of the Mandates plan has recently been published in England by "Political and Economic Planning." It says that:

International agreement is needed on the interpretation of the trusteeship principle itself. This would be best accomplished by the promulgation of a Colonial Charter. Such a Charter should be neither detailed nor lengthy. It need affirm only the following points: (1) that colonial dependencies are held in trust; (2) the primary aim of the trusteeship is to enable the dependencies to attain self-government as rapidly as possible; (3) the second major aim is the development of colonial territories primarily for the benefit of their own inhabitants; (4) the trusteeship is exercised jointly by all countries included in the international organization, but delegated, as far as administrative responsibilities go, to powers with colonial experience; (5) no inherent or permanent inequality exists between races or peoples, and equal status and equal opportunity for all is a goal to be realized as speedily as possible; (6) all nations adhering to the international organization shall have equality of economic opportunity in the colonies, and also of all other opportunity, subject only to the need for maintaining efficient administration.*

The same group well defines the aim of colonial policy in tropical dependencies:

* *Planning*, No. 184, January 20, 1942.

The aim should be to substitute for the chaos resulting from nineteenth-century imperialistic colonial expansion a system designed to eliminate the jealousies of the industrially advanced nations, to promote the development of tropical areas in the interests primarily of their own populations, but also of the rest of the world, and to facilitate the progress of the non-self-governing territories toward self-government. If it is essential for world prosperity that the rate of tropical development should be quickened, it is equally essential for any stable peace settlement that the thorny political problem of colonies should find a solution.

6. *"Sixth Point"*—DESTRUCTION OF NAZI TYRANNY, AND FREEDOM FROM FEAR AND WANT

> *"After the final destruction of the Nazi tyranny, they hope to see established a peace which will afford to all nations the means of dwelling in safety within their own boundaries, and which will afford assurance that all the men in all the lands may live out their lives in freedom from fear and want."*

"Final destruction of Nazi tyranny"—which seems essential if native Africans are to be protected against the extreme racial doctrines stated in *Mein Kampf* and other Nazi utterances—should pave the way for an end of the vicious principle and method of "might makes right," which today seem to threaten all peoples. "Dwelling in safety within their own boundaries" and "assurance that all the men in all the lands may live out their lives in freedom from fear and want" are important statements. As indicated in the discussion of the Fifth Point, there has been long-time anxiety as to the possession of their land—a "haunting fear" that it may be taken away from them—and also fear of the constant infringement on their personal freedom. This has kept Africans in many territorial areas in a deplorable state of insecurity. In addition to these limitations there have been the fears associated with witchcraft and many other forms of superstition. Much of the African heritage is rooted, as Lord Hailey states, "in the influence of the spirit world on daily life and in the importance attached to the use of magic." Surely the objective of "freedom from fear and want" for the African people is comprehensive and realistic. It must include every type of human relationship—economic, social, educational, and religious.

To make the ideal more realistic let us use some imagination in looking at the world from the standpoint of a thoughtful African who knows that a foreign Power is in possession of his territory and is largely responsible for determining its destiny and his welfare. To him "freedom from fear" may well mean fear that the old cultures, arts, and institutions of the past, which tradition has handed down, may be lost, and nothing suitable to their folkways substituted; fear that his family may lose their lands to Europeans who wish them for coffee growing or some other purpose for which they are especially suited; fear that young people will be drawn away from the old restraints of tribe, clan, and family, and placed in dangerous new surroundings in distant parts of Africa in mining or other industrial operations; fear that the "overlord" does not really mean what he says as to help in fitting him for self-government in a better state than he has ever known; fear that the vote that he or his representative has given for the chieftainship may be overthrown by the Government in favor of someone who is more tractable; fear that he will not get his share of the benefits from public works, and educational, health, and social-welfare services, supported in considerable part by native taxation; fear that the introduction of modern "civilization" may upset domestic economy and tradition. It would be unfair to say that such fears are generally justified, but we must have enough imagination to see that they are often real.

"Freedom from fear and want." As Africa is not, on the whole, a land with a rich soil, and as methods of agriculture are generally primitive, a large proportion of Africans are still living on the borderland of want. They fear the day when their lack of ready cash will be so great that they cannot secure the simple implements, tools, and seeds needed for productive agriculture. They fear that they will not have the money to meet the taxes that are imposed. They fear that their children may want medical attention and education. They fear, especially in industrial centers, where subsistence farming is impossible and where wages are low, that they cannot provide their children with nourishing food.

If President Roosevelt is right in saying that one third of

the American people had been "ill-fed, ill-clad, ill-housed," surely the proportion is very much greater in Africa, even considering the simple wants of the native population. The wolf is more frequently at the door, and to be relieved of "fear and want" would be an indescribable boon. The goal is practicable under an intelligently conducted economic and social system.

7. *"Seventh Point"*—FREEDOM OF THE SEAS AND OF TRAVEL

"Such a peace should enable all men to traverse
the high seas and oceans without hindrance."

Though Africa—outside of Egypt and South Africa—has practically no ships fitted to traverse the oceans, the Africans and their friends depend upon the high seas and air lines for contact with the achievements and the inspirations of other continents. During the early centuries Africa lived too much alone, and—outside of Mohammedan influences in the North—too far removed from the great trends and exchanges of civilization, especially those of science, education, art, and religion. While the isolation had advantages in permitting the Africans to develop their own native culture, the exclusion from worthwhile developments in Europe, Asia, and America has retarded participation in the advance of civilization. International commerce in such ways as will improve the economic status of the native African and be fair to all nations and groups, as well as international travel to broaden horizons, are highly important.

This will help accomplish the purpose outlined by Professor DuBois in a suggestive memorandum prepared for the Committee, in which he says that "The great problem facing the World is to achieve such wide contact of human cultures and mutually beneficent intercourse of human beings as will gradually by inspiration, comparison and wise selection evolve the best civilization for the largest number of human beings." To accomplish this purpose, which involves international travel and exchange of views, he says that "there is need of a great crusade, a religious mission. . . ." This is absolutely true, although it does not require that all human groups should adopt the same customs and beliefs.

In this connection it is hoped that those parts of Africa which place hindrances in the way of visits by entirely responsible educated American Negroes may change their policies. There is no serious trouble in most colonies, but the existing situation in this respect in the Union and some other areas has caused an unfortunate impression in thoughtful circles in this country. It has only been with great difficulty, and due to the earnest efforts of a few liberally minded statesmen, that it has been possible to make any exception to the Union's practice of excluding the residence of Negro American missionaries or the visits of Negro American students. As a help to making this possible, all organizations in the United States which have anything to do with Africa should use special care to send out as their agents, representatives, and missionaries—both white and colored—men and women who will be constructive and helpful in their attitude on complex social problems.

8. "Eighth Point"—ABOLITION OF FORCE AND PROVIDING PERMANENT SYSTEM OF SECURITY

> "They believe that all of the nations of the world, for realistic as well as spiritual reasons, must come to the abandonment of the use of force. Since no further peace can be maintained if land, sea or air armaments continue to be employed by nations which threaten, or may threaten aggression outside of their frontiers, they believe, pending the establishment of a wider and permanent system of general security, that the disarmament of such nations is essential. They will likewise aid and encourage all other practicable measures which will lighten for peace-loving peoples the crushing burden of armaments."

"For realistic and spiritual reasons, [all nations] must come to the abandonment of the use of force" is an inspiring pronouncement by the representatives of such powerful nations. "For spiritual reasons" is of special significance to those who firmly believe that in the long view such reasons are the most realistic of all. Only as mankind has faith in the Divine Order and in the sacredness of human personality can there be faith that humanity will ultimately acquire an attitude of mind that will hate war and "come to the abandonment of the use of force" in the settlement of international affairs.

To achieve this goal will require a long period of education, in which a specially heavy responsibility will rest on the people and Government of the United States, to help plan and carry out some effective method to prevent the international economic rivalries of the past and to assure collective security. The United States can never again be selfishly isolationist. The various experiences—both favorable and unfavorable—of the League of Nations, the World Court, and the International Labor Organization should, with our aid, point the way to some plan that will conserve their advantages without their limitations. Furthermore, under a practical program of gradual but real disarmament brought about by faith in the spiritual verities, by a realization that competitive armament resulting in war can only end in the destruction of civilization itself, and by education and constructive effort, the world can achieve the overthrow of the principle that "might makes right" and carry out the implications of the belief in the Fatherhood of God and the Brotherhood of Man.

The Committee, being opposed to the imperialistic use of the troops of any race anywhere, is naturally opposed in principle to use of conscripted troops from African colonies in Europe or other continents, or of similar troops from Europe or other continents in African colonies—except as they may be members of an international police force.* In this connection Africa might well make its contribution to the attempt to prevent future wars by endeavoring to restrict its troops to policing and the maintenance of order. The large use in Europe and elsewhere of native conscripted troops from North Africa (Algiers) and Senegal has been open to criticism both on the part of Africans and Europeans. It should, however, be remembered in fairness to the French that these Negro soldiers are French citizens from the "colony" area and that this conscription does not apply to the ordinary "unassimilated" native population.

There are certain other implications of this point with reference to African conditions which seem worthy of special mention. After referring to "all of the nations of the world" it

* There is nothing in this statement that is intended by the Committee as a criticism of the military efforts being made by the United Nations in the present crisis to prevent the conquest of Africa and the world by aggressive Totalitarianism under the lead of Nazi Germany.

speaks of the need of their establishing "a wider and permanent system of general security." This, taking into account also the reference under the Fifth Point to "the fullest collaboration between all nations in the economic field," clearly looks to some world organization at the close of the war.

The Committee is convinced that the new world order will involve more limitations than we have had in the past in the scope of national political sovereignty everywhere. This should be borne in mind as we face the future of African states. In the politico-military sense they should, and probably will, along with other states, have less exclusive self-determination than in the past—that is, looking forward to the time when African states will have a status similar to other states. Such considerations lead to a realization that, although it is right and proper that Africans should be encouraged to look forward to having a much larger share in determining their own policy, this must always be subject to the general plans for world collective security and policing that are decided upon. In a word, each nation, race, creed, or other constituted minority, should have full cultural autonomy, but this should not involve complete self-determination in the political field, as this would result in the revival of extreme forms of nationalism, which must be discouraged. After outlining the need of imposing limitations on political state sovereignty so as to secure collective security, Professor Malinowski writing to the Committee rightly said: "The nation as the culturally integrated group, that is integrated by language, tradition, way of life, and its specific institutions, must be given more and not less freedom."

Furthermore, in the interest of international coöperation within Africa it would be of the greatest importance if there could be more contact and interchange of views between people of different colonies, not only of those under a single European Power but between responsible leaders in French, British, Belgian, and Portuguese colonies. At present there is all too little knowledge by one group of what other groups are doing. It is particularly important that government officials, especially Commissioners of Native Welfare and some of the higher officials, should meet to pool their information and wisdom from time to time. There has been a beginning of intercolonial meetings in the past by the Governor's Conferences in the British colonies and protectorates in East Africa coming together in Nairobi, and similarly in the Governor's Conferences in West Africa at Lagos, but it would be helpful to go further, extending the membership and the scope of subjects discussed. For instance, the French and Belgians have contributions to make to the British, and vice versa. In the past the difficulties and expense of travel have been prohibitive, but the improvements in transportation which the war is bringing about will have their permanent effect, and there are places, such as Elizabethville, for example, where it would not be impossible to get important groups from different parts of Africa together. It would also be helpful if representative native Africans could be invited to take part in the discussions. Such a gathering might well be the precursor of a future African Congress, and this in turn might in time lead to General Smuts's dream of a United States of Africa. It must be realized, however, that such a dream could never become highly significant unless its governing bodies include native as well as European members.

The effect of the war has already been to draw most of those parts of Africa south of the Sahara closer together, especially in the field of economic coöperation. An East African Economic Council was established in 1940. Since that time there have been other important intercolonial trade developments, especially between the Free French territory, the Belgian Congo, and the Union of South Africa, and even between Kenya and the Congo.

In keeping with this general idea of interchange of opinion, few things have been of more significance to Africa than the LeZoute Conference in Belgium on "The Christian Mission in Africa," held in 1926. This was highly important in bringing government officials, especially from French, British, and Belgian colonies, together, along with missionaries, representative Africans, and American white and colored people interested in Africa. The results at LeZoute in developing a wise policy for native education, public health, and other social-welfare services, were notable. It would be distinctly worth while if such a conference—organized on the broadest possible lines so as to include representatives of all important national, racial, and religious groups interested in Africa—could be held again a few years after the war, preferably in Africa itself.

CHAPTER III

Comparison of Various Peace Plans and Their Application to Africa

The significance of the Atlantic Charter is emphasized by the numerous peace pronouncements recently made by social and religious organizations in the United States and Great Britain. Conscious of mistakes and injustices of peace negotiations in the past, and of the failure to carry out some of their constructive suggestions, students of international relationships are eagerly exploring the essentials for a sound and lasting peace when the horrors of this present war are ended. Historic records and recent experience reveal that the welfare of Africa has been often neglected in the proposals and plans for peace. But Africans and their friends assume that Africa is included in the Roosevelt-Churchill declaration that "peace will afford to all nations . . . assurance that all the men in all the lands may live out their lives in freedom from fear and want."

In view of the vital implications of the declaration by the official spokesmen of the two great democracies as confirmed and supplemented by the "Twenty-Six Nation Agreement," it is important to ascertain the relationship of such official pronouncements to the views and convictions expressed by representative social and religious leaders and organizations interested in world problems. Do the official declarations reflect the ideals and basic beliefs of the two nations and of the people in general? The answer to this searching question requires an examination of various significant peace plans. Among those recently proposed, the following are under such distinguished and authoritative sponsorship as to merit the special consideration of those whose major interest is in the improvement of economic and social conditions:

President Roosevelt—"The Four Freedoms."
British "Ten Points" by Anglicans, Catholics, and Nonconformists.

Pope Pius XII—"Peace and the Changing Social Order."
American Friends Service Committee—"Dynamic Methods
    and Peace."
National Study Conference, convened in March, 1942, at
    Delaware, Ohio, by the Federal Council of Churches'
    "Commission to Study the Bases of a Just and Durable
    Peace"—Statement of Guiding Principles.

For the purposes of this discussion it seems desirable to sum-
marize all the aims of the various plans and relate them to the
welfare and destiny of Africa. To this end, the points have been
assembled under five comprehensive aims:

1. SPIRITUAL BASIS OF PEACE

"For realistic as well as spiritual reasons, [all nations] must
come to the abandonment of the use of force." This is the one
definite reference to the "spiritual" in the Roosevelt-Churchill
Declaration, although "freedom of religion" was added when
this was ratified by the Twenty-Six Nations Agreement. In a
sense it is the climax of the "Eight Points." Naturally, Pope
Pius and the British Christian leaders emphasize the imperative
necessity of acknowledging the "unchangeable order of God,"
and the "holy and unshakable rules of divine law" in human
affairs. British leaders urge that the "resources of the earth be
used as God's gifts to the whole human race." The Pope proclaims that "Goods were created by God for all men." American churchmen, in their National Study Conference, proclaimed
as their first guiding principle:

WE BELIEVE that moral law, no less than physical law, under-
girds our world. There is a moral order which is fundamental and
eternal, and which is relevant to the corporate life of men and the
ordering of human society. If mankind is to escape chaos and recur-
rent war, social and political institutions must be brought into
conformity with this moral order.

President Roosevelt's "freedom of every person to worship
God in his own way" is emphatically an essential to the higher
life of man. Nothing is more fundamental in human relationships than the ethical and religious attitudes of individuals
and groups toward each other. Nothing is more realistic in
human affairs than faith in the universe and faith in the

Divine Order. Surely peace proposals must be rooted in the spiritual faiths of mankind and must guarantee religious freedom. As missionaries are primarily concerned with the spiritual and ethical elements of life, their rights to serve the African people should be guaranteed. It is in accordance with the American Bill of Rights, whose sesquicentennial we have just celebrated, that religious freedom should be the first mentioned, although in Africa it has been less overlooked than some other fundamental rights.* This should involve toleration of and freedom for all religions, both native and foreign, with due appreciation of the vital importance of religion, especially of the Christian religion, in developing and maintaining ethical standards; and of the rights of all missionaries both in preaching and education—all subject only to the usual qualification that practices inconsistent with social welfare may be disallowed. The freedom granted missionaries carries with it a heavy responsibility. They should remember that they are primarily the representatives of the churches, and that although loyal to their respective governments, they should not use their freedom for nationalistic propaganda or exploitation, as has occasionally been charged.

Missionaries of one group should always show respect and consideration for those of other groups, and there should be as large a degree of coöperation in organizing and carrying on their work as the tenets of the various religious bodies permit. They should also work in sympathetic coöperation with the representatives of Government and with the tribal authorities. It is also just as important that they should have training in African studies before going to Africa, as in the case of government officials. Conferences between missionaries of the same area with each other and with missionaries of different areas, and occasional visits of inspection from responsible persons in the home land, are also distinctly worth while.

2. RIGHTS OF THE INDIVIDUAL AND THE FAMILY

The "Four Freedoms" as proclaimed by President Roosevelt are strong and definite in their advocacy of the rights of the individual:

---

* This is guaranteed by the Berlin Convention of 1885.

"Freedom of speech and expression."

"Freedom of every person to worship God in his own way."

"Freedom from want."

"Freedom from fear."

British Christians declare:

"Every child, regardless of race or class, should have equal opportunities for education."

"The family as a social unit must be safeguarded."

"The sense of a divine vocation must be restored to man's daily work."

The Pope proclaims:

"The power of the state does not imply a power so extensive . . . that public authority can interfere with the evolution of the individual. This would mean falling into the error that the proper scope of man is society, that society is an end in itself."

Said the National Study Conference:

"WE BELIEVE that the right of all men to pursue work of their own choosing and to enjoy security from want and oppression is not limited by race, color or creed. The rights and liberties of racial and religious minorities in all lands should be recognized and safeguarded. Freedom of religious worship, of speech and assembly, of the press, and of scientific inquiry and teaching are fundamental to human development and in keeping with the moral order."

On the long view, the preservation and development of individuality is the ultimate test of freedom. Intimately and vitally related to the rights of the individual are the rights of the family. The menace of dictatorship and totalitarianism is particularly in the destruction of individuality and of inherited family responsibilities. Lasting peace must guarantee personal freedom and a genuine regard for the individual and the family. All this needs special emphasis in Africa, where the large majority of people is governed by nations whose capitals are far distant in another continent.

3. ECONOMIC WELFARE AND RIGHTS

"No aggrandizement of property," "access to trade and resources on equal terms," "collaboration in the economic field to secure improved labor standards, economic advancement and social security"—these are the economic objectives of the Atlantic Charter. British Christians urge that "the extreme inequality of wealth should be abolished," "that the resources of the earth should be used with due consideration for the needs of present and future generations." The American Friends Service Committee insists that "all nations shall be assured equitable access to markets." Pope Pius declares any "so-called civil progress as unnatural which renders private property void of significance." One of the guiding principles of the Delaware Conference was

that economic security is no less essential than political security to a just and durable peace. Such security nationally and internationally involves among other things the use of material resources and the tools of production to raise the general standard of living. The possession of natural resources should not be looked upon as an opportunity to promote national advantage or to enhance the prosperity of some at the expense of others. Rather such possession is a trust to be discharged in the general interest.

In such peace aims both governmental and non-governmental representatives united in considering economic rights as essential to a just and lasting peace.

Freedom from want and the guarantee of economic security are the fundamental rights of individual and community. Adequate food, clothing, and dwelling are elemental necessities of all. No peace is permanent without the provision of access on equal terms to all resources necessary to existence, comfort, and security. Such a policy requires that special attention be given to the question of land use—that no native African fitted to support himself by agriculture be denied access to land adequate in extent and quality—and to the whole matter of protecting more fully the interests of the African worker.

4. INTERNATIONAL COÖPERATION

International coöperation as an imperative peace aim is urged or implied throughout the "Eight Points." The ideal of "collaboration between all nations" is repeated in varying forms in the Atlantic Charter, especially in the reference to a "wider and permanent system of general security." The most definite statement on the subject is the declaration of the British Christian leaders that "international institutions must be created or recast to insure the loyal and faithful execution of international agreements." The American Friends Service Committee urges international mandates, arbitration, general disarmament, and the conviction that "economic and social policies which affect other nations must be determined in international consultation." The appalling destruction of life and property throughout the world makes effective international coöperation imperative in removing the causes of war if what we call civilization is to be preserved. "We believe," said the American churchmen at their National Study Conference,

that the principle of cooperation and mutual concern, implicit in the moral order and essential to a just and durable peace, calls for a true community of nations. The interdependent life of nations must be ordered by agencies having the duty and the power to promote and safeguard the general welfare of all peoples. A world of irresponsible, competing and unrestrained national sovereignties whether acting alone or in alliance or in coalition, is a world of international anarchy. It must make place for a higher and more inclusive authority.

5. DISARMAMENT AND THE ABOLITION OF FORCE IN THE SETTLEMENT OF INTERNATIONAL DISPUTES

The eighth objective of the Atlantic Charter is both emphatic and definite in the declaration that "all nations of the world must come to the abandonment of the use of force." Equally definite are the British Christian leaders—including Anglicans, Catholics, and Non-conformists—that "disarmament must be mutually accepted, organic and progressive, both in letter and spirit." Civilization must effectively abandon the method and principle "that might makes right." The reëmergence of this principle in world affairs is the tragedy of this generation and indeed of the century. Past efforts to abolish the use of force as "an instrument of national policy," as provided for in the Kellogg-Briand Pact, have failed, but the attempt must be earnestly made again. On the matter of armaments, the National Study Conference declared that military establishments should be internationally controlled and be made subject to law under the community of nations. For one or more nations to be forcibly deprived of their arms while other nations retain the right of maintaining or expanding their military establishments can only produce an uneasy peace for a limited period. Any initial arrangement which falls short of this must therefore be looked upon as temporary and provisional.

The cruelty and injustice inherent in the policy of Nazism, Fascism, and Japanese militarism call emphatically for progressive disarmament after peace has been effectively reëstablished.

6. GENERAL CONCLUSIONS

Now that the objectives of the five peace plans have been grouped under five general aims, the significance of these aims for the formulation of the ultimate peace terms, bearing in mind the needs of the world and especially the welfare of the African people, may be considered. The following observations are submitted as a help in answering this important question:

The essential wisdom of the peace plans under consideration is assured by the elemental character of the general aims which they believe that peace should guarantee. The review of the five aims seems sufficient to confirm the truth of this observation in relation to Africa.

Another evidence of the wisdom of the peace plans is the substantial agreement of the objectives as proposed by the Atlantic Charter, the President's Four Freedoms, the British Christian leaders, the Pope Pius Declaration, the American Friends Service Committee, and the National Study Conference. Such harmony of convictions reflects the sincerity and unity of the divergent groups now advocating these fundamentals of a lasting peace.

The final and searching test of the sincerity and effectiveness of these peace plans from the standpoint of this Committee is the extent to which they are to be applied in behalf of Africa and Africans. Surely the official spokesmen of the great democracies and the representatives of the great religions are including Africa and Africans in their proclamation that peace should afford to all nations the assurance "that all men in all lands may live out their lives in freedom from fear and want."

CHAPTER IV

Basic Rights and Social Essentials for African Welfare

With full appreciation of the peace aims of the Atlantic Charter and the similar declarations of the great social and religious organizations, it seems now desirable to record the basic rights and social essentials necessary to the welfare and full development of the African people. Even though such a summary requires a repetition of some of the peace aims already discussed, such repetition is justified in order to make sure that the record of rights and social essentials may be based on the actual conditions and needs of the African people.

1. BASIC RIGHTS OF NATIVE AFRICANS

In this brief summary it is obvious that only the more elemental rights can be listed. We should also remember that all rights involve responsibilities, and that African and European should unite in emphasizing both.

It should be stated at the outset that it is easier to enumerate basic rights than to insure them. Various devices have been adopted by Colonial Powers and by the Union of South Africa to accomplish this purpose. For instance, the Belgian Congo has a "Commission for the Protection of Natives" established by charter. Its President is the Procurator General of the Appeal Court at Leopoldville, and there are eighteen members nominated by the King from residents in the colony qualified to judge of native interests. The Commission must meet annually and prepare a report. It is empowered collectively and individually to report any abuses and examples of illegal treatment. Somewhat similarly, each British colony and self-governing dominion has either a commission, department, or secretary for Native Affairs. All of these plans are good, but this Committee is of the opinion that they need implementing by the international inspection of the conduct of native affairs by some such body as the Permanent Mandates Commission or its representatives. In the case of the Union of South Africa, Liberia, and

Ethiopia, such inspection would have to be at the request of the government concerned. In the case of the mandated territories the plan, if adopted by the Peace Conference, should be put into effect automatically. In the case of all other European colonies and protectorates, quite irrespective of whether they are under the regular Mandates System or not, it would help greatly if the Home Government invited such inspection and report by the international mandate group of impartial, experienced, and sympathetic students of government and of native affairs. But even if the international system of mandate inspectorates is not adopted by any given European Power, much can be said in favor of the British Secretary of State for the Colonies, or the corresponding official in other countries, adopting a systematic national inspection plan—something like that of France—so that the Home Government might have regular reports on conditions by experts from outside the colony. It would be understood that such inspectors would be expected to report particularly on the observance of native rights and the advancement of native welfare.

The basic rights—which need special emphasis in the case of the African—may be thus enumerated:

(1) Economic Rights—The Land Problem; Wages

Of the numerous economic rights to which the Africans are entitled, land rights are probably the most vital. Primitive people are vividly conscious of their dependence on the soil. In their contacts with the more powerful peoples of Europe, Africans have been too often unjustly deprived of their land. The land of Africa ought to be considered the property of the permanent residents of Africa of whatever race, subject to the usual right of eminent domain. This and other natural resources should be considered as primarily national assets to be safeguarded and developed in the interest of the African people of present and future generations. The guarantees of land rights should include at least three provisions, namely:

(a) Such a distribution of land as will meet the present and future needs of the African people.

(b) Strict governmental supervision of land transactions to protect native Africans from the abuses often connected

with the alienation of the land to Europeans or privileged Africans.

(c) Encouragement of the proper use of land as the basis
of the native way of life, including methods to prevent
soil erosion and to improve agriculture, as well as adequate limitation of land cultivation for extra colonial
commercial purposes so as to protect the normal activities and relationships of the community.

It is recognized that the land problem is especially acute
where climatic conditions permit European residence, such as
in the Union of South Africa, Southern Rhodesia, and Kenya.
Here difficult problems of adjustment arise which will require
the most careful attention of Government to protect native
interests. By common consent the problem is the most serious
in the Union, which contains almost 90 per cent of Europeans
living in the section of Africa—that south of the Sahara—with
which this Report deals. Senator Rheinallt Jones—one of the
four Europeans elected to the Union Parliament through the
native franchise—in a recent issue of *Race Relations News*
(November, 1941), has outlined the complicated problem in the
Union in a way which represents the point of view of the more
liberal statesmen and publicists in that part of Africa. He says:

There is a growing tension among the Chiefs and people in the
Native areas of the Union. They are profoundly disappointed and
chagrined over the Government's land settlement policy. The situation calls for careful handling. The main facts are:—

1. Although the Native Trust & Land Act of 1936 has laid down
that 7¼ million morgen* more land may be "released" for Native
occupation, the land which the S.A. Native Trust has so far acquired
(3 million morgen), has been found to be heavily populated by
Africans already, so that the tribes have been greatly disappointed
to find that the relief from land shortage in the Reserves that they
had hoped for is not forthcoming. Those already on this land are
now tenants of the Trust.

2. The Government has decided that, as even when the 7¼ million morgen have been acquired, there will still be a great shortage
of land for Native occupation, allotments on the land acquired by
the Trust must be restricted to 5 morgen arable land, and pasture
for 10 head of large stock (or 20 small). The Chiefs and people

* A morgen equals about two thirds of an acre.

complain bitterly that they cannot make a living on these allotments.

3. The Chiefs and people are angry because the Trust will not let them buy the land by tribal levies (as they have done in the past) but charges an annual rent of £1 10s. 0d. per allotment in perpetuity. They do not appreciate the fact that the rent goes to the Trust for the development of Native areas.

4. The Trust (i.e. the Native Affairs Department) insists that the administration of the new lands shall be in the hands of the Trust and not in those of tribal authorities, who complain further that their people on Trust land are being divorced from them, and that the Chiefs are ignored by the Trust officials.

5. The Trust has issued stringent regulations against the cutting of trees in the Reserves, and on Trust farms, and has imposed a tariff of charges for wood taken to build houses, cattle kraals, etc. The people, however, hold that trees, like water, are for common use.

6. The Trust is also taking measures to restrict the number of cattle in the Reserves and on Trust land. This is fiercely resented. The Chiefs and people say "not too much cattle but too little land."

7. The employment of Europeans, instead of Africans, as overseers, foremen, etc., on Trust land is strongly opposed, and there are many complaints of their harsh and overbearing way of dealing with both chiefs and people.

8. As against these complaints, the Department points to the impoverished lands of the Reserves, which are at present over-occupied by their human and cattle population, and which must somehow be saved. This involves the closing of grazing and ploughing ground for years at a time. The new land acquired by the Trust must also be protected from getting into the condition in which the Reserves are now. This requires closer control than the tribes have been used to.

It is manifestly impossible for this Committee to enter here in any detail into the solution of so complicated a problem, but this must receive constructive consideration by responsible statesmen or it will develop into a situation involving not only grave injustices to the African population but friction so serious as to be most embarrassing to the European population itself.

A living wage for all employed men and women should also be considered as a basic economic right. The matter is discussed elsewhere. Suffice it here to add that it is impossible for the

African to attain to a decent standard of living while the general scale of wages for labor continues so inadequate. Even in Johannesburg under urban conditions wages are so low that according to the South African Institute of Race Relations, in its April, 1942, issue of *Race Relations News*, "even with the strictest economy in essentials the average family can never make its budget balance."

(2) Personal Freedom

The right of personal freedom is among the most searching tests of the democratic way of life. This right should be interpreted to include President Roosevelt's "Four Freedoms"— Freedom of Speech; Freedom of Religion; Freedom from Want; and Freedom from Fear. These Freedoms emphatically imply free labor, a modification of the tax system wherever necessary to eliminate its use in the exploitation of native labor, the abandonment of Pass Laws—at least in their present form—and the limitation of forced military service, in accordance with the best colonial tradition, to such terms as are applicable to all other groups of the population. These matters have already been developed in discussing the application of the "Fifth Point" of the Atlantic Charter to Africa.*

(3) Native Participation in Government

During the last century European nations or people have by various methods secured control of all Africa, except the Republic of Liberia, the Empire of Ethiopia, temporarily under external military control, and Egypt. The ruthless conquest of Ethiopia within the last decade has aroused the African people to bitter feelings and to acute anxiety as to their present and future security. This has made them increasingly eager to have a larger share in the determination of governmental policy. They appreciate the growing change of emphasis from exploitation to trusteeship, or better, guardianship, but they want this to imply definitely that even wardship is a temporary status having as one of its major purposes to help prepare the native population for eventual self-government. In this respect African leaders are beginning to share the attitude of nationals in other

* See *supra*, II, 5.

continents, especially in their desire for self-expression, self-realization, and self-determination.

There is increasing evidence that responsible European statesmen are giving heed to these matters. For instance, Lord Hailey, whose remarkable *African Survey* has been frequently quoted in this Report, made an address at the United Empire Society meeting in London on October 28, 1941, in which he discussed the interpretation of the word "trusteeship." He said that "the British would not regard themselves as fulfilling their duty as trustees, unless they endowed the Natives of the Dependencies with such self-governing institutions as will ultimately fit them to attain a position of political independency."

There are three major forms of government participation which seem of special importance as far as native Africans are concerned. These are "indirect rule"; representation in the legislative and other councils of the colonies; and membership in the Civil Service.

(a) Indirect Rule

This is a form of colonial government which has been put into practice increasingly by European Powers in Africa in recent decades, and which has reached its highest development in such colonies and protectorates as Nigeria (where it was first initiated), Uganda, and Tanganyika. Under this policy a tribe, through its traditional form of government—slightly modified in most cases to meet modern conditions—administers practically all local matters under its own chiefs and councils, subject to certain safeguards in the interest of the rank and file of the native population. The councils are supervised by European administrators—Residents, Provincial and District Commissioners. Indirect rule does not generally extend policy-making powers on important matters to local tribal authorities. An interesting and authoritative statement regarding its meaning and significance is contained in the official report, *British Cameroons*, 1924. Significant statements are the following:

The belief which underlies this policy is that every system of government, if it is to be permanent and progressive, must have its roots in the framework of indigenous society.

European standards and methods must be introduced in the form and measure in which they can profitably be grafted on to the pre-existing stock.

This report dismisses as impracticable and undesirable from the viewpoint of African welfare the policy of carrying on the major work of local administration by European officials. It states that the policy of direct European rule, if it were possible, "might be humane, incorruptible, and efficient. It would also be alien, exotic, and impracticably expensive."

Indirect rule has the advantage of being directly related to the historic past of the native people, and encourages them to be proud of their institutions and to develop them in an effective way. It carries a significant appeal to the colonial Power in that it is a cheaper and more expedient method of providing for the control of native groups, and at the same time obviates certain difficulties and dangers from an administrative standpoint. It also involves a considerable measure of local self-government with relatively little interference from without. It has, however, certain disadvantages in that it does not apply very effectively to detribalized Africans who are so numerous in and near the older sections of large European settlement; that it appeals mainly to the more conservative groups in the native population; that it does not do much to adjust native people to the requirements of government under the colonial form of administration; that it represents tribal rather than broader colonial African interests; that there is danger of the native unit of government not being given sufficient independent authority; and that in some instances also, as colonial peoples come to realize that the European official and not the tribal authority is their supreme arbiter, they cease to extend to their traditional rulers and institutions that respect and loyalty which they have customarily received.

In Uganda the Buganda under their King or Kabaka, and with a strong parliament, have a treaty with Great Britain giving them a significant measure of control of their own affairs, which they look after, on the whole, admirably. The states of Toro and Bunyoro are also given large opportunity to determine their own local policies under their own administration.

The policy of indirect rule has been adapted in some places to a larger constituency than a single "kingdom," perhaps the most effective type of organization of this character being the

Bunga or General Council in the Transkei Territory of the Union of South Africa. This council has under the British Resident considerable powers of administration over its own affairs; its Assembly Hall is a place of dignity; its business is carried on with effectiveness; and the native population takes much pride in it.

A somewhat similar but much less effective recent development to meet modern conditions is that of the "Natives Representative Council" in the Union of South Africa, which has been planned by the Government in connection with the Union policy of segregation, so as to give the native African population a form of representation in a national council of its own. Its powers are, however, only advisory, and although it serves a useful function it does not, and will not, satisfy the aspirations of the South African native people. The meeting of the Council in the fall of 1941 considered some eighty-four motions suggested by African members. These dealt with such varied matters as education, land, agriculture and stock limitation, wages, miners' phthisis, housing, trade unions, farm labor, status of chiefs, food prices, social welfare, representation on municipal councils, pass laws, taxation, and police raids. The membership consists of twenty-two members—twelve being elected by native vote, four nominated by the Government, the Secretary of Native Affairs (who acts as Chairman), and, without vote, the five Chief Native Commissioners. The native population of the Union also votes for four Senators chosen from the European population to represent them in Parliament. Their choices have been admirable, and this particular plan, as far as it goes, is working well. This is in addition to four Senators nominated by the Governor-General in Council for their acquaintance "with the reasonable wants and wishes of the non-European races." The Native Affairs Commission also strives to protect native interests, but neither here nor in most other parts of Africa is it (or the corresponding Secretariat of Native Affairs) a bi-racial body on which the African people are represented except in minor positions.

(b) Membership in Colonial Councils

"Indirect rule" is undoubtedly the best of the existing forms of colonial government to meet the local needs of many tribal groups and should be further developed. But the educated African Negro naturally and rightly wishes to go further and to play a part in the administration of the colony of which his tribe is a part, especially in two ways—first, through adequate and effective representation on the Legislative Council, and second, through the holding of responsible positions in the various services of the Government.

As to the former, it must be remembered that it is a feature of the organization of most British Crown Colonies, mandated areas, and protectorates, and that it is the main source of law in a given territory, as distinct from the French and Belgian method of legislating by ministerial decree. In most of the British colonies in Tropical Africa a beginning has been made by having some native members of the Legislative Council nominated by the Government, but this does not go far enough to meet the reasonable expectations of Africans in those places where there is an educated and responsible native leadership. The beginnings of elective representation in some of the West African colonies are encouraging, and it is desirable that the principle be established everywhere, and extended where it is already in existence. Probably Nigeria and Sierra Leone have gone further than any other British colonies in this direction. The former has four elected and seven appointed native members of its Legislative Council, though this is considered far from adequate by the articulate African population of this dependency. How the electorate should be constituted is a matter about which no American committee can be dogmatic. It would doubtless vary in different colonies and in different areas of the same country, and be dependent partly on the progress of education and of other factors. It would also in many cases be "indirect" through election by tribal and other councils. The essential point is that the native people should have in all Legislative Councils, as they already have in some British and French colonies on the West Coast, not only representatives nominated by the Government, but also even more of their own direct choice, or chosen by their duly constituted electors, and that such representatives should increase in number with the years.

The councils of administration of the French Sudan, the Ivory Coast, French Guinea, and Dahomey have each contained three elected native subjects as members; furthermore, about ten of the forty-four members of the Advisory Council of Government to the Governor-General of the West Coast have been Africans. In Senegal the Africans originating in the four communes have long exercised the right to vote upon the same basis as Europeans. A Negro, Monsieur Blaise Diagne, held the position of deputy from Dakar in the French Chamber for many years and served as Under Secretary of the Colonies. The privilege of voting only extends to people who are *originaires* of the communes referred to.

Natives in these communes also largely control the elections to the General Council and some Municipal Councils, as they outnumber the Europeans in this section of West Africa. This Senegal situation is unique and is due to historical reasons dating back many generations. There can be no question, however, but that the native electorate should be, and will be increasingly, represented on various governmental councils in all the colonies.

Lord Hailey, as one of the most experienced and broad-minded of British administrators, coming to Africa from India, is right when he says, "It is increasingly clear that Africans must before long be given a material addition to their very limited representation in the Legislative Councils." Representative native Africans who have conferred with the Executive Committee in connection with the preparation of this Report have emphasized this point, and with much justice. Stress has been laid upon it above in discussing under the Atlantic Charter (II, 3) the development of self-government in Africa.

(c) Membership in the Civil Service

Here is found both a great need and a great opportunity for expansion. There is a legitimate demand in every colony for developing the "intermediate" service through trained Africans who should gradually supplant most of the Civil Servants from abroad. The European Civil Service staff is generally highly responsible, and the gradual transition to a Native Civil Service will be difficult, and may carry with it at first some decrease in efficiency, but it is an essential goal. The "hesitation" in the employment of Africans in the administrative service, "save as clerks or in some other subordinate capacity," to which Lord

Hailey calls attention, must be overcome for reasons of justice, as well as of colonial economy because of the high expense of salaries and necessary travel and furlough expenses for Europeans living in the tropics. There is no reason why immediate further steps should not be taken in this direction.

Belgium has recently adopted as a part of its policy that Africans rather than Europeans should be appointed to such positions in the Civil Service—thus far mostly minor—as they are thought qualified to fill. This is doubtless due partly to considerations of economy and partly to a realization of what constitutes a fair and wise program in dealing with the African population. There is need for a clear-cut statement of policy by every Colonial Power on this matter. It will do more than almost anything to meet the legitimate criticism of educated Africans, who are increasingly dissatisfied with their lack of adequate official participation in public affairs. It will require many readjustments, especially in larger emphasis on the educational training of native Africans for effective leadership. It should carry with it certain real advantages not only by satisfying the legitimate aspirations of the native people, but by giving the Government the services of men qualified to deal sympathetically with Africans.

(d) Note on New Free French Policy in Relation to Other Colonial Policies

The general attitude of the British, French, Belgian, and Portuguese Governments, and the Government of the Union, towards participation by the Africans in public affairs is well known. The principal difference in the past—outside of the Union with its rigid segregation policy—has been between the French and British points of view. The former have, in general, stood for a highly centralized government with a uniform policy decided upon in Paris and considering the French African colonies as almost part of France; permitting the population of the four communes of Senegal to choose a deputy in the French Chamber; emphasizing the use of the French language; discouraging indirect rule; and making a sharp line of distinction between the limited élite, with many privileges, and the masses of the people. The French—whatever the defects of their governmental policy—are to be commended for practising less racial discrimination than most Anglo-Saxons. In fact, the Latin peoples, because of various historic factors, seem in some ways in advance of Anglo-Saxons in this respect.

The British Government has, on the other hand, generally stood for decentralization; emphasis on indirect rule; the use of the vernacular; encouraging Africans to remain Africans and to be proud of their race rather than to wish to become British; and adjusting the character of government to the special needs of different tribes and groups. This has been made possible by its high grade personnel. Each national policy has its advantages and disadvantages.

With these differences of point of view it is interesting to note what is happening in French Equatorial Africa and the neighboring mandated Cameroons under the Free French (de Gaullists) as they may be destined to have a large influence.

The beginnings seem auspicious, especially in comparison with Totalitarian developments in French Africa under the Vichy régime. The Free French Governor, with long experience in the French Colonial Service, issued in the fall of 1941 a *Circulaire générale sur la politique indigène en A.E.F.* The fundamental principles, which have been approved by the local authorities and by a new Consultative Commission (including not only Government authorities but five Roman Catholic bishops, a Protestant pastor, officers of the Chamber of Commerce, and various public officials), involve emphasis on the need for reform, especially by abandoning the old system of great concessions and their attendant economic exploitation; by the improvement of native education; and by the much greater emphasis on the traditional native institutions of the country. The last point is specially stressed. The Governor refers with approval to Lyautey's statement that there is in every society "a ruling class" born to direct, without which nothing can be accomplished, and says that the important thing is to find out the traditional chiefs and "notables" of the tribe wherever the African has not been detribalized by urban conditions, and to give them larger powers. He calls special attention in this connection to the success of the British in Nigeria and of the French in Morocco, in their policy of "indirect rule." "The Colony," he says, "is made up of two stable elements: French sovereignty and Native authority issuing from the soil itself."

He adds: "Administrators are the *representatives* of French sovereignty. Chiefs are the *holders* of local authority. Respect and obedience are due to the former because of their function, to the latter because of their birth." He also calls attention to the fact that the chief is not a functionary but "an aristocrat" accustomed to rule, and one whom his people respect, and it is better to give local power to traditional rulers, even if they make mistakes, than to impose a new system upon them. Great emphasis is consequently placed on the education of chiefs. The Governor-General feels that in the past the idea of the *élite*, although there is much good in it, has received relatively too much emphasis, as it is too apt to involve such superficial features of culture as European manners, language, and dress, without going very deep. The new emphasis on "indirect" rule will not, however, interfere with the development in towns and in the colony of representative institutions in which educated natives, the so-called *notables évolués*, will play their part. A part of this whole philosophy is the feeling that the French African policy of the past has been given too much to "individualism" and not enough to meeting the social needs of the mass of the people in their own communities, and the training and support of their chiefs.

In general this modern French policy—recommended many years ago by experienced French colonial administrators, such as M. Delafosse and M. Labouret—which appears to be about midway between the old French and the present British policy, although nearer the latter, is given in this phrase: "Instead of vague and ill-adapted ideas which appear to associate certain Natives to the government of all of France, or of the empire, we will devote ourselves without any demagogy and with the assurance of doing good to transform them from now on into excellent citizens of their own country."

(4) Self-development and Coöperation

Opportunity for adequate self-development may well be considered a basic right of the individual, for where such opportunities are lacking, either because of serious limitations of educational facilities or environment, no individual can attain to his highest ends. Furthermore, the coöperation of others more advanced and in a position to help the individual to develop his own powers, should be considered as closely related. Every person's development requires sympathetic aid from others. Such coöperation, however, means nothing unless the individual is willing to exert himself and gain the most possible from it. As to coöperation, the principle is capable of wide extension—coöperation with individuals, coöperation with economic processes, coöperation between social groups however differentiated. The testimony of history is that peoples and nations have required the help and coöperation of others for their evolution through the various stages of civilization. Self-development is only one half of the wheel of progress. Coöperation is the other half. Both elements are necessary to genuine and permanent advancement. In Africa these two essentials are specially imperative. The heritage of native cultures and the potentialities of the African peoples must be recognized. Their need for coöperative relationships with other peoples must also be included in the program for their full development. It may be a frequently made statement, but it is none the less worthy of repetition, that "working *for* Africans" is no longer adequate; "working *with* Africans" is the ideal of sincere and effective democracy.

Here is must be realized that although this Committee does not accept the doctrine of "superior" and "inferior" races, as far as potentiality under favorable conditions of development is concerned, it recognizes that nations and people differ greatly in their special characteristics, talents, and interests; that some are today much more advanced than others; and that it is the duty and privilege of the more advanced groups to aid those less advanced. This should not be done with any feeling of superiority, but in the spirit of brotherhood and full realization that the so-called backward peoples (in terms of European civilization) have much to teach the more sophisticated, and vice versa. The aim should be to have potential equality between peoples result ultimately in actual equality.

American and African experience shows the great value of developing sympathetic understanding and coöperation between whites and blacks as brought about by the commissions on interracial coöperation. These organizations, which started in the United States after the first World War, have done much to bring the two major racial groups in our population into sympathetic understanding, especially in Southern towns and cities.

Made up as they are of representative citizens, white and Negro, and meeting from time to time for frank discussion, they have largely avoided theoretical questions and have devoted themselves to the concrete problems of developing more sympathetic coöperation in their own communities, especially in such matters as the improvement of local housing, the abolition of lynching, the development of Negro schools and social-welfare services, and the protection of civic rights. Too much credit cannot be given to the South African Institute of Race Relations, with its British, Dutch, and other membership, for its fearless championing of the rights of the native population and of various other non-European groups. Its recent activities have included serious investigations of such subjects as native land policy; social and economic conditions of Indians in Natal, and the Cape Coloured population; the examination of legislative and administrative measures before Parliament; the rendering of legal aid to the poor of all races; the consideration of industrial problems, including African workers' organizations and the use of non-Europeans in skilled trades; the problems of social welfare, including such matters as housing, nutrition, training of non-Europeans for social and health work; the development of non-European education and library service; publication of *Race Relations*, and of statements, pamphlets, and reports intended to influence public opinion in adopting a more constructive native policy; and the frank discussion of the whole question of interracial coöperation, including the formation and guidance of various joint councils. The Institute has become the recognized center for studies and the carrying out of constructive programs of this character in the interest of the native peoples of South Africa. It has not been able to carry out all of its plans, but it has developed strong support for its courageous and far-sighted program in influential university and other circles, and is accomplishing important results. The extension of its activities, or the development of similar agencies in all other sections of Africa, is highly desirable. The local branches of the Institute form excellent forums for the frank discussion by representatives of the two major racial groups of the most pressing problems of interracial adjustment and the advancement of native interests.

Another form of coöperation of vital help to the African in

securing adequate opportunities for self-development is that provided by sympathetic groups in Europe interested in native welfare. This can be shown through official and unofficial groups. Belgium has had for twenty years a highly influential Belgian Colonial Congress which meets from time to time and has exercised considerable influence of a constructive character over colonial policies. It has published many valuable brochures. As a result of his careful study incorporated in his *Native Problem in Africa*, Dr. Buell praises the "serious and intelligent thought . . . paid in Belgium to the colonial question."

In England there has also been a very keen and intelligent interest in colonial problems and in the welfare of the native population. This resulted in the establishment in 1923 by the Secretary of State for the Colonies of the "Advisory Committee on Native Education in the British Tropical African Dependencies." This Committee's name has been changed, and its scope has latterly been extended beyond Africa, but it still takes a keen interest in African problems. There are also many volunteer groups such as the long-established Anti-Slavery and Aborigines Protection Society. Such groups are highly useful in calling attention to African conditions and to governmental policies which independent citizens conversant with Africa believe to need modification. Indeed, it is a matter of vital importance that both semi-official and independent groups in the colony-controlling Powers, namely, England, France, Belgium, Portugal, and Spain, should be constantly on the alert to try to suggest ways in which conditions can be improved.

The International Institute of African Languages and Cultures is also a highly important institution rendering large service in the fields covered by its name.

The elemental rights of the African people have thus been grouped and summarized under four comprehensive headings: Economic Rights, Personal Freedom, Native Participation in Government, and Self-development and Coöperation. Obviously, each of these rights implies many others too numerous to be listed in this brief summary. In the consideration of rights for Africa and Africans, the basic conviction is that lasting peace and real progress must be rooted in full justice for all concerned.

2. SOCIAL ESSENTIALS

In the long view the welfare of the African people requires adequate provision for the organization and maintenance of an effective program for the development of community essentials. Such a program must include the combined and coöperative services of both governmental and private organizations.

(1) Summary of Essentials

Obviously, the so-called "community essentials" are closely related to the elemental rights and peace aims discussed at length in this Report. In some instances the development of the essentials has preceded the formal recognition and announcement of the rights. In other instances the proclamation of the rights has helped to create public opinion favorable to their formal adoption. Whatever the relationship, an adequate and effective development of the essentials in community life is vital to the welfare of the African people. Briefly outlined, these essentials are:

Adequate provision for the health and sanitation of every community.

Activities and movements to enable the people to know and to master the economic resources, in particular the agricultural and climatic ones, of the local environment from which a community must obtain its livelihood.

Facilities to encourage the people to acquire a knowledge and mastery of a decent and comfortable domestic life, without degradation or exploitation of women and children, on which race vitality and advancement so largely depend.

Conditions favorable to the friendly and coöperative attitude of racial and social groups however differentiated in origin and status.

Arrangements and organizations for recreation and for the cultural development of the people in body, mind and spirit, including a recognition of the values in native culture and the inspiration of education and religion.

Sincere determination to develop an educational system, adequate in quantity and quality, to enable all the people to give full expression to their physical, mental, cultural, and spiritual potentialities, including those of effective leadership.

(2) Essentials Demanding Special Emphasis

These "essentials" are all referred to in their appropriate places in this Report, but some of them are so basic as to demand special consideration here.

(a) Health and Hygiene

The importance of health, as an objective of missionary and government effort, has been recognized in the institution of dispensaries, hospitals, and health departments. Medical missionaries and medical officers have rendered a remarkable service in many parts of Africa. They were almost everywhere the pioneers, but the field is so vast that it is now recognized that Government must play the largest part in its development.

The question of health is particularly important in a continent like Africa where the population is inadequate to meet its needs of development and where the ravages of malignant tropical diseases are so devastating. These epidemics—in many cases preventable—can hardly be imagined by those who enjoy the health conditions of civilized Western countries. Accurate statistics covering Africa as a whole are not available, but in contrast with death rates of twelve to fifteen per thousand in England and America, the death rates in many primitive communities in Africa have been estimated to range from fifty to a hundred per thousand. The contrast in infant mortality is even more striking. Whereas the death rates in England and America for infants under one year of age range from sixty to a hundred per thousand, in Africa the infant rate is believed to range several times as high. Under such conditions the importance of education in matters of health becomes imperative.

There is space in this Report merely to outline the three major needs in the African health field: (1) *the improvement of public health services;* (2) *the training of African health officers and doctors;* and (3) *health education.*

As to the *first,* much has been done in almost every colony, especially those of Great Britain, France, and Belgium, and in the Union of South Africa. But when it is realized that such diseases as yellow fever, typhoid, typhus, dysentery, bubonic plague, silicosis, smallpox, tuberculosis, typhoid fever, malaria, yaws, sleeping sickness, venereal diseases, parasitic worm diseases, and leprosy are either latent or prevail in large areas, and that most of the native population is ignorant of the essentials of hygiene and health, it must be emphatically recognized that only beginnings, although excellent beginnings, have been made. In this work the Government is taking the lead, with some of the large mining companies, such as those of Great Britain and Belgium, and the missions—both Catholic and Protestant—supporting them effectively, but the problem is a vast one, as it involves in the end providing elementary dispensary and sanitary services for tens of thousands of villages as well as central hospital and laboratory facilities, and competent supervision.

As to the *second*, the Belgian Congo, the Anglo-Egyptian Sudan, the French African possessions in the West Coast, and Uganda, have been among the areas that have shown special concern for the training of native medical assistants. Such assistants are now being trained at Dakar in French West Africa—which has a long-established and well equipped Medical School, with related departments of Pharmacy, Midwifery, and Veterinary Science—Yaba in Nigeria, Mulago in Uganda, Leopoldville in the Belgian Congo, and Fort Hare in the Union of South Africa. The general testimony is that they are efficient in their limited fields. There is also need to develop the fully qualified native medical practitioner, but unfortunately there is at present no place in Africa where Africans can receive at all adequate training with hospital experience, except Khartoum, Dakar, and perhaps Kampala in Uganda. But none of these is sufficiently advanced. Those who have received a medical degree have generally been educated at the University of Edinburgh in Scotland, or at one of the French universities, or, in a few cases, in the United States.*

There are colonies, such as French Equatorial Africa, without a single native medical doctor. On the other hand, there are colonies on the West Coast with a considerable number who have demonstrated their capacity and usefulness. Africa will

* While this Report has been passing through the press the gratifying news has been received that the University of Witwatersrand at Johannesburg is about to provide for the education of native African doctors. Arrangements have been made for a suitable hostel for students, and the Government is providing some scholarships. The laboratory work will be carried on in the University Medical School. This is an important victory, crowning the efforts of a decade led by the South African Institute of Race Relations.

need the leadership of European medical men for many decades to come, but the work of reaching the native communities must be carried on increasingly by trained native assistants and practitioners with more adequate facilities provided for their training.

As to the *third*, health as an objective in education is only beginning to be recognized. The potentialities of the school not only for the prevention of disease but for the building up of the physical welfare of the community are not adequately reflected in the school curriculum. This indifference is doubtless the result of the incidental value which the educational world has often attached to health as a school objective. Programs of hygiene and of sanitation in civilized communities have evolved with great rapidity. A few years ago the chief concern was the curing of disease. This has been followed by widespread campaigns for the prevention of disease and epidemics, such as yellow fever, malaria, hookworm, and sleeping sickness. There is now the third stage, namely, the building up of bodily health so that the full measure of manhood and womanhood may be realized in an extension of life and in the development of physical capacities.

Many native schools do not share in the benefits of campaigns for the prevention of disease. Statistics issued in the last three years by the British Registrar-General's office are almost dramatic as indications of the progress made in the elimination of disease when effective health measures are introduced. But as long as the school systems of civilized countries frequently do not advocate the potentialities of health education for the general improvement of society, it is not surprising that African schools should be lacking in this respect. Furthermore, it must be urged that Tropical Africa can less afford to neglect any forms of health propaganda than Western countries with their multiplicity of social organizations supplementing the school.

Not only are health campaigns and education necessary for the native population, but also in the interest of Europeans. The people of the United States have latterly come to realize that the existence of slums in our big cities, whether occupied by white or colored, are not only centers of vice and sickness, desolating the dwellers in them, but that they are centers from which contagion spreads to well-to-do groups in the whole community. As long as there are unsanitary "locations" from which native domestics come to white homes, just so long will the white people themselves suffer. The health campaign is essential as a matter of fairness to the Negro, protection to the whites, and in the interest of Africa generally.

The value of adequate nutrition to meet the main deficiencies in an economical but adequately balanced diet for the native population is specially important and requires more attention than it has received. It might properly come in for a share of some of the funds for scientific research in the colonies recently voted by the British Parliament.

(b) Womanhood and the Home

Every phase of colonial welfare is dependent on the healthful and normal development of the home and family life of the native people. The conservation of human life, so essential not only to the labor supply but to public welfare generally, is more intimately dependent on home activities than on those of the hospital and clinic. Government, native leaders, settlers, and traders should therefore be actively interested in all that pertains to the homes of Africa. The desirable qualities of character can be better cultivated in the right type of home than elsewhere. Here youth may be taught a sense of responsibility, the place of leadership and authority, as well as of loyalty and obedience, and the practice of thrift and industry. Missionaries can make large use of the home in the inculcation of high ideals and in the maintaining of religion at the heart of everyday life. In the home may be developed a spirit of service to others, a love of the beautiful and the good, and an appreciation of spiritual values. Where the cohesive forces of tribal life have been disrupted by modern conditions of industry and Western civilization, it is essential that every effort should be made to protect womanhood and the family structure. We have dealt briefly with housing problems in a previous section.*

(c) Education and Religion

The development of all phases of education is of vital importance.

Elementary Education. The need of further extending ele-

* See *supra,* II, 5, (4).

mentary education is paramount. The practice followed in the British and Belgian colonies of having this in the vernacular whenever practicable is a wise one. It is only through such use in elementary teaching—based on vernacular textbooks—that this can be accomplished, and that the native people can be given a sense of pride, and a deep and intelligent interest in tribal welfare. But the vernacular needs supplementing, at least in all fields of secondary education, by the European language of the colony, so that pupils may have a large field of printed literature open to them and may be fitted for governmental and other responsibilities. A large literate population is essential if the trained African leaders are to secure adequate support and if wise policies are to be adopted. With this in mind, Governments may well consider the experiments in mass education recently introduced in China and India. These should be adapted to the needs of Africa. There is also vital need of emphasis on adult education so that the older elements in the population may not be too far removed from the knowledge and point of view of the youth who receive a modern training. Furthermore, if the leaders of the future are to continue to develop after the completion of their institutional education, libraries open to native Africans must be largely increased in number, resources, and service, as well as more and better special literature provided for their purpose.

Agricultural and Industrial Training. The first step toward agricultural instruction as an educational aim is the development of a real appreciation of its importance in Africa. One of the unfortunate results of the education so far given there has been all too often the depreciation of agriculture in native opinion. However unintentional and incidental this result has been, it has been nevertheless frequently found. The sin has been rather of omission than of commission. The school program has in some places been so largely devoted to the conventional elements of the school curriculum as to cause Africans to think that agriculture is not really basically important. The responsibility for this unfortunate result cannot be placed upon the school alone. Modern civilization and some of the agencies of the Christian Church must share it, although a number of Protestant and Catholic missionaries, such as Father Bernard Huss of South Africa, have been leaders in agricultural education. There is probably no more vital problem of education than that of helping society to understand the primary importance of agriculture to human affairs, and to aid in its development. This will require the thorough training not only of practical farmers, but also of scientific leaders in all fields related to Africa, such as education, research, and extension work. This last named is a matter of special importance. The possibility of adopting in Africa the plan for interesting youth in agriculture and home life through boys' and girls' clubs deserves consideration.

Africans are primarily dependent on agriculture—the occupation of the overwhelming majority. Agricultural education—based on a sound knowledge of biology and the soil, and closely related to community needs as in the case of the Jeanes Schools —should correspondingly receive large consideration in school plans. While Africans have learned much through centuries of experience, there is much more to be learned through scientific study of the possibilities of the soil, and the best methods of its use, as well as of the whole field of animal husbandry. The radical changes as regards land tenure and consequent limitation to smaller acreages, the new conditions of marketing, additional wants of individual and family life, the demands of Government for taxes, and numerous other changes brought about by the entrance of Western civilization into Africa, all combine to create a perplexing agricultural situation which is baffling to the native population. In addition to these real discouragements to agriculture, there are the enticements of large industrial operations maintained by European capital. The lure of new experiences and of cash wages, the desire to share in the activities of the Europeans in control, and the active systems of recruitment are attracting large numbers from the soil to the artificialities and dangers of labor compounds and urban centers.

The distinctly educational value of suitable mechanical training is enormously increased in Africa by the need for every form of industrial development. Primitive Africa lacks roads, railroads, bridges, boats, all types of vehicles, farming implements, machinery, household utensils, and an endless variety of things that may well be considered essential to modern civilization. The large physical resources of Africa must remain relatively undeveloped until the industrial facilities are provided and skilled labor is available. Any large-scale importation of skilled labor into Africa is not justifiable as a permanent policy. The native Africans must be taught to share this responsibility and in the course of time be prepared to undertake it. There are sufficient examples of skilled native workmen to prove that they can and will respond to opportunities for such training.

Secondary and Higher Education. Secondary and higher education are essential to provide trained leadership in all fields. For example, knowledge of the physical sciences is necessary to understand and develop the great resources of soil, minerals, and animal life in Africa. Thus the native Africans will not only be freed from the fear of superstitions, but will also be given a command of their environment that will be of value to themselves and to their country. The campaigns for hygiene and sanitation required in Africa cannot be effectively carried on without the aid of a native leadership trained in the sciences. Similarly, the adequate development of the social and religious life of the millions of Africa awaits native ministers, priests, and teachers who—in addition to being trained in their own field of work—have an adequate and accurate knowledge of social forces. In all this there is need for acquaintance with anthropology and ethnology, tribal folk-lore, the history of civilization, and the great literature of the world. The type of education developed should in most cases allow youth, while learning new subjects, methods, and attitudes, to remain in touch with their own traditions, and so make them capable of participating effectively in the compound culture which is developing in Africa. In this connection educational leaders should make more of a point than they generally have in the past of securing advice from the most responsible local African tribal authorities—a plan carried out effectively in one or two places in East Africa.

Native Africans must be increasingly trained for posts in the Civil Service, in commerce, in medicine, in law, in agriculture, in engineering, in economic and industrial problems, and in other fields. To advance these forms of education more scholarships should be provided at home and abroad to carefully selected and qualified students of proven character, and opportunities assured them for their employment on the completion of their studies, whenever their records warrant it. The experience of history, the wisdom of science, and the inspiration of literature and art (including of course African art) will be required by native leadership to guide and direct Africans through the perplexing processes of evolution from primitive stages of life to those of modern civilization—processes necessitated by overwhelming forces, both beneficial and disruptive.

In this field of higher education for native Africans there has been much progress recently. Fort Hare College in the Union of South Africa (closely related to the admirable Lovedale School), Achimota in the Gold Coast (whose Council of fifteen members has the encouraging requirement that it must include at least six Africans), Gordon College in Khartoum, and Makerere in Uganda, all provide higher education in institutions supported in whole or in part from Government funds. There is need for a similar institution for the French-speaking Africans of the Congo and the West Coast, where there is nothing higher than an excellent institution of the *lycée* type, in Dakar. Belgium has been specially backward in this matter. Fourah Bay College in Sierra Leone (affiliated with Durham University), although a missionary institution, has had a long and honorable career, and is largely responsible for the considerable number of Africans from its colony who have gone on to England for higher university courses. It should also be remembered that the universities of South Africa have no legal color bar and that from two of them, namely, the University of Witwatersrand and the University of Cape Town, some native African students have been graduated, while others have secured degrees from the University of South Africa, an examining but not a teaching institution.

General Considerations. All departments of education are making progress, but Government, in keeping with some farsighted official pronouncements, should increasingly recognize its fundamental responsibility either to provide adequate educational facilities itself or to aid more generously well-established and responsible private agencies in providing them. All future progress of the native African will depend to a large extent on Government's effective attitude in this matter of education, and this in turn will depend primarily on three factors—a clearer vision as to Africa's future; provision for competent leadership; and improvement in economic conditions. Incidentally, the experience of the United States in the development of Negro education has clearly shown that such education is, on the long view, distinctly worth while economically, and in every other way, to the community as a whole. Where the Negroes or any other disadvantaged group have their educational facilities increased in ways related to their needs it means an improvement in their economic status. This in turn means an increase in their buying power, which improves local financial conditions for all concerned. Of course it also means— which is of supreme importance—a development of cultural and spiritual values, and of opportunities for useful self-support and service.

An African student in this country, Mr. Ako Adjei of the Gold Coast, in a memorandum submitted to the Committee, shows his deep concern as to larger educational facilities for his people. He says:

The education Africa needs: Africa is crying for education—the light of civilization. What we need, and what we are asking for, is the kind or type of education which makes it possible for a people to utilize the resources of their country to make life better, not only for themselves but also for all people in the world. And by resources, I mean both the human as well as the material wealth of a country. Thus Africa needs the kind of education that will help its people to develop their lands and build and live in better homes and rear healthy families under healthy conditions. This includes education of the hands, the head and the heart, and the study of the various professions which are also necessary for the proper functioning of a modern society. . . .

The need for missionaries of civilization: Africa needs a new type of missionaries. These we may call "missionaries of civilization." They include qualified medical doctors of all kinds, teachers of trade and the industrial arts, women teachers of home economics and child welfare, nursing, business, education and all the various vocational subjects which are taught in the different vocational and industrial schools of this country. In the past this kind of vocational education has been ignored in African education, or very little interest was stimulated in it. The responsibility lies on the governments and the various foreign Christian missions, now operating in Africa, to give serious consideration to this problem in their plans for post-war educational enterprise in Africa, Africa needs the services of educators and other missionaries of civilization who understand the meaning of life and who do appreciate the value and the significance of an alien culture which is different from their own. . . .

He also makes a special appeal for provision to enable educated Africans to come to this country for the purpose of studying the coöperative movement here and in Nova Scotia.

As there are relatively few rural regions of Tropical Africa away from the main lines of communication where over one out of ten Africans receives even an elementary education, the problem is enormous—far beyond the scope of the missions, which have done such heroic work. It is a task which must be undertaken by Government not only through more and better schools but through adult education, radio, village readers— which play such a large part in India and have been successfully tried in Tanganyika—agricultural demonstration work such as has proved so helpful in our Southern States, and the larger use of the lantern, the motion picture, and the broadcast. The Department of Industrial Research of the International Missionary Council has made some interesting films, especially appropriate for African use under the so-called Bantu Educational Kinema Experiment. It would be difficult to overestimate the importance of the potential influence of the cinema in Africa. Up to the present time American films have all too often made a bad reputation, and have done much to discredit this country in the eyes of thoughtful Africans. American philanthropy might well give further aid to the development of educational films for use in African communities.

No better statement of educational policy for Tropical Africa has ever been issued than that adopted by the British Colonial Office's "Advisory Committee on Native Education in the British Tropical African Dependencies" in March, 1925. It is important as representing the goal of British policy. It is too long to be reproduced in full, but its paragraphs on "Adaptation to Native Life" and "Religion and Character Training" are specially worth quoting:

Education should be adapted to the mentality, aptitudes, occupations and traditions of the various peoples, conserving as far as possible all sound and healthy elements in the fabric of their social life; adapting them where necessary to changed circumstances and progressive ideas, as an agent to natural growth and evolution. Its aim should be to render the individual more efficient in his or her condition of life, whatever it may be, and to promote the advancement of the community as a whole through the improvement of agriculture, the development of native industries, the improvement of health, the training of the people in the management of their own affairs, and the inculcation of true ideals of citizenship and service. It must include the raising up of capable, trustworthy, public-spirited leaders of the people, belonging to their own race. Education thus defined will narrow the hiatus between the educated class and the rest of the community whether chiefs or peasantry. As a part of the general policy for the advancement of the people every department of Government concerned with their welfare or vocational teaching—including especially the departments of Health, Public Works, Railways, Agriculture—must co-operate closely in the educational policy. The first task of education is to raise the standard alike of character and efficiency of the bulk of the people, but provision must also be made for the training of those who are required to fill posts in the administrative and technical services, as well as those who as chiefs will occupy positions of exceptional trust and responsibility. As resources permit, the door of advancement, through higher education, in Africa must be increasingly opened for those who by character, ability and temperament show themselves fitted to profit by such education.

Religion and Character Building. The question of religion and character building is dealt with equally effectively in the Advisory Committee's report:

The central difficulty in the problem lies in finding ways to improve what is sound in indigenous tradition. Education should strengthen the feeling of responsibility to the tribal community, and, at the same time, should strengthen will power; should make the conscience sensitive both to moral and intellectual truth; and should impart some power of discriminating between good and evil, between reality and superstition. Since contact with civilization—and even education itself—must necessarily tend to weaken tribal authority and the sanctions of existing beliefs, and in view of the all-prevailing belief in the supernatural which affects the whole life of the African it is essential that what is good in the old beliefs and sanctions should be strengthened and what is defective should be replaced. The greatest importance must therefore be attached to religious teaching and moral instruction. Both in schools and in training colleges they should be accorded an equal standing with secular subjects. Such teaching must be related to the conditions of life and to the daily experience of the pupils. It should find expression in habits of self-discipline and loyalty to the community. With such safeguards, contact with civilization need not be injurious, or the introduction of new religious ideas have a disruptive influence antagonistic to constituted secular authority. History shows that devotion to some spiritual ideal is the deepest source of inspiration in the discharge of public duty. . . .

In actual practice the religious provisions in Government Schools generally involve Mohammedan teaching in Mohammedan areas and Christian instruction elsewhere.

Perhaps the best statement noticed with reference to the important place which religion should have in the program of native education is one made a few years ago by Louis Franck, Minister of the Belgian colonies. It carries special weight in view of his high reputation as a man and an administrator. He gave it as his opinion that "it is necessary to rely on evangelization for moral education. Nothing permanent will be done without it. This conviction is independent of every consideration of religious faith or dogma. It is based on this observation —that native life is profoundly penetrated by religious sentiment and dominated by mystery"—"pour l'education morale c'est sur l'évangelisation qu'il faut compter. On ne fera rien de permanent sans elle. Cette conviction est indépendante de toute considération de foi ou de dogme. Elle est basée sur cette observation que la vie indigène est profondement penetrée de religiosité, et dominée par le mystère."

It is hard to over-estimate the contribution which Christian missions have made and are making to education in Africa. Missionaries have done more than any other group to reduce the languages to writing; to provide the foundations of educational textbooks and literature; and, prior to the recent increase of the social-welfare activities of the State, to develop education and medical work. They have also been active in preventing the exploitation of the native population, and in aiding in various other ways in the extension of civilization.

In this connection it is interesting to know that substantial parts of the Bible have been translated into about 250 of the 700 languages of the continent, and that, as Lord Hailey states,

"It is the most widely read book in Africa." It is stimulating to think of the possibilities which follow from the fact that the majority of the native people of Africa who receive an education are being trained through Christian teaching—either with the New Testament or the Catechism as the basis.

Education of Resident Europeans in Native Life and Race Relations. No discussion of education for native Africans would be satisfactory without at least a passing reference to the importance of placing greater emphasis in schools and colleges for Europeans in Africa on African traditions, customs, etc. In other words, it is a matter of vital importance that European youth growing up in Africa should have a sympathetic understanding of Africans, their history, traditions, beliefs, and points of view. The Universities of Cape Town and Witwatersrand (Johannesburg) have done much to encourage this movement. Americans may well endorse it, for the Southern States of this country have profited greatly during the past quarter of a century by the movement started in the South itself to study Negro and interracial relations objectively and sympathetically. Much of the progress made has been due to the efforts of those farsighted men and women from all parts of the country who have tried to take the "Negro problem" out of the field of the emotions and make it a matter of objective study, just as one would study any other social problem. It is particularly important in white schools that false theories of race should be exposed. Emphasis may well be placed on the teaching of St. Paul on Mars Hill that "God that made the world and all things therein . . . hath made of one blood all nations of men for to dwell on all the face of the earth, . . ." (Acts 17, 24-26)

CHAPTER V

Summary of Major Findings and Recommendations

1. FINDINGS

Among the Committee's major findings are the following:

That Africa today should be the subject of intelligent study in this country for many reasons, but especially because it is the ancestral home of one tenth of our population, and that it is a continent of vast possibilities and difficult problems, and of vital concern to the United Nations in the present war.

That Africa still represents the largest undeveloped area in the world, with mineral deposits, agricultural land, waterpower, forest and wildlife resources of importance, all of which are decreasing in value because of careless or reckless use or exploitation; and that these resources need development for its own defense and welfare.

That all of the areas except the four independent states of the Union of South Africa, Egypt, Ethiopia, and Liberia, are under European control; while of those named the first is a member of the British Commonwealth of Nations, the second and third are under forms of British influence, and the last has close historical relations with the United States.

That the policies of the various European powers in control differ greatly—the most fundamental difference being between the British, who stand very largely for "indirect rule" by native chiefs, "kings," and councils, and the development of the native population without losing touch with their own languages and best traditions; and the French, who stand for highly centralized rule and the purpose of making Frenchmen of Africans; and that each system has its advantages and limitations.

That of the European nations the French are probably the ones that practice the least racial discrimination, and give a striking example in their educational system and their Civil Service of European and African studying and working together.

That the colonies and protectorates controlled by the British

Colonial Office have in general (with only one or two exceptions) adopted in the interest of the native population, the basic and progressive social-welfare ideals, of the Mandate and "guardianship" systems, and that they are all staffed by a Civil Service which has made an enviable reputation for public integrity and personal character.

That the Mandates System established after the last war has proved of great value, with its basic requirements, its hearings before the International Mandates Commission, and its published findings on reports from the Mandatories, although the system needs supplementing by regular international inspection and report.

That during the past twenty years, under the influence of the Mandate idea of trusteeship, and other forces, there has been substantial progress in most parts of the continent in dealing with problems of native rights and native welfare.

That Europe's connection with Africa has been due to many historical factors, good and bad, such as the slave trade (in the early days), the abolition of the slave trade (in later years), the promotion of legitimate trade and commerce, the exploitation of African resources for European and American profit, the spread of Christian missions (with their manifold educational and other activities), European settlement, and national prestige.

That the impact of Western civilization on the primitive culture of Africa has created extremely difficult problems, with resulting credits and debits.

That the native people, although differing widely in their stages of culture, interests, and talents, have large potentiality, and that there is in every colony a steadily increasing group of educated Africans competent to take positions of additional responsibility.

That the missionary societies, both Protestant and Catholic, have in many instances led the way in education, medicine, and other fields, and such organizations as the Institute of Race Relations in the Union of South Africa, have done much for the protection of Africans' rights and interests.

That America has a large interest in Africa—missionary, financial, educational, scientific, and otherwise—all increased by the fact that we have the largest educated Negro population in the world, and by the further fact that war conditions involving the United Nations are relating this country increasingly to Africa.

That although the slave trade has been abolished and some of the more serious abuses of industrial exploitation have been reduced, largely as a result of the efforts of the International Labor Organization, the African laborer is still extremely poor, generally receives but a pitiful wage in proportion to corporation profits, and inadequate attention to his housing and other social welfare needs.

That, speaking generally, race friction exists in the most serious form in those areas where there is a large settler population living on the soil, such as in the Union of South Africa, Southern Rhodesia, and Kenya.

2. RECOMMENDATIONS

The Committee realizes the extreme complexity of African problems, and that it is far easier to give advice when one is without direct responsibility for government. It nevertheless feels that a Report on the Problems of Africa, the War, and Peace Aims would have little significance without specific recommendations, presented in a spirit of modesty and fairness.

(1) Political Conditions

Among the Committee's major recommendations are the following:

That the lessons of the recent military defeats in Malaya, Singapore, Java, and Burma—resulting partly, in the opinion of many European authorities, from a lack of more general coöperation between the native population and the Europeans in control—emphasize the vital importance of prompt steps to give colonial peoples a larger and more responsible share in the government of their country, in order that it may not be said that measures adopted to meet legitimate native aspirations have been "too little and too late."

That although the Atlantic Charter, even in the expanded form adopted in the Twenty Six Nation Agreement, is inadequate in certain respects, especially in its failure to provide for a world organization to promote collective security, it represents a substantial step forward, and that the "Eight Points" of the Charter should all be applied to Africa in keeping with the broad humanitarian and democratic principles enunciated.

That the goal of ultimate self-government should be definitely accepted in every colony, and that the controlling governments should show themselves both willing and eager to fit the African people for larger and larger participation in their own affairs both through "indirect rule" and through direct representation in government councils.

That every effort should be made to secure the best public opinion of the African population when any changes in governmental control or policy are contemplated.

That in every colony steps should be immediately taken to provide adequate native representation in the Legislative Council (or what corresponds to it), including some African members elected directly, or by qualified African electors, or by Tribal Councils, and that such membership should steadily increase with the years.

That immediate steps should be taken to throw open more positions in the Civil Service in every colony to competitive examinations in Africa—making ability and not color the basis of choice—looking forward to the time when most Civil Service posts shall be held by Africans.

That the word "guardianship" is better than trusteeship as applied to an African territory under Mandate control as it rightly implies that the relationship is not permanent but has as its purpose the fitting of the ward for self-government as soon as his education and experience permit.

That the Mandate ideal of the vital importance of native rights, welfare, and development should be applied in all African territory controlled by European powers and should be adopted by the independent African states.

That all European colonies in Africa should be willing, even when they continue under separate European administration, to submit to international inspection and report.

(2) Social-economic Conditions

That it is a matter of vital importance that all forms of racial discrimination based on the Nazi "Herrenvolk" idea should be eliminated, and that instead of looking upon different races as "superior" or "inferior" they should rather be considered as "advanced" or "retarded."

That all forms of industrial color-bars are as indefensible in Africa as they are in the United States, and that such as exist should be eliminated.

That the improvement of the economic status of native Africans is a matter of prime importance and one which must be approached from many sides.

That special attention should be given to the fundamental problem of land to make sure that Africans have adequate land of a good quality for all their needs, and that this land is not alienated from them in the interest of Europeans, Americans, or privileged Africans, and that the native farmers be protected from the destruction of their own lands by the effective demonstration of proper practices in land use.

That everything possible be done through governmental controls to prevent the exploitation of the mineral, water, plant, animal, and soil resources, by the adoption of a sound conservation policy looking to the future as well as the present welfare of the inhabitants.

That, as agriculture is the primary occupation of the overwhelming majority of Africans and largely the basis of their economic security, everything possible should be done to improve methods and practices of land management and of soil and crop conditions by education and action in such fields as scientific agriculture, forestry, and irrigation.

That there is need in every colony of larger emphasis on education directly related to the needs of the people, and on training for effective leadership in education, family life, medicine, agriculture, the ministry, public life, economic and industrial planning, and other fields.

That social anthropology should be studied more, thereby making more satisfactory the adjustments between Western and African cultures.

That education should be based on the vernacular supplemented in its later stages by the European language of the nation concerned, and that in addition to the conventional forms, various attempts at mass education through radio, motion pictures, etc., should be adopted.

That the health problems of Africa are exceptionally serious and demand more attention through education and health campaigns than has yet been given to them so as to eliminate some of the most dreaded forms of sickness and pests.

That everything possible should be done by voluntary corporate action and by the adoption of wise governmental controls to prevent the exploitation of the African in industry; to give him a larger wage; and to provide for him better housing and recreational facilities.

That the principles of self-development and of coöperation are both highly important, so that everything should be done to encourage the African to develop his own capacities, and to aid him in this development and in the improvement of native conditions through various forms of interracial coöperation— valuable to white and black alike.

That in view of many serious defects in our treatment of the Negro in the United States, we should approach the problems of race relations in Africa with humility, but with the confident belief that as they have been and are being steadily improved here and in some parts of Africa, so will they be steadily improved in all parts of Africa under the impact of Christian and humanitarian ideals.

(3) *American Relations with Africa*

That the Government of the United States, being already a party to many treaties and conventions dealing particularly with Africa and the protection of its native people, has assumed certain responsibilities which it cannot escape; and should not only continue to participate actively in international conferences but also in other projects dealing with Africa.

That American financial and business interests with investments in Africa should be specially careful to see that African labor is treated fairly as to methods of employment, wages, living conditions, etc.

That the people of the United States should be willing, both through philanthropic and missionary societies, to devote more attention and more financial aid to Africa than in the past.

That our Government should stand ready to unite with other nations in some world organization (including a Mandates System) which will promote collective security and see to it that the provisions of the Atlantic Charter are duly implemented so as to protect the interests of Africans, who should be given some form of representation in connection with the Peace Conference.

That our Government should also be willing to aid in such ways as Liberia may desire, in improving its social-welfare activities, especially in matters of health, education, and agriculture.

That the Government should consider establishing in the State Department a separate Division with most of its personnel having African experience, to deal with African-American affairs, as the system of the past, by which Africa has been dealt with as part of the work of the Near East Division or of the West European Division, seems inadequate for the present and future.

That the Government of the United States should consider the possibility of aiding after the war "to a limited extent," and through some such plan as that of the Lend-Lease Act, certain parts of Africa, such as Ethiopia, which has suffered so cruelly from the war, and Liberia, with which the United States has a mutually friendly historic bond, to encourage the development of public works, education, and health and social-welfare services.

Africa, a Brief General Description

The great continent, question-mark in form, stands between the Occident and the Orient. It is evidently one of the world's great battlegrounds because of its strategic position and resources.

Africa, according to Dr. Thomas Jesse Jones, "formerly the Great Dark Continent" and the "Continent of Great Misunderstandings," is now the "Continent of Great Opportunities" and the "Continent of Great Responsibilities." These four words—Darkness, Misunderstanding, Opportunities, Responsibilities—vividly suggest the evolution of Africa from the limitations of primitive life to the complexities and influences of Western civilization, and to a worthy rank among the continents of the earth. The undeveloped resources and the real awakenings in Africa are guarantees of significant developments. The scientific and altruistic approach to its countries and to the people is dispelling the over-emphasis on Africa as a sportsman's paradise, and the haunting fear of disease connected with it, and revealing the normal Africa of large and little-developed economic resources, beautiful scenery, and native people of much potentiality.

The general physical features of Africa may be briefly described. It is the second largest of the continents. The northern extremity is about on the latitude of Washington, D. C., the southern extremity on that of Buenos Aires. The northern part is mainly low and its center taken up with the Sahara Desert. In the heart of the continent is the Congo basin with its vast tropical forests. The remaining parts of Africa are largely plateaux with a narrow coastal plain which provides very few good harbors. This fact was largely responsible for Africa's long isolation. Much of the area is of the semi-arid savannah type. Lord Hailey, in *An African Survey*, thus describes its general features:

A continent which stretches for 5,000 miles from the Mediterranean southwards across the Equator to 35 degrees south, and for 4,500 miles from Dakar in the west to Guardafui in the east, naturally exhibits a wide variety in climate and in vegetation. But the great mass of Africa lies in the tropics; it is only in the north-western and southern extremities and in a few areas of high altitude that temperate climates exist. It may be possible to ski close to the line of the equator on the slopes of Mt. Kenya, or to find a perfect winter climate in South Africa; but, taken as a whole, Africa is the most tropical of the continents, and it is only a relatively small area which offers conditions comparable to those of Europe, or has proved suitable for European settlement.

Of great importance is the spine of the continent which is east of the center, extending down from Ethiopia into the Union of South Africa and including the highest mountain, Kilimanjaro, in Kenya, 19,010 feet, and Mt. Kenya, as well as the Great Lakes. There are many great rivers, especially the Nile, Congo, Niger, and Zambesi, although none is navigable for any long distance by large ships. They play, however, a very important part in transportation, which is in most places inadequate, owing to poor roads and few railroads. They are also large potential sources of hydro-electric power, which will doubtless be used for many factories and other industrial developments in the future.

1. AREAS, GOVERNMENTS, POPULATIONS

The continent of Africa is too vast and varied for an adequate summary of areas, populations, and confusing diversity of government. However, the following statistics give some hint of the continental dimensions, the substantial populations, and the perplexing and erratic divisions of foreign governments ruling the native peoples of the continent.

1. The total area is twelve and a quarter million square miles— three times the size of Continental United States, and twice that of Europe, and the total population is about one hundred and forty million people.*

2. This is divided into two main regions:

a. *Mediterranean* Africa, including Egypt, closely related both to Asia and Europe, as well as to Africa, has an area of two million square miles and a population of almost forty million.

b. Africa *south of the Sahara Desert*, which is frequently regarded as the "Real Africa," has an area of ten and one fifth million square miles and a population of about ninety-five million. Of this section the *Union of South Africa*, an independent nation differing widely from the remainder in government, economic status, and population, has an area of almost half a million square miles and a popu-

* Lord Hailey, *An African Survey*, p. 107, says:

Dr. R. R. Kuczynski estimates that the total population of the continent, shown in the *Statistical Year Book of the League of Nations* for December 31, 1934, as 145,054,000, may be as low as 138,100,000 or as high as 163,300,000; and though the margin of error is large, it is not greater than that for Asia or South America.

lation of about nine millions, of whom over two millions are white, three quarters of a million mixed, and one fourth of a million are Asiatics. The remainder are mostly Negroes of the Bantu group. We are concerned in this Report with (b) in its two major divisions of Tropical Africa and South Africa.

3. The diversity of governments is of very unusual importance in the interpretation of African conditions and African welfare. The general facts are:

a. Six European nations, including their descendants in South Africa, rule an area of eleven and one half million square miles and a population of about one hundred and thirteen millions.

b. The mandates, included in the colonial system listed above, and made up of Tanganyika, South-West Africa, and the other colonies taken from Germany at the close of the first World War, have an area of a million square miles and a population of about thirteen millions. Great Britain, France, Belgium, and the Union of South Africa are the Mandatory Powers. When in the course of the years African states become autonomous, most of those which are now British colonies, protectorates, or mandated areas will doubtless become members of the British Commonwealth of Nations. It is possible that other European Colonial Powers may develop some similar system.

c. The independent or quasi-independent countries (in addition to the Union of South Africa—a member of the British Commonwealth of Nations) are Egypt, Ethiopia, Liberia, with an area of three-fourths of a million square miles and a population of twenty-one millions. Egypt, with its historic tradition of an ancient civilization, and its face toward Europe and Asia, is marked by conditions which are on the whole so different from those of Africa south of the Sahara as scarcely to fall within the scope of this Report.

d. The Anglo-Egyptian Sudan is a condominium in which the Governor-General, who has charge of the administration, is appointed by Egypt with the assent of Great Britain.

4. Probably most significant of all is the distribution of areas and peoples among the European Powers in Africa. The figures represent conditions prior to the second World War.

	Area		Population	
British (including the Union of South Africa, now self-governing)	4	millions	52	millions
French	4	"	35	"
Belgian	1	"	13	"
Portuguese	3/4	"	7	"
Italian	4/5	"	2 1/3	"
Spanish	1/6	"	1	"

It is important to note the distribution of the above areas and peoples between Africa south of the Sahara and Mediterranean Africa. This may be seen by studying the map at the end of the Report. It will be noticed that whereas the French territory is divided between the Mediterranean and Equatorial regions, all of the Belgian and all of the Portuguese territory, if the islands in the Atlantic are excluded, and almost all of the British, is south of the Sahara.

5. From the above facts, the following observations as to the governments are significant:

a. That the British (including the British and Dutch of the Union of South Africa) govern one fourth of the area and almost one third of the population of Africa.

b. That the French (including the Free French in French Equatorial Africa) govern one fourth of the area and almost one fourth of the population of all Africa. However, a third of the area under French rule, and a third of the population, are in Mediterranean Africa.

c. That the Belgians govern one thirteenth of the area and about one tenth of the population.

d. That the Portuguese—the first European power to have large colonial possessions in Africa—still control about one eighteenth of the area and one nineteenth of the population.

e. That Italians and Spanish rule the remaining areas and populations in smaller proportions.

f. That "Mediterranean Africa" is governed by Egypt, France, Italy, and Spain.

g. That the Independent Governments—outside of the Union of South Africa—rule only about one sixteenth of the area and less than one sixth of the population of Africa. Ethiopia and Liberia, however, have only one thirtieth of the area and one twentieth of the population of all Africa.

While these statistics present some conception of the quantitative diversity of governmental controls in Africa, they are very inadequate descriptions of the qualitative diversity of governmental policies and methods. Indeed, the qualitative differences are far too numerous and wide to be accurately outlined in this Report. However, the following comments seem to be necessary to supplement the statistical facts already presented:

1. That British control in Africa differs widely and includes Crown Colonies, Protectorates, Mandates, and semi-Dominion in Southern Rhodesia. The Union of South Africa—controlled mainly by people of Dutch and British descent—is a self-governing and independent Dominion within the British Commonwealth of Na-

tions. Despite the wide divergence of these controls, there are some uniformities of attitude and trends, such as the encouragement of "indirect rule" by native peoples, the use of the vernacular, and the gradual adoption of the principle of trusteeship, which is especially marked in British Crown Colonies, mandated areas, and protectorates. Some of these, such as Nigeria, Uganda, Sierra Leone, and Tanganyika, show indirect rule at its best.

Nyasaland is a good example of a well-governed protectorate, with a native population of a high type, excellent missions, fertile soil, and some beautiful scenery. The attempt to amalgamate the Rhodesias with Nyasaland, under a single governor, has been frequently discussed, but most impartial authorities interested in native welfare fear that it might result in the more rigid segregation policies of the south extending northward, and consequently being disadvantageous to the Africans.

2. That the French colonies are fairly uniform in governmental policy and administration, with a strong tendency to require centralization of authority, and French as the only official language. A unique feature is the development of a "native *élite.*" What effect the present control of Equatorial Africa by the Free French forces may have on ultimate French policy it is hard to determine. Its tendencies have been discussed above.*

3. That all of the mandated areas belonged to Germany prior to the last war and were removed from her control by the Treaty of Versailles. An illuminating statement based on a broad study of the documents and actions of the German Government, and of various Nazi groups, regarding the Africa of the future, in case of a German victory, is given in an article by Heinz Soffner in *The Commonweal,* May 29, 1942. It is entitled "Hitler in Africa."

4. That the references to Liberia, Ethiopia, and Egypt as "Independent Governments" require the following explanations:

a. Egypt is *legally* independent, but at present is practically under British domination. In time of peace, the British have retained the right of maintaining certain armed forces in the Suez Canal area. In time of war, the King of Egypt is obliged by treaty of alliance to furnish to the British "on Egyptian territory . . . all the facilities and assistance in his power, including the use of his ports, aerodromes, and means of communication," and to take appropriate administrative and legislative measures, including the establishment of martial law and an effective censorship.

b. Ethiopia, until conquered by Italy, was ruled by an Emperor whose authority was largely distributed among local chiefs. Since

* See *supra,* IV, 1, (3), (d).

the defeat and elimination of the Italians, the Emperor has returned to Ethiopia, and his country has been duly recognized. On January 31, 1942, an "Agreement and Military Convention between the United Kingdom and Ethiopia" were signed at Addis Ababa by the Emperor Hailé Sellassié and Major-General Sir Philip Euen Mitchel representing the United Kingdom. This recognizes Ethiopia as being "now a free and independent state," and reëstablishes diplomatic relations between the two countries. The Agreement shows that the independence of Ethiopia is subject to many of the features of a British Protectorate, as Great Britain is to provide advisers as well as certain police officers and some judges and magistrates, and the Emperor agrees to appoint no other advisers except after consultation with Great Britain. The British Government makes large grants to the Emperor "in order to re-establish his administration." In any case where a foreigner is a party before one of the courts, at least one British judge must be among those on the bench. The Emperor further agrees "not to conduct any external military operations which, in the opinion of the General Officer Commanding-in-Chief the British forces in East Africa, is contrary to the joint interests of Ethiopia and the United Kingdom."

The Agreement is to remain in force until replaced by a "Treaty for which His Majesty, the Emperor, may wish to make proposals." If not so replaced within two years it may be terminated at any time by either party giving three months notice to the other. In the Military Convention signed at the same time, the British Government agrees to provide at its own cost "a Military Mission for the purpose of raising, organizing and training the Ethiopian army." The Convention specifies the privileges of the British army during the period of occupation.

c. Liberia is an independent Republic under its own constitution. There is relatively little participation by the native peoples outside of the coastal area in governmental affairs, as the virtual control of the government is in the hands of the Americo-Liberians, a small group of about 12,000 people, aided by a few Negroes who have come from neighboring African colonies and from the West Indies. This situation has, however, been somewhat modified by considerable intermarriage between Americo-Liberians and the indigenous native population. The unfortunate conditions which led to the League of Nations investigation of forced labor and other conditions a decade ago have improved in recent years, thanks largely to the more effective administration under President Barclay, the friendly coöperation of the United States Department of State and its representatives in Liberia, and the economic and other advantages which have come through the Firestone Plantations Company.

d. It is necessary to note that the independent status of these three countries does not mean that their social and economic condition is satisfactory. On the contrary, the facts indicate that Liberia and Ethiopia are in many respects more lacking in the essentials of social welfare than most of the colonies under European control.

2. RESOURCES AND TRADE

Dr. Emory Ross, having spent twenty-five years in the Belgian Congo—the heart of Africa—after describing eloquently the material and human resources of the continent, says in *Out of Africa*:

Our vaunted modern industry is dependent on Africa. Our two million tons of tin plate every year are boiled in African palm olive. Our mass production technique depends on African cobalt, that indispensable ingredient for the making of high speed tool steel. And it is only the Congo which blocks Canada from developing a monopoly of this metal for the whole world!

The earth's largest known resources of copper lie in Africa; . . . The world's well known and late departed gold standard was dependent upon Africa, which furnished most of the gold, and still continues to do so more profitably than ever. Africa bores the very bowels of the earth with drills pointed with diamonds; and African diamonds are among the largest ever found and cut.

The quoted statement gives a fair general picture of the large dependence of the world on African resources, although cobalt is mined extensively in some places outside of Africa, and there are substitutes for the making of certain steel tools. Dr. Ross might also have added that Africa provides about one third of all the world's production of chrome ore and of vanadium, and about one fifth of its manganese.

Even more impressive than the Gold ridge of Johannesburg, the Diamond fields of Kimberly, the Copper plateaux of the Katanga and Rhodesia, the Radium of the Congo, and the innumerable other precious metal resources of Africa, are the potentialities of African soil—if rightly treated—under climatic conditions ranging from the tropical to the temperate zone.

In this connection it must be remembered that Africa has over one fourth of the potential crop land of the earth and the most extensive tropical region of any continent. Of the total area, however, over a fourth is either desert, or relatively dry savannah not capable of extensive cultivation, and large parts of the remainder have suffered from soil erosion, or are subject to serious droughts and pests such as the locusts which destroy crops and the tsetse fly which is the cause of sleeping sickness. But the continent is vast in extent and has large possibilities for certain crops, under proper control and cultivation. For example, Dr. Homer Shantz, Plant Specialist in the U. S. Department of Agriculture, gives the following striking illustration of soil possibilities in a supplementary chapter prepared by him for the Phelps-Stokes Report on *Education in East Africa*:

The cultivated acreage of East Africa, exclusive of South Africa, could in time almost equal that of the United States of America, an area three and a half times the total surface of the United Kingdom and Ireland.

East Africa north of the Transvaal contains 300,000 square miles of high plateaux free of tropical heat and tropical diseases, and capable of producing the crops of the temperate zone.

The most important agricultural products of Africa are thus summed up by the same author:

The forest and agricultural possibilities of Africa have scarcely been touched. The forests include large quantities of timber which could be made into articles of commercial value or shipped to other countries for manufacture. No more valuable or varied timber lands are to be found than the vast forest areas of Central Africa, rich in both dye woods and cabinet woods. There are extensive valleys, plains and plateaux producing a variety of vegetables, grains and fruits, and capable of much larger production under proper cultivation. South Africa produces tons of wheat, maize, Kaffir corn, potatoes, oats, barley, and tobacco, and great quantities of fruits, including grapes, peaches, pears, melons and other products. In Angola there are coffee, sugar, cocoanuts, vegetable oils, maize, yams, tomatoes, peanuts, melons, oranges, lemons, limes, pineapples, bananas, peppers, and tobacco. The extensive plateaux of the colony combine quantities of both the tropical and temperate zones, grain, vegetables, and fruits of great variety and excellent quality. West Africa is known for its immense production of palm oil, cocoa and rubber. The areas devoted to cotton are increasing with great rapidity, and promise to rival the great cotton-producing sections of the world.

It will be seen from the above that there are still large undeveloped resources. Indeed, in comparison with the other great continents of the world Africa may be considered the undeveloped continent, and this in spite of all the money that has gone into African mining, trade, and commerce in recent years. It is its relatively undeveloped condition and its enormous tropical area—the largest in any continent—that are largely responsible for its commercial interest to the outside world. Africa's share of international trade in the last year for which statistics are readily available (1938) was 7 per cent, and her share in the world's primary production 3 per cent.* The last percentage could be greatly increased to the benefit of Africa itself with proper attention to agriculture. Her latent riches are at least sufficiently significant to have resulted, according to Frankel's *Study of Capital Investment in Africa*, in an investment of nearly $6,000,000,000 of foreign capital up to the end of 1936, of which investment, however, about 40 per cent was in the Union of South Africa. Even the distant Japanese find the trade of Africa a matter of significance. Their imports in several colonies are well over 20 per cent of the total imports. As the economic resources of the native population improve, its capacity to produce will likewise improve, and therewith should come an improved standard of living.

3. AFRICAN PEOPLE AND THEIR POTENTIALITY

(1) Characteristics of Africans

The terms Africans, native Africans, native people, and native population, are used in this Report instead of the old term Natives, which is going out of use as it is thought to have implications which may be open to criticism. The native people of Africa seem to have been derived from three principal stocks, namely, Bushman, Negro (including Bantu), and Hamite. The Hottentots are believed to be a mixture of stocks in which Bushman and Hamite predominate. The Bushmen and Hottentots are both few in number and are confined to the South. It is with the *Negro* group that we are primarily concerned in Tropical and Southern Africa. The purest Negro tribes are found in the West between the mouth of the Senegal River and the eastern frontier of Nigeria, but the *Bantu* people of the East and South are mainly of Negro blood, and the Nilotic people of the Nile Valley are largely Negroid. The two major groups, the relatively pure Negro and the Bantu, each represent about 40,000,000 people. The former are mainly agriculturists, the latter combine agriculture with cattle raising— cattle being the most prized form of wealth and intimately connected with religious observances. Almost all Negroes in Africa are engaged primarily either in agriculture or in pastoral life, living in rural regions, although in parts of West Africa, especially Nigeria, there are some large towns. The number living mainly on the chase is much smaller than generally realized. The density of the population varies, but in West Africa it is generally from twenty-five to sixty-five per square mile. This also holds for most

* These figures are from *Europe's Trade*, published by the League of Nations in 1941.

of the region of the Union, but in Eastern and Central Africa it is generally much less, from five to twenty-five per square mile.

Madagascar has a different population, not being of the Negro type, but related to the Malay and the Polynesian.

The relation between African tribes and languages is complicated and cannot be entered into here. Suffice to say that there are about seven hundred languages in Africa. Insufficient attention has been paid in the past to the study of anthropology, especially social anthropology, for without a knowledge of the beliefs, customs, traditions, and practices of a native tribe it is almost impossible for the Government or the missionary to deal wisely with its members. A Report of this character can give no attention to anthropological details. They are extremely complicated, but the members of this Committee wish to record their conviction as to the vital importance of studies of social anthropology and the need of bearing more in mind native beliefs and customs in adjusting modern European forms of government to Africa. For an example taken almost at random, the actions and reactions of many Bantu people will remain a closed book to the administrator or the missionary, and he will be unable to deal with his people wisely, if he has not a thorough and sympathetic understanding of *lobolo* (bride price) and of their whole attitude toward cattle.

The indigenous religions of Africa, in addition to Mohammedanism and Christianity, take various forms in which ancestor worship generally plays some part. There is also general belief in the spirit world—the spirits being of all types, evil disposed, well disposed, or indifferent. Witch doctors play a large part. There is also very often a belief in a higher personal power on which an historic religion, such as Christianity or Mohammedanism, may build. An authority on African religions makes this statement regarding underlying factors in the indigenous religious beliefs:

In fact, from one end of Africa to the other we meet, overgrown by a more or less confused mass of strange superstitions, the essential ideas of that which everywhere has been looked upon as the primitive religion: an unseen God, Master of all things, and Organizer of the world; the survival of the human soul, under a form not clearly defined; at times, the idea of reward and punishment in the other world; the existence and activity of spirits, some of whom help men while others deceive them; prayer, sacrifice, the need of a worship; the sacred nature of a fruit, a tree, or an animal; the duty of abstaining from certain actions, of practising self-restraint; the idea of sin, of the power left in man to wipe out its stain, etc. The sum total of this evidence—and the list might be prolonged—more or less clear, distinct, or scattered, collected from tribes of different origin which cannot possibly have met for centuries, leaves us convinced that at the beginning of the formation of the black race there were common beliefs and practices, such as are found at the beginnings of every human race, and on which Christianity itself rests, as we have it to-day.*

There are two main forms of native religion:

Animism. This is the main feature of the religion of most Negro and Bantu people, being based on the distinction between matter and spirit, and implying a belief in beings which have no affinity to any definite thing in the world of nature, but are endowed with a higher power.

Fetishism. The word "fetish" is derived from the Portuguese and signifies some material object to which a mysterious influence is assigned. Images, stones, trees, huts, bones, or other objects may become fetishes. This form of belief is specially prevalent in West Africa.

It is the opinion of competent authorities that the native religions will gradually be superseded by one of the two theistic missionary faiths, Christianity or Mohammedanism, which are at present contending for leadership in several parts of Equatorial Africa. Both have done much for the native African and count today millions of loyal converts from among them. The latter are mostly north of the Equator; the former, both Roman Catholics and Protestants, are scattered everywhere in constantly increasing groups.† One of the authors of this Report, in a recent trip through British and Belgian dependencies in 'Africa, met nine colonial governors, all of whom expressed appreciation of the work of Christian missionaries, and the belief that they have made and are making an invaluable contribution to African welfare. This is the prevalent opinion among civil servants in all colonies, although a few who have served in Mohammedan areas emphasize that this religion is especially fitted to meet African needs.

In dealing with the African people we must always remember the important part played historically by family, clan, and tribe. The African, especially when he has not received a European type of education, is much less of an "individual" and much more of a social being than the average Westerner. This is why the detribalized African, one of the inevitable results of industrialization in parts of Africa, is in a position so disadvantageous to himself and to the community. This problem demands most careful and sympathetic consideration. Everything possible must be done to maintain

* Article "Africa," (3), in *The Catholic Encyclopedia*, I, 185.
† See *supra*, IV, 2, (2), (c).

the tribal unit where this is feasible, creating interest in its history and making it a basis of pride for future development. Indirect rule does much to preserve many of the best features of tribal community life, but to prevent the extremes of tribalism it is also necessary to bring the tribes into relationship with broader social and governmental units.

No intelligent understanding of present and future Africa can be had without a realization of tribal differences and customs and their significance, which there is no time to enter into here. But there are, speaking generally, certain basic traits of character, such as family loyalty, courtesy, kindness, sense of humor, honesty, patience, courage, and a combination of essential democracy with due recognition of authority, that are fine foundations on which to build.

(2) *African Potentiality*

Perhaps the most unfortunate of all the misunderstandings about Africa is the assumption that most Africans do not give promise of development sufficient to warrant confidence in them and efforts for their development. The fact of the matter is that there has been an inadequate appreciation on the part of the Government and also, in some cases, on the part of missionaries, of the latent potentiality of Africans. This impressed Americans at the LeZoute Conference some fifteen years ago and was partly responsible for the policy adopted by one of the foundations in making possible the visits of African leaders to the United States—one of the major purposes being to demonstrate the progress made by the descendants of African Negroes in this country.

The old theory that African peoples were all children who would always remain children is not tenable. One of the encouraging results of the visits of African educators to the United States has been to help them realize the potentiality latent in the Negro. They have been impressed by the fact that so many of the outstanding leaders of our Negro Americans are very dark, with little or no admixture of white blood. It is highly important that this potentiality of the native African should be emphasized, as it will influence the whole point of view of governments in their African policy.

A good statement as to African potentiality is found in a book published last year in London by Joyce Cary, entitled *The Case for African Freedom*. In it the author, who spent about fifteen years in the British Colonial Service in Nigeria and had many assignments in the remote regions where he was virtually alone with the native people, says:

. . . But the general point, that the African is capable of equal education and responsibility with Europeans, is beyond argument, to anyone who deals with realities, that is, who has known real Africans. The Mahomedan judge, subtle and learned, the great chief with his political shrewdness, the hospital assistant, the village headman, the lorry driver, the sergeant-major; put any of them into a white skin and they would take their place, in the same rank of European society, on equal terms. They would appear like the rest, the lawyer among lawyers, the chief among statesmen, the government clerk among officials; the sergeant-major among that natural aristocracy of the soldiers of career—the non-commissioned officers.

Racial differences may be deep but no race exists, except perhaps a few remnants of the primitive bushmen, which is not capable of that degree of education and responsibility necessary to carry on the modern state.

Mr. Cary, after referring to the African capacity for growth, and for worthy citizenship, adds:

It is obvious that such a development will take a very long time. But to see that it is possible is important because it alters the whole approach to the African problem. . . . The only safe and wise course in African native districts is to hand over power gradually and continuously so that native responsibility increases at about equal speed with economic political development.

This seems to be an admirable statement of a difficult problem.

Two South Africans with long experience in watching native Africans in court have rendered their testimony. Sir Thomas Graham, a well-known judge, said "that he had formed the definite conviction that there was no substantial difference in natural ability between the White and the Black." Mr. Peter Nielsen is equally emphatic:

I have listened to thousands of old Native men of many different tribes in my time, I have heard them speak their inmost thoughts, not through interpreters—who ever learned anything through an interpreter?—I have studied these people in and out of Court, officially and privately, in their kraals and in the veld during many years, and I say that I can find nothing whatever throughout the whole gamut of the Native's conscious life and soul to differentiate him from other human beings in other parts of the world.

To go to another part of Africa, General Mangin, one of the best-known Commanders of French African troops, bears this witness:

The Negro is probably as competent as the white man to handle the scientific instruments of civilization. . . . I do not deny that he still has to be educated. What I do maintain is that he has qualities of head and heart which ought not to be treated as negligible. He is by nature good and faithful and endowed with a sense of honour, and if he is really given the chance, he will reach a high level. There is an *élite* in the black world capable of excelling in all regions of human intelligence.*

The endeavor to prove the inferiority or equality of Africans in comparison with other peoples of the world is of relatively little value in determining policies concerned with their development, and can never be fairly used to justify the denial of educational or other opportunities to any group. In this connection the following clauses from the statement adopted by the American Anthropological Association in 1938 are worth quoting:

Race involves the inheritance of similar physical variations by large groups of mankind, but its psychological and cultural connotations, if they exist, have not been ascertained by science.

Anthropology provides no scientific basis for discrimination against any people on the ground of racial inferiority, religious affiliation, or linguistic heritage.

Probably the most authoritative summary of conclusions in the field of comparative intelligence of whites and blacks is that which appears in the *Journal of the Royal African Society* for January, 1938, by Messrs. W. B. Mumford and C. E. Smith of the University of London Institute of Education. This reviews the scientific tests of over a century, beginning with those by Spurzheim in 1815. Here is the conclusion: "On the basis of the foregoing notes it is suggested that there is little evidence to date in support of the conclusion that any particular race is inferior in mental capacity to any other race, or that there are fundamental racial differences in mental processes." The present distribution of the African groups through the various stages of human society, whether that stage be primitive or civilized, is a natural condition that has found duplication at some time in all civilized races. It must be remembered that civilization is a relative term, and that many African tribes have developed native cultures which, although very different from our own, are nonetheless highly significant and in some respects well fitted to their needs. To combine the best in native customs and in Western civilization is difficult but not impossible.

It is especially important that Europeans and Americans should bear in mind that Africans have developed types of culture and

* These quotations are taken from Dr. Edwin W. Smith's *The Golden Stool*, pp. 86, 91.

civilization of their own, manifesting themselves in forms of political organization and community life in many ways well adapted to their needs. They have also made a specially important contribution in the field of art.

The potentiality of the African people is clearly shown by their native tribal chiefs and other leaders, by the response to the efforts of missions and governments, and by their ability to adapt themselves to the needs of modern industry. There are physicians, teachers, lawyers, and ministers, who have completed the requirements of European universities and are practising their professions creditably. In some sections such as the Gold Coast native business men have had notable success. While the number of these well-trained and effective leaders is small, it is sufficient to prove the capacity of the people. For definite examples of the potentiality of native Africans in achievement both within and without the tribal group, we may turn, for instance, to great chiefs, such as Moshesh of Basutoland, Behanzin of Dahomey, and Khama of Bechuanaland; church administrators and leaders, such as the Catholic Bishops Kiwanuka of Uganda and Faye of East Africa, and the Anglican Bishop Crowther; other ministers of the gospel, such as Canon Apolo, Mr. Dube (father and son); business men, such as Peter Thomas of Lagos; doctors of medicine, such as the Zulu Dr. Gumede; teachers and educational leaders, such as Dr. Aggrey of Achimota, Dr. Jabavu and Dr. Z. K. Matthews of Fort Hare; statesmen and leaders in public life, such as the present Mukama of the Bunyoro, the Treasurer of the Buganda; Sir Apolo Kagwa, once Prime Minister of Uganda, and René Maran of Senegal. Nigeria has had an unusual number of Africans of responsible leadership, not only among the emirs of the North but among the people living near the coast. Among these have been Messrs. Herbert Macauley, C.E., a respected exponent of native public opinion; Nnamdi Azikiwe, Editor of the influential *West African Pilot*; and Eyo Ita, an educator—the last two having studied in the United States. These are typical of what native Africans of character and ability can accomplish.

That some of these have made creditable records at British, French, and American universities is well known. The clerical tasks of government, industry, and commerce are largely and increasingly entrusted to young Africans. The mechanical operations on railroads and in construction are more and more being taken over by African workmen, except in those few territories where it is not permitted. Every mission gives emphatic testimony to the value of the native teachers, priests, and ministers. In view of the inadequacy and lack of adaptation of educational facilities in Africa, it is greatly to the credit of native Africans that some of their number have been able to achieve success in every colony.

Nor are the possibilities of the Africans to be judged only by the progress of those who have entered the ranks of Western civilization, whether in Africa, Europe, or America. An adequate study of the tribal customs and capacities of those who are still in pre-literate or "primitive" stages will more and more reveal the fact that the present condition of the masses of the African people is relatively normal and comparable with other peoples at the same stages of development. Their folk-lore, their handicrafts, their music, their sculpture, their forms of government, their linguistic powers, all are substantial evidence of their capacity. Goldsmiths, copper and iron workers, weavers of cotton and wool, and those skilled in pottery, leather, wood, and ivory may be found. There is evidence of considerable knowledge of agriculture and, even though the results are often crude, there are definite indications of capacities which manifest themselves in varied fields of activity in different tribes. Every student of Africa is impressed by the fine qualities developed by widely separated groups such as the Mandingos of the Northwest, the Yoruba of the West Coast, the Zulus of the Southeast, the Kavirondos and Buganda of the East—to mention only a few of many.

4. NON-EUROPEAN IMMIGRANT COMMUNITIES

These communities are composed mainly of Arabs or descendants of Arabs, and East Indians. Most of the former are located in North and Northeast Africa, of the latter in South and East Africa. The Indians are engaged chiefly in trade and commerce. In addition to these Asiatic groups, the population of South Africa includes three quarters of a million so-called "Coloured" people, who are of mixed white, Malay, and African origin, rather sharply differentiated from the natives by public opinion, customs, and language. The following quotations from Lord Hailey's *African Survey* present the principal facts concerning the Arabian and Indian communities in Africa:

The Arab Community. The importance of the Arab immigration belongs largely to the past. By the twelfth century Arabs had established themselves in a number of points of trading vantage as far south as the Zambesi outlets. . . . In 1832 the reigning Sultan of Oman transferred his court to Zanzibar and extended his authority to parts of the mainland now included in Kenya and Tanganyika. . . . On the mainland the Arabs are to-day most prominent in Kenya, where the 1931 census recorded 12,166 Arab residents. Their position has been recognized by the nomination of an Arab to the

legislative council, and the institution of separate Arab schools. . . .
But the Arab has neither the political flair nor the aptitude for
trade possessed by the Indian; unlike the latter, therefore, he seldom
exhibits himself as a political or economic competitor to the European. . . .

The Indian Community. There has been intercourse between
India and Africa throughout history. . . . When the Portuguese
reached East Africa in the late fifteenth century, Indian traders were
already there, and it was an Indian who piloted Vasco da Gama on
his first voyage across the Indian Ocean. This Indian commercial
community continued to prosper in Zanzibar throughout the seven-
teenth and eighteenth centuries, under both Portuguese and Arab
rule; . . . In 1863 there were 5,000 or 6,000 Indians on the island
and on the mainland territories of the Sultan, and almost the entire trade of these territories, estimated at more than £1,500,000
annually, passed through their hands. . . .

In view of this long historical connexion, it is not surprising that
Indians emigrated in large numbers to Africa when the development of sea transport stimulated colonization, and large areas of
Africa came under British rule. To-day there are large Indian communities in South Africa, Kenya, Uganda, Tanganyika, Zanzibar,
and Portuguese East Africa. In smaller numbers Indians are to be
found trading in the Rhodesias, Nyasaland, and British Somaliland. . . .

The population of the larger communities is as follows:—South
Africa: The Asiatic population in the Union in 1936, of whom the
great majority were Indians, was 219,928—less than one-ninth of
the European population, and approximately one-forty-third of the
whole; Kenya: The estimated Indian population in 1936 was
38,325, of whom more than half are engaged in commerce; Tanganyika: The number of Indians increased from 9,400 in 1921 to
23,400 in 1931; Uganda: The estimated number of Asiatics in 1935
was 14,860, predominantly Indian but including a number of
Arabs and Goans.

Arabians, East Indians, and various other Near East middlemen
serve a certain useful purpose, but in many cases undoubtedly interfere with the development of trade and small business enterprises by
native Africans.

5. EUROPEAN SETTLERS AND OTHER RESIDENTS

(1) General Situation

No description of Africa would even approximate giving a fair
picture without reference to the European residents. It is generally
estimated that of the total population of about 140,000,000 in the
continent about 5,000,000, or only one in thirty, is European. This
includes Europeans of all groups—settlers, missionaries, government

officials, businessmen, engineers, and other residents. Of these, approximately 2,250,000 live in that part of Africa with which this Report is especially concerned, that is, Africa south of the Sahara, and of this number slightly over 2,000,000 are residents of the Union of South Africa. These figures are important, as in no other nation or colony in that part of Africa with which the Committee is concerned does the European population bear anything like so large a relationship to the native people. The figures of European population as given by Hailey for 1935-36 are as follows:

Angola	30,000	Northern Rhodesia	9,913
Basutoland	1,434	Nyasaland	1,781
Bechuanaland	1,899	Ruanda-Urundi	893
Belgian Congo	18,680	Sierra Leone	718
Cameroons, British		South-West Africa	31,049
Mandate	354	Southern Rhodesia	55,419
Cameroons, French		Swaziland	2,735
Mandate	2,257	Tanganyika	8,455
French Equatorial Africa	4,463	Togoland, British	
French West Africa	19,061	Mandate	43
Gambia	217	Togoland, French	
Gold Coast	2,800	Mandate	418
Kenya	17,997	Uganda	1,994
Mozambique	10,000	Union of South Africa	2,003,512
Nigeria	5,246		

This table is highly suggestive, for from the standpoint of this Report, which devotes much attention to the native population, friction and serious difficulty occur in almost direct relation to the percentage of Europeans to the total population. It may be said that, speaking generally, the portions of Africa in which most friction exists are Kenya with a population of about 18,000 Europeans, as well as about 38,000 East Indians and a considerable number of Arabians, and the Union of South Africa with the neighboring Rhodesias and South-West Africa.

(2) South Africa and Kenya

The British Government at home is in a difficult position, and it requires tact and courage to deal with those British groups in the colonies that have made it their permanent home and wish to keep the native Africans very definitely segregated "in their place." Fortunately, however, there are in all the colonies many white officials and some settlers deeply interested in native welfare, and there are evidences that conditions are improving. As the Union of South Africa is an independent nation, it has to work out its own problem of race adjustment, but the Kenya problem is one which seriously concerns the British Government, as it is a Crown Colony. Somewhat similar but less acute problems exist in the neighboring British mandate of Tanganyika and in the Rhodesias. In such regions the land question is always more or less acute—the Africans feeling that the Europeans take most of the desirable lands, and that what is set aside for native reserves is frequently inadequate in amount and inferior in quality.

The Union of South Africa is outside of the tropical region, and is generally considered as a European nation transplanted to Africa, with its 2,000,000 Europeans, who have developed a history, literature, and art of their own, and have excellent universities. Its problems are extraordinarily complicated on the racial side, in fact among the most complicated in the world. There is first of all the problem of adjustment between European groups. According to a recent census about 57 per cent were of Dutch descent, 34 per cent British descent, and 9 per cent miscellaneous. This problem also to some extent comes down to a contest between the rural groups, which are mainly Dutch—that is, Boers speaking Afrikaans—and the urban groups, which are mainly British. Then there is the problem of adjustment between the Europeans, the numerous East Indians, and the several hundred thousand "Cape Coloured" of mixed African, Malay, and European stock. In addition there are some 6,000,000 Bantu and other native groups. The policy of the Government is frankly one of racial segregation, including a good deal of repression as far as the native population is concerned.

The courage of those European liberals in the Union who see the danger of the existing policy of African segregation and repression is to be heartily commended. They know that no race can be kept permanently down, and that the extremes of the color bar, such as those which exclude skilled African labor from the mines of the Rand, can, unless corrected, result only in bitterness and ultimately in strife. There have been industrial strikes in the past, and they know that they will become more serious in the future if present policies persist without recognition of the right of the Negro in industry to go as far as his capacity permits. It is well known that racial and color solidarity has a tremendous emotional appeal, and that it is dangerous to permit it to have any justification for falling under the influence of radical agitators. Consequently, looking at history in the large, the true conservatives in South Africa are the present-day liberals in the matter of race relations.

It is heartening to know that the Christian Council of South Africa has arranged for a conference in July at the South African Native College in Fort Hare in which the theme is to be "Christian

Reconstruction . . . in South Africa." Some 150 delegates are expected, of whom it is hoped that from a fourth to a third may be African, Coloured, and Indian delegates. Such interracial gatherings are full of significance and encouragement for the future peace and welfare of South Africa.

That the white people of South Africa have a very serious and difficult problem cannot be questioned. Their desire to maintain their own high standards of living is commendable. That they have a real fear of what might happen to their children and their standards of life if segregation were broken down, is indisputable. So is the fact that tens of thousands of them are deeply interested in the welfare of the black man, but the fact remains that the restrictive policy adopted towards Africans, especially if it is extended to other parts of Africa, is full of danger.

In recent years, and especially since the delivery of Field Marshal Smuts's address on Trusteeship in January of this year, there have been some encouraging developments in the Union as far as native welfare is concerned. For instance, the Government has quadrupled its grants to native education since 1920, and those for the year 1942-43 are far higher than any previous year.

In Kenya settlers have a basis of justification for their desire to secure adequate land, as they were induced in many cases to come to Kenya by offers of undeveloped lands which had little or no native population and were considered vacant. They have settled there and consider it their permanent home. So that they have rights that must be recognized, and an important contribution to make to the welfare of the native people of the colony, must be taken for granted, but it is clear that trouble of the general character that exists in South Africa will become serious if the rights of Africans are not adequately protected, and if they are restricted from entering certain industrial and agricultural pursuits for which they are fitted.

Two quotations from recent official British Government statements should give hope in this most difficult and complicated of the British African colonial fields. The Devonshire White Paper of 1923 stated that:

primarily Kenya is an African territory, and His Majesty's Government think it necessary definitely to record their considered opinion that the interests of the African natives must be paramount, and that if and when those interests of the immigrant races should conflict, the former should prevail. . . . In the administration of Kenya His Majesty's Government regard themselves as exercising a trust on behalf of the African population, and they are unable to delegate or share this trust, the object of which may be defined as the protection and advancement of the Native races.

This theory was also the basis of the Hilton Young Commission of 1930, which took the ground that "the creation and preservation of a field for the full development of Native life is a first charge of any territory," but declared that this is not "incompatible with the common duty of any government to promote the development of the resources of the territory and the prosperity of its inhabitants, including the immigrant communities within it." The native labor situation in Kenya has been discussed in an earlier section—II, 5, (2).

The situation in Kenya is reproduced in some of its features in Northern and Southern Rhodesia, in both of which there is an influential group of settlers which appears at times more insistent upon protecting its own rights than those of the native population. This situation was brought out in a striking form in an interchange of letters in 1930 between the settler members of the Legislative Council of Northern Rhodesia and the British Colonial Office. The members of the Council, strongly objecting to the theory of the paramountcy of native rights in the Colony, addressed Lord Passfield as follows:

British colonists . . . hold that the British Empire is primarily concerned with the furtherance of the interests of British subjects of British race and only thereafter with other British subjects, protected races, and the nationals of other countries, in that order. . . . To British settlers the paramountcy of the native appears to be incompatible with justice. To subordinate the interests of civilized Britons to the development of other races, whose capability of substantial advancement has not been demonstrated, appears to be contrary to natural law.

Lord Passfield's reply, sent through the Government of Northern Rhodesia, represents what has been in general the broad and considerate policy of the Colonial Office. While not disregarding the rights of European settlers in the Colonies, this has been that the British Government must always give prime consideration to the welfare of the native people who originally occupied an African territory and who are in the large majority among its inhabitants. The Colonial Secretary wrote:

I have to request that you will inform the Signatories that I have received and examined their representations; and that it is unnecessary to discuss them since the views expressed are wholly irrecon-

cilable with the considered policy of His Majesty's Government
. . . a conference can serve no useful result and therefore I do not
feel justified in placing the expense of a deputation on the funds of
the Protectorate.*

This exchange of letters throws a flood of light on the difficulties
of the situation in those parts of Tropical Africa where there is a
considerable population of Europeans—whether British, Dutch
or other—living on the land. The settler members of the Legislative Council did not, of course, represent the point of view of all
European residents in the Colony but it is probably fair to infer
that they did substantially represent a considerable segment of
public opinion.

It is impossible to say how many of the Europeans in Africa are
engaged in government service, but statistics from a few representative colonies will give some indication. For instance, according to
Hailey's figures for Nigeria and the British Cameroons, the total
is 2,048 (the largest in any British African colony); in Sierra Leone,
215; and in Kenya (including some men who render service also
in Uganda), 1,362. The largest numbers are under Administration;
Railways and Transportation; Medical and Health Service; Public
Works; Military and Police; Agriculture, Veterinary, and Forestry
Services; Education; Judicial-Legal Departments. The mere enu-
meration of these groups shows the manifold services provided and
their complexity.
The figures are high in comparison with places like India,
where the number of British in the Civil Government is under
a thousand, but this is due to the fact that up to the present
there has been no large group of educated Africans who could be
drawn upon. Obviously the key positions involving expert knowledge and training must be filled from abroad until qualified native
Africans are available. It must also be remembered that many of
the territories are very large in extent. Nigeria, for instance, with
the small adjoining British-mandated Cameroons, includes 370,000
square miles, or well over twice the size of all the New England
and Middle Atlantic States put together.

The number of missionaries in Africa is relatively large. The
latest figures show that Protestant foreign mission staff workers
in Africa, including Madagascar, were 8,447. The total number of
foreign Catholic priests is reported to be 5,010, with 3,495 lay
brothers and 10,892 sisters. The recent increase in native mission-

* Hinden, Rita. *Plan for Africa*, pages 37 and 38; quoting *Correspondence
with regard to Native Policy in Northern Rhodesia*, 1930.

aries is particularly important. The Catholic Church now reports 429 native priests. It is the conviction of most broad-minded missionaries that Africa can only be completely evangelized by native Christians, and that a major emphasis of the foreign staff should be on the thorough training of native clergy and teachers.

The helpful and hampering activities of economic groups have been mentioned in other chapters of this Report. Grateful acknowledgment must, however, be made to the thousands of able, conscientious, sympathetic, and far-sighted government officials and employees, both European and native, and to the devoted and competent Christian missionaries, both Protestant and Catholic, who have learned African languages, endured the threats of tropical life under primitive conditions, and won the confidence of the native people. These two groups deserve a word of special commendation, for they have generally served with real devotion and have often been pioneers of enlightenment in remote regions.

Terms of the Mandate System*

1. ARTICLE 22 OF THE COVENANT OF THE LEAGUE OF NATIONS— MANDATORIES

1. To those colonies and territories which as a consequence of the late war have ceased to be under the sovereignty of the States which formerly governed them and which are inhabited by peoples not yet able to stand by themselves under the strenuous conditions of the modern world, there should be applied the principle that the well-being and development of such peoples form a sacred trust of civilization and that securities for the performance of this trust be embodied in this Covenant.

2. The best method of giving practical effect to this principle is that the tutelage of such peoples should be entrusted to advanced nations who, by reason of their resources, their experience or their geographical position, can best undertake this responsibility, and who are willing to accept it, and that this tutelage should be exercised by them as Mandatories on behalf of the League.

3. The character of the mandate must differ according to the stage of the development of the people, the geographic situation of the territory, its economic conditions and other similar circumstances.

4. Certain communities formerly belonging to the Turkish Empire have reached a stage of development where their existence as independent nations can be provisionally recognized subject to the rendering of administrative advice and assistance by a Mandatory until such time as they are able to stand alone. The wishes of these communities must be a principal consideration in the selection of the Mandatory.

5. Other peoples, especially those of Central Africa, are at such a stage that the Mandatory must be responsible for the administration of the territory under conditions which will guarantee freedom of conscience and religion, subject only to the maintenance of public order and morals, the prohibition of abuses such as the slave trade, the arms traffic and the liquor traffic, and the prevention of the establishment of fortifications or military and naval bases and of

---

* These have been copied from Appendixes XI and XII, in Volume I of Buell, *The Native Problem in Africa.*

military training of the natives for other than police purposes and
the defence of territory, and will also secure equal opportunities for
the trade and commerce of other Members of the League.

6. There are territories, such as Southwest Africa and certain of
the South Pacific Islands, which, owing to the sparseness of their
population or their small size, or their remoteness from the centres
of civilization, or their geographical contiguity to the territory of
the Mandatory, and other circumstances, can be best administered
under the laws of the Mandatory as integral portions of its territory
subject to the safeguards above mentioned in the interests of the
indigenous population.

7. In every case of mandate, the Mandatory shall render to the
Council an annual report in reference to the territory committed
to its charge.

8. The degree of authority, control or administration to be ex-
ercised by the Mandatory shall, if not previously agreed upon by the
Members of the League, be explicitly defined in each case by the
Council.

9. A permanent Commission shall be constituted to receive and
examine the annual reports of the Mandatories, and to advise the
Council on all matters relating to the observance of the mandates.

2. TYPICAL MANDATE AGREEMENT—WITH GREAT BRITAIN FOR EAST AFRICA

The Council of the League of Nations:

Whereas by Article 119 of the Treaty of Peace with Germany
signed at Versailles on June 28th, 1919, Germany renounced in
favour of the Principal Allied and Associated Powers all her rights
over her oversea possessions, including therein German East Africa;
and

Whereas, in accordance with the treaty of June 11th, 1891, between Her Britannic Majesty and His Majesty the King of Portugal,
the River Rovuma is recognised as forming the northern boundary
of the Portuguese possessions in East Africa from its mouth up to
the confluence of the River M'Sinje; and

Whereas the Principal Allied and Associated Powers agreed that,
in accordance with Article 22, Part I (Covenant of the League of
Nations), of the said treaty, a mandate should be conferred upon
His Britannic Majesty to administer part of the former colony of
German East Africa, and have proposed that the mandate should
be formulated in the following terms; and

Whereas His Britannic Majesty has agreed to accept the mandate
in respect to the said territory, and has undertaken to exercise it on

behalf of the League of Nations in accordance with the following provisions; and

Whereas by the afore-mentioned Article 22, paragraph 8, it is provided that the degree of authority, control or administration to be exercised by the Mandatory, not having been previously agreed upon by the Members of the League, shall be explicitly defined by the Council of the League of Nations;

Confirming the said mandate, defines its terms as follows: . . .

Article 3.

The Mandatory shall be responsible for the peace, order and good government of the territory, and shall undertake to promote to the utmost the material and moral well-being and the social progress of its inhabitants. The Mandatory shall have full powers of legislation and administration.

Article 4.

The Mandatory shall not establish any military or naval bases, nor erect any fortifications, nor organise any native military force in the territory except for local police purposes and for the defence of the territory.

Article 5.

The Mandatory: a

(1) shall provide for the eventual emancipation of all slaves and for as speedy an elimination of domestic and other slavery as social conditions will allow:

(2) shall suppress all forms of slave trade;

(3) shall prohibit all forms of forced or compulsory labour, except for essential public works and services, and then only in return for adequate remuneration;

(4) shall protect the natives from abuse and measures of fraud and force by the careful supervision of labour contracts and the recruiting of labour;

(5) shall exercise a strict control over the traffic in arms and ammunition and the sale of spirituous liquors.

Article 6.

In the framing of laws relating to the holding or transfer of land, the Mandatory shall take into consideration native laws and customs, and shall respect the rights and safeguard the interests of the native population.

No native land may be transferred, except between natives, without the previous consent of the public authorities, and no real rights over native land in favour of non-natives may be created except with the same consent.

The Mandatory will promulgate strict regulations against usury.

Article 7.

The Mandatory shall secure to all nationals of States Members of the League of Nations the same rights as are enjoyed in the territory by his own nationals in respect of entry into and residence in the territory, the protection afforded to their person and property, the acquisition of property, movable and immovable, and the exercise of their profession or trade, subject only to the requirements of public order, and on condition of compliance with the local law.

Further, the Mandatory shall ensure to all nationals of States Members of the League of Nations, on the same footing as to his own nationals, freedom of transit and navigation, and complete economic, commercial and industrial equality; provided that the Mandatory shall be free to organise essential public works and services on such terms and conditions as he thinks just.

Concessions for the development of the natural resources of the territory shall be granted by the Mandatory without distinction on grounds of nationality between the nationals of all States Members of the League of Nations, but on such conditions as will maintain intact the authority of the local Government.

Concessions having the character of a general monopoly shall not be granted. This provision does not affect the right of the Mandatory to create monopolies of a purely fiscal character in the interest of the territory under mandate, and in order to provide the territory with fiscal resources which seem best suited to the local requirements; or, in certain cases, to carry out the development of natural resources either directly by the State or by a controlled agency, provided that there shall result therefrom no monopoly of the natural resources for the benefit of the Mandatory or his nationals, directly or indirectly, nor any preferential advantage which shall be inconsistent with the economic, commercial and industrial equality hereinbefore guaranteed.

The rights conferred by this article extend equally to companies and associations organised in accordance with the law of any of the Members of the League of Nations, subject only to the requirements of public order, and on condition of compliance with the local law.

Article 8.

The Mandatory shall ensure in the territory complete freedom of conscience and the free exercise of all forms of worship which are consonant with public order and morality; missionaries who are nationals of States Members of the League of Nations shall be free to enter the territory and to travel and reside therein, to acquire and possess property, to erect religious buildings and to open schools throughout the territory; it being understood, however, that the Mandatory shall have the right to exercise such control as may be necessary for the maintenance of public order and good government, and to take all measures required by such control.

Article 9.

The Mandatory shall apply to the territory any general international conventions already existing, or which may be concluded hereafter, with the approval of the League of Nations, respecting the slave trade, the traffic in arms and ammunition, the liquor traffic, and the traffic in drugs, or relating to commercial equality, freedom of transit and navigation, aerial navigation, railways, postal, telegraphic, and wireless communication, and industrial, literary and artistic property.

The Mandatory shall co-operate in the execution of any common policy adopted by the League of Nations for preventing and combating disease, including diseases of plants and animals.

Article 10.

The Mandatory shall be authorised to constitute the territory into a customs, fiscal and administrative union or federation with the adjacent territories under his own sovereignty or control; provided always that the measures adopted to that end do not infringe the provisions of this mandate.

Article 11.

The Mandatory shall make to the Council of the League of Nations an annual report to the satisfaction of the Council, containing full information concerning the measures taken to apply the provisions of this mandate.

A copy of all laws and regulations made in the course of the year and affecting property, commerce, navigation or the moral and material well-being of the natives shall be annexed to this report.

Article 12.

The consent of the Council of the League of Nations is required for any modification of the terms of this mandate.

Article 13.

The Mandatory agrees that if any dispute whatever should arise between the Mandatory and another Member of the League of Nations relating to the interpretation or the application of the provisions of the mandate, such dispute, if it cannot be settled by negotiation, shall be submitted to the Permanent Court of International Justice provided for by Article 14 of the Covenant of the League of Nations.

States Members of the League of Nations may likewise bring any claims on behalf of their nationals for infractions of their rights under this mandate before the said Court for decision. . . .

List of American Organizations Specially Interested in Africa

1. PHILANTHROPIC, EDUCATIONAL, AND OTHER FOUNDATIONS AND SOCIETIES*

Carnegie Corporation of New York, 522 Fifth Avenue, New York, N. Y.

Rockefeller Foundation, 49 West 49th Street, New York, N. Y.

The Guggenheim Foundation, Carnegie Hall, New York, N. Y.

Phelps-Stokes Fund, 101 Park Avenue, New York, N. Y.

Mary Esther Bedford Fund, c/o Dr. W. B. Mumford, Southport, Conn.

Africa Bureau, 156 Fifth Avenue, New York, N. Y.

Council on African Affairs, 8 W. 40th St., New York, N. Y.

New York State Colonization Society, 49 West 49th Street, New York, N. Y.

American Colonization Society, c/o Mr. James B. Reynolds, President, Transportation Building, Washington, D. C.

Trustees of Donations, Mr. George G. Wolkins, Secretary, 50 Congress Street, Boston, Mass.

American Aid for Ethiopia, 156 Fifth Avenue, New York, N. Y.

2. MISSIONARY ORGANIZATIONS

(1) Protestant Societies

Foreign Missions Conference of North America, 156 Fifth Avenue, New York, N. Y.: member boards and agencies which maintain relations with Africa:

United Church of Canada, 299 Queen St., W., Toronto, Canada

Woman's Missionary Society of the United Church of Canada, 96 Wellesley Building, Toronto, Canada

General Conference of the Seventh-Day Adventists, Takoma Park, Washington, D. C.

American Baptist Foreign Mission Society, 152 Madison Avenue, New York, N. Y.

* This list does not include organizations in the general international field. There is an African Students' Association. Address c/o International House, New York, N. Y.

Woman's American Baptist Foreign Mission Society, 152 Madison Avenue, New York, N. Y.

Lott Carey Baptist Foreign Mission Convention, 1505 11th St., N. W., Washington, D. C.

Foreign Mission Society of the National Baptist Convention, 701 S. 19th St., Philadelphia, Pa.

Foreign Mission Board of the Southern Baptist Convention, 610 E. Franklin St., Richmond, Va.

Foreign Mission Board of the Brethren in Christ Church, Mount Joy, Pa.

Foreign Mission Board of the Brethren in Christ Church, 1925 E. 5th St., Long Beach, Calif.

General Mission Board of the Church of the Brethren, 22 S. State St., Elgin, Ill.

Foreign Mission Society, United Brethren in Christ, 1410 U. B. Bldg., Dayton, Ohio

Woman's Missionary Association, United Brethren in Christ, 1412 U. B. Bldg., Dayton, Ohio

Domestic, Frontier and Foreign Missionary Society, United Brethren in Christ, 407 U. B. Bldg., Huntington, Ind.

Women's Missionary Association, United Brethren in Christ, 411 U. B. Bldg., Huntington, Ind.

Christian and Missionary Alliance, 260 W. 44th St., New York, N. Y.

American Board of Commissioners for Foreign Missions, 14 Beacon St., Boston, Mass.

Missionary Board of the Church of God, Gospel Trumpet Co., Anderson, Ind.

Mission Board of the Evangelical Free Church of America, 1630 Farragut St., Chicago, Ill.

United Christian Missionary Society, Missions Bldg., Indianapolis, Ind.

Department of Missions, Protestant Episcopal Church in the U. S. A., 281 Fourth Avenue, New York, N. Y.

Missionary Society of the Evangelical Church, 1900 Superior Ave., Cleveland, Ohio

Evangelical Free Church of the U. S. A., 306 N. Rockford Ave., Rockford, Ill.

Board of Foreign Missions, Evangelical Synod of N. A., 1720 Chouteau Ave., St. Louis, Mo.

American Friends Board of Missions, 101 S. 8th St., Richmond, Ind.

Board of Foreign Missions of the Augustana Synod, 415 Harvard St., S. E., Minneapolis, Minn.

Friends Africa Gospel Mission of Kansas Yearly Meeting, Stafford, Kan.

Board of Missions of the Church of the Lutheran Brethren, Fergus Falls, Minn.

Board of Foreign Missions of the Norwegian Lutheran Church in N. A., 425 S. 4th St., Minneapolis, Minn.

Board of Foreign Missions, United Lutheran Church in America, 18 E. Mt. Vernon Place, Baltimore, Maryland

Women's Missionary Society, United Lutheran Church in America, 717 Muhlenberg Bldg., Philadelphia, Pa.

Congo Inland Mission, 1300 W. 72nd St., Chicago, Ill.

Board of Foreign Missions of the Pennsylvania Conference of the Mennonite Brethren, in Christ, Box 294, Emaus, Pa.

Board of Missions and Church Extension of the Methodist Church, 150 Fifth Avenue, New York, N. Y.

Woman's Division of the Board of Missions and Church Extension of the Methodist Church, New York, N. Y.

Foreign Missionary Department of the African Methodist Episcopal Church, 112 W. 120th St., New York, N. Y.

Woman's Parent Mite Missionary Society of the African Methodist Episcopal Church, 419 Alger Ave., Detroit, Mich.

Foreign Mission Board, African Methodist Episcopal Zion Church, 1421 U St., N. W., Washington, D. C.

Woman's Home and Foreign Missionary Society, African Methodist Episcopal Zion Church, 1919 Bainbridge St., Philadelphia, Pa.

General Missionary Board of the Free Methodist Church of North America, Winona Lake, Ind.

Missionary Society of the Wesleyan Methodist Connection in America, 222 S. Clemens Ave., Lansing, Mich.

General Council of the Assemblies of God, 336 W. Pacific St., Springfield, Mo.

Church of the Nazarene, 2923 Troost Ave., Kansas City, Mo.

Hephzibah Faith Missionary Association, Tabor, Iowa

Board of Foreign Missions, Presbyterian Church in the U. S. A., 156 Fifth Avenue, New York, N. Y.

Executive Committee of Foreign Missions of the Presbyterian Church in the U. S., Post Office Box 330, Nashville, Tenn.

Committee on Woman's Work, Presbyterian Church in the U. S., Henry Grady Bldg., Atlanta, Ga.

Board of Foreign Missions of the United Presbyterian Church in North America, 1505 Race St., Philadelphia, Pa.

Women's General Missionary Society of the United Presbyterian Church of North America, 5542 Hampton St., East Liberty Station, Pittsburgh, Pa.

Christian Reformed Board of Missions, 745 Benjamin Ave., Grand Rapids, Mich.

Scandinavian Alliance Mission in North America, 2839 McLean Avenue, Chicago, Ill.

Evangelical Mission Covenant Church of America, 1005 Belmont Ave., Chicago, Ill.

Other Protestant mission boards and agencies working in Africa:

Canada Yearly Meeting of Friends, Pickering, Ontario, Canada

Unevangelized Fields Mission, 1162 N. 63rd St., Philadelphia, Pa.

Africa Inland Mission, Home Council for North America, 373 Carlton Ave., Brooklyn, N. Y.

Berean African Mission, 407 University Bldg., Denver, Colo.

American Missionary Association, 287 Fourth Avenue, New York, N. Y.

Agricultural Missions, Inc., 156 Fifth Avenue, New York, N. Y.

Evangelical Congregational Church, Missionary Society, 317 Maclay St., Harrisburg, Pa.

Congo Gospel Mission, 245 N. Villa Ave., Villa Park, Ill.

Gospel Missionary Society, Inc., 17 Court St., New Britain, Conn.

Gospel Missionary Union, 1841 E. 7th St., Kansas City, Mo.

United Free Gospel and Missionary Society, 285 Larimer Ave., Turtle Creek, Pa.

Eastern Mennonite Board of Missions and Charities, Box 23, Akron, Pa.

Mennonite Brethren in Christ, United Missionary Society, 483 S. Paddock St., Pontiac, Mich.

General Church of the New Jerusalem, Bryn Athyn, Pa.

Pentecost Faith Mission, R. 1, Bedford, Ind.

Pentecostal Assemblies of the World, 1902 N. Capitol Ave., Indianapolis, Ind.

Pentecostal Holiness Church, Box 762, Oklahoma City, Okla.

The Evangelization Society of the Pittsburgh Bible Institute, 12 Congress St., Pittsburgh, Pa.

Sudan Interior Mission, 156 Fifth Avenue, New York, N. Y.

South Africa General Mission, 23 Flatbush Ave., Brooklyn, N. Y.

Unevangelized Africa Mission, Box 27, Garden Grove, Calif.

Unevangelized Tribes Mission, 147 W. School Lane, Germantown, Philadelphia, Pa.

Sudan United Mission, 47 Petman Ave., Toronto, Canada

Seminaries placing Emphasis on Preparation of Missionaries for
Africa:

Africa Department, Kennedy School of Missions, Hartford Seminary Foundation, Hartford, Conn.

Stewart Missionary Foundation for Africa, Gammon Theological
Seminary, Atlanta, Ga.

Scarritt College for Christian Workers, Nashville, Tenn.

(2) Catholic Societies

The Fathers of the Holy Ghost, Headquarters, 1615 Manchester
Lane, N. W., Washington, D. C. V. Rev. George J. Collins,
C.S.Sp., Provincial.

The Congregation of Mariannhill Missionaries, 23715 Ann Arbor
Trail, Dearborn, Mich. V. Rev. Joseph Reiner, C.M.M., Provincial.

The Society of African Missions, St. Ignatius Novitiate African
Missions, Silver Spring, Md. V. Rev. Ignatius Lissner, S.M.A.,
Provincial.

Society of the Divine Word, St. Mary's Mission House, Techny, Ill.
V. Rev. Charles Michel, S.V.D., Provincial. (This conducts St.
Augustine's Seminary, Bay St. Louis, Miss., where American
Negroes are prepared for work in Africa as well as in this
country.)

Missionary Sisters of Our Lady of Africa, 319 Middlesex Avenue,
Metuchen, N. J. Mother Theodora, Superior. (This is the only
house in this country. It is, however, a very large organization,
some 1,500 Sisters. Founded in Algeria in 1869. They are also
called the White Sisters.)

Franciscan Missionaries of Mary, 399 Fruithill Avenue, Providence,
R. I. Mother Mary Hildegardis of Jesus, Provincial. (These Sisters work in Uganda and other parts of Africa.)

The National Society for the Propagation of the Faith, 109 East 38th
St., New York, N. Y. Rt. Rev. Msgr. Thomas J. McDonnell,
National Director.

3. Embassies, Legations, and Consulates from Africa or from Countries Having African Territory

Belgium: Belgian Embassy, Washington, D. C.

Egypt: Egyptian Legation, Washington, D. C.

France: French Embassy, Washington, D. C.

Great Britain: British Embassy, Washington, D. C.

Portugal: Portuguese Legation, Washington, D. C.

Spain: Spanish Embassy, Washington, D. C.

Union of South Africa: Legation of U. of S. A., Washington, D. C.
Ethiopia (Consulate General), 78 Water St., New York, N. Y.
Free French Delegation, 626 Fifth Avenue, New York, N. Y.
Liberia (Consulate General), 25 Beaver St., New York, N. Y.

4. LIBRARIES, MUSEUMS, AND UNIVERSITIES

No comprehensive study of African collections and facilities for instruction on African history and problems in this country is available. A few institutions are, however, worthy of special mention:

The Schomburg Collection of Negro Literature in the New York Public Library, 135th Street Branch, is probably the most inclusive of its character, covering the Negro in the United States, Africa, and other parts of the world.

The John G. White Collection of the Cleveland Public Library is also worthy of note. The Library of Congress and the Library of Harvard University are also specially rich in African material. So are the Foreign Missions Libraries connected with the Union Theological Seminary, New York, the Yale Divinity School, New Haven, and the Kennedy School of Missions, Hartford.

Similar important collections are found at Atlanta, Fisk, and Howard Universities, Hampton Institute, and in other places.

Several museums lay special emphasis on African art or African ethnology. Among these are the Brooklyn Museum of Arts and Sciences, the American Museum of Natural History in New York, the Field Museum of Chicago, the University of California Museum of Anthropology, the Peabody Museum of Archaeology and Ethnology at Harvard University, the Buffalo Museum of Science, the Museum of the University of Pennsylvania, and that of Lincoln University. The Museum of Modern Art in New York has been specially interested in exhibits of African art.

The Department of History of the University of California, Southern Branch, under the leadership of Professor Frank J. Klingberg, has been specially interested in studies regarding the Negro both in Africa and the United States. The same is true of Atlanta, Fisk, and Howard Universities.

The University of Pennsylvania has this year introduced courses of study, under the direction of Dr. Heinz Wieschoff, in African languages, including Fanti, Haussa, Swahili.

5. TRANSPORTATION COMPANIES WITH AFRICAN CONNECTIONS

American South African Line, 26 Beaver St., New York, N. Y.
American West African Line, 17 Battery Place, New York, N. Y.
Pan American Airways System, 135 East 42d St., New York, N. Y.

Selected African Bibliography*

1. BACKGROUND SOURCES

Africa (A social, economic and political geography of its major regions). London, Methuen, 1934.

Africa Answers Back. Akikik Nyabango. London, Routledge, 1936.

African Questions at the Paris Peace Conference. G. L. Beer. New York, Macmillan and Co., 1923.

African Republic of Liberia and the Belgian Congo, The. (2 vols.). Based on the Observations Made and Material Collected during the Harvard African Expedition, 1926-1927. Edited by Richard P. Strong. Cambridge, Harvard University Press, 1930.

Ashanti. R. S. Rattray. New York, Oxford University Press, 1924.

Belgian Congo and the Berlin Act, The. A. B. Keith. New York, Oxford University Press, 1919.

Bibliography of the Negro in Africa and 'America, A. Monroe N. Work. New York, The H. W. Wilson Company, 1928.

Bisoro Stories. Akikik Nyabango. London, Blackwell, 1937.

Black Folk: Then and Now. William Edward Burghardt DuBois. New York, Henry Holt & Co., 1939.

Dual Mandate in British Tropical Africa, The. F. D. Lugard. Edinburgh, William Blackwood & Son, 1926.

East Africa and Its Invaders. R. Coupland. Oxford, Clarendon Press, 1938.

Empire and Commerce in Africa: A Study in Economic Imperialism. Leonard Woolf. London, Allen and Unwin, 1920.

Ethiopia—A Pawn in European Diplomacy. Ernest Work. Ashville, Ohio, Pickaway County News, 1935.

Ethnology of Africa. W. D. Hambley. Chicago, Field Museum, 1930.

European Imperialism in Africa. Halford L. Hoskins. New York, Henry Holt & Co., 1930.

Exploration of East Africa 1856-1890. R. Coupland. London, Faber & Faber, 1939.

Germans in the Cameroons, The, 1884-1914. Harry R. Rudin. New Haven, Yale University Press, 1938.

* This Bibliography, prepared in the main by the African Bureau through the kindness of Dr. Emory Ross, merely covers the most generally useful modern works on that part of Africa dealt with in this Report—Africa south of the Sahara—especially with reference to native problems.

Golden Stool, The. Edwin W. Smith. London, Holborn Publishing House, 1926.

History of Abyssinia, A. A. H. M. Jones and Elizabeth Monroe. New York, Oxford University Press, 1935.

History of the Gambia, A. J. M. Gray. Cambridge, University Press, 1940.

History of South Africa, A. E. A. Walker. London, Longmans Green, 1940.

History of South Africa: Social and Economic, A. C. W. de Kiewiet. London, Oxford University Press, 1941.

Hunger and Work in a Savage Tribe. Audrey I. Richards. London, Routledge, 1932.

Intervention and Colonization in Africa. Norman Dwight Harris. New York, Houghton Mifflin Co., 1914.

Liberia. (2 vols.). Sir Harry Johnston. New York, Dodd Mead & Co., 1906.

Liberia—Old and New. J. L. Sibley and Diedrich Westermann. Garden City, N. Y., Doubleday, Doran, 1928.

Life of a South African Tribe, The. Henri A. Junod. London, Macmillan and Co., 1927.

Native Problem in Africa, The. (2 vols.). Raymond Leslie Buell. New York, Macmillan and Co., 1934.

Native Races of East Africa. W. D. Hambly (in his Native Races of the British Empire, Vol. 3). New York, Oxford University Press, 1921.

Opening Up of Africa, The. Harry H. Johnston. New York, Henry Holt & Co., 1911.

Partition and Colonization of Africa, The. Charles P. Lucas. New York, Oxford University Press, 1922.

Problèmes Coloniaux d'Hier et d'Aujourd'hui. Georges Moulaert. Bruxelles, L'Edition Universelle, 1940.

Real Abyssinia, The. C. F. Rey. Philadelphia, J. B. Lippincott.

Statesman's Year-Book, The. M. Epstein, editor. London, Macmillan and Co., Limited, 1941. [This contains good bibliographies.]

Story of an African Chief. Akikik Nyabango. New York, Scribners, 1935.

Sudanese Kingdom, A. C. K. Meek. 1931.

Suppression of the Slave Trade in the United States, The. William Edward Burghardt DuBois. New York, Longmans, Green & Co., 1896.

Vue Generale d'Histoire d'Afrique. Georges Hardy. Paris, 1922.

2. Education and Religion

Africa and Christianity. Diedrich Westermann (Duff Lectures). London, Oxford University Press, 1937.

African Beliefs and Christian Faith. Edwin W. Smith. London, United Society for Christian Literature, 1936.

African Ways and Wisdom. T. Cullen Young. London, United Society for Christian Literature, 1937.

Africans Learn to Be French. W. Bryant Mumford in consultation with Major G. St. J. Orde-Brown. London, Evans Brothers, Limited, 1935.

Aggrey of Africa. Edwin W. Smith. New York, Friendship Press, 1936.

Bibliography of African Education, A. Howard Drake. Aberdeen, The University Press, 1942.

Chaga Childhood. A Description of Indigenous Education in an East African Tribe. O. F. Raum, Ph.D. Oxford University Press, 1940.

Christian Mission in Africa, The. Edwin W. Smith. London, The International Missionary Council, 1926.

Christianity and the Race Problem. J. H. Oldham. London, Student Christian Movement, 1924.

Clash of Colour, The. Basil Mathews. London, United Council for Missionary Education, 1924.

Consider Africa. Basil Mathews. New York, Friendship Press, 1935.

Education in Africa. A Study of West, South and Equatorial Africa by the African Education Commission (1920-21) . . . Report prepared by Thomas Jesse Jones. New York, Phelps-Stokes Fund, 1922.

Education in East Africa. A Study of East, Central and South Africa by the Second African Education Commission (1923-24) . . . Report prepared by Thomas Jesse Jones. New York, Phelps-Stokes Fund, 1925.

Education of a Primitive People. Albert D. Helser. New York, Fleming H. Revell Co., 1934.

Education of the South African Native, The. Charles T. Loram. New York, Longmans, Green & Co., 1917.

Evangelisation of Pagan Africa, The. J. Du Plessis. Cape Town and Johannesburg, J. C. Juta & Co., Ltd., 1929.

Lovedale, South Africa: The Story of a Century, 1841-1941. Robert H. W. Shepherd. Lovedale, C. P., The Lovedale Press. 1941.

Native African Medicine. George Way Harley, M. D. Cambridge, Mass., Harvard University Press, 1941.

Religion of Lower Races as Illustrated by the African Bantu, The. Edwin W. Smith. New York, Macmillan and Co., 1923.

Remaking of Man in Africa, The. J. H. Oldham and B. D. Gibson. London, Oxford University Press, 1931. (Now out of print.)

School in the Bush, The. A. Victor Murray. London, Longmans, Green & Co., 1929.

Soul of the Bantu, The. W. C. Willoughby. New York, Doubleday, Doran & Company, 1928.

Ten Years in the Congo. W. E. Davis, M.D. New York, Reynal & Hitchcock, 1940.

World Dominion Series, published by the World Dominion Press, London:

   A Missionary Survey of French, British, Spanish and Portuguese West Africa and Liberia. J. J. Cooksey and Alexander McLeish. 1931.

   A New Day in Kenya. Horace R. A. Philip. 1936.

   Angola, the Land of the Blacksmith Prince. J. T. Tucker. 1933.

   Congo, Past and Present. Alfred R. Stonelake. 1937.

   Great Emancipation, A: A Survey of Nyasaland. W. J. W. Roome. 1926.

   Light and Darkness in East Africa. Compiled and edited by Alexander McLeish. 1927.

   Nigeria, The Land, the People and Christian Progress. J. Lowry Maxwell. 1925.

   Portuguese East Africa. Eduardo Moreira. 1936.

   Religion and Civilization in West Africa. J. J. Cooksey and Alexander McLeish. 1931.

   Tanganyika and Its Future. D. Julius Richter. 1934.

   Way of the White Fields in Rhodesia, The. Edwin W. Smith. 1928.

3. Late Economics, Politics, Social, and General

Africa and the World Conflict. Louis E. Frechtling. Foreign Policy Report, Vol. XVII, No. 15, October 15, 1941.

Africa Emergent: A Survey of Social, Political and Economic Trends in British Africa. W. M. Macmillan. London, Faber & Faber, 1938.

African and the Cinema, The. L. A. Notcutt and G. C. Latham. London, The Edinburgh House Press, 1937.

African Labourer, The. G. St. J. Orde-Brown. New York, Oxford University Press, 1933.

African Survey. Lord Hailey. London and New York. Oxford University Press, 1938.

African Today, The. Diedrich Westermann. London, International Institute of African Languages and Cultures, 1934.

Africans and British Rule. Margery Perham. African Welfare Series. London, Oxford University Press. 1941.

An Essay on the Economics of Detribalization in Northern Rhodesia. Part I. G. Wilson. Rhodes-Livingston Institute, 1941.

Bantu Are Coming, The. Ray Phillips. New York, Richard R. Smith, 1930.

Bantu in the City, The. Ray Phillips. Lovedale Press, Lovedale, South Africa, 1938.

Behind God's Back. Negley Farson. New York, Harcourt, Brace & Co., 1941.

Black Problem, The. D. D. T. Jabavu. Lovedale, C. P., The Book Department, 1920.

Case for African Freedom, The. Joyce Cary. London, Secker & Warburg, 1941.

Colonial Policy and the Christian Conscience. J. W. C. Dougall. International Review of Missions, October, 1941, pp. 477-492.

Colonial Problem, The. Royal Institute of International Affairs. New York, Oxford University Press, 1937.

Colour Bar in East Africa. Norman Leys. London, Hogarth Press, 1941.

Colour Problems of South Africa, The. Edgar H. Brookes. Lovedale Press, 1934.

Dakar, Outpost of Two Hemispheres. Emil Lengyel. New York, Random House, 1942.

"Democratise the Empire!" W. M. Macmillan. London, Messrs. Kegan Paul, 1942.

East Africa. Elspeth Huxley. London, Collins, 1941.

Freedom for Colonial Peoples. An essay in *Programme for Victory.* W. M. Macmillan. London, Routledge, 1941.

French Colonial Empire, The. Information Department Papers, No. 25. London, Royal Institute of International Affairs, 1940.

Future of the Colonies, The. In *Planning* (published by "Political and Economic Planning"), January 20, 1942.

History of Native Policy in South Africa from 1830 to the Present Day, The. Edgar H. Brookes. Pretoria, J. L. Van Schaik, Ltd., 1927.

Italian Colonial Empire, The. London, Royal Institute of International Affairs, 1940.

Modern Industry and the African. J. Merle Davis. London, International Missionary Council, 1932.

Native Labour in South Africa. Shiela T. van der Horst. London, Oxford University Press, 1942.

Native Policy in Southern Africa. Ivor L. Evans. New York, Macmillan and Co., 1934.

Northern Rhodesia: Report of the Commission appointed to inquire into disturbances in the Copper Belt, July, 1940. Lusaka, Government Printer.

Out of Africa. Emory Ross. New York, Friendship Press, 1936.

Plan for Africa. Rita Hinden. London, George Allen and Unwin, Ltd., 1941 (mainly about Northern Rhodesia and the Gold Coast).

Portrait of a Colony, the Story of Natal. A. F. Hattersley. Cambridge, University Press, 1940.

Position of Colonies in a British Commonwealth of Nations. Lord Hailey (The Romanes Lectures). London, Oxford University Press, 1941.

Race Problems in the New Africa. W. C. Willoughby. New York, Oxford University Press, 1934.

Renascent Africa. Nnamdi Azikiwe. Lowestoft, M. F. Robinson & Co. Ltd. Library Press [1937].

South Africa: People, Places and Problems. William Hurbutt Dawson. New York, Longmans, Green & Co., 1925.

South African Native Policy and the Liberal Spirit. Being the Phelps-Stokes Lectures delivered before the University of Cape Town. R. F. Alfred Hoernlé. Lovedale, The Lovedale Press, 1939.

Union's Burden of Poverty, The. J. D. Rheinallt Jones and R. F. Alfred Hoernlé. Johannesburg, South African Institute of Race Relations, 1941.

Western Civilization and the Natives of South Africa. Isaac Schapera. London, Routledge, 1934.

4. PERIODICALS

Africa. Published quarterly (1927-1940). London. Oxford University Press. (Temporarily discontinued.)

African Morning Post. Published daily. Accra, Gold Coast.

African Observer, The. Published monthly. Bulawayo, Southern Rhodesia.

African World. Published weekly. London.

Anti-Slavery Reporter and Aborigines Friend. Published quarterly. London, Anti-Slavery & Aborigines Protection Society.

Bantu Mirror, The. Published weekly. Bulawayo, Southern Rhodesia.

Bantu Studies. Johannesburg, University of the Witwatersrand Press.

Books for Africa. Published quarterly. London, International Committee on Christian Literature for Africa.

Colonial News Bulletin. London, Colonial Department, Institute of Education, University of London.

Colonial Review. Published monthly. London.

Congo Mission News. Published quarterly. Leopoldville, Conseil Protestant du Congo.

East Africa and Rhodesia. Published weekly. London.

L'Evangile en Afrique. Published bi-monthly. Leopoldville, Conseil Protestant du Congo.

International Review of Missions, The. Published quarterly. London.

Journal of Negro History, The. Published quarterly. Washington, D. C., The Association for the Study of Negro Life and History, Inc.

Journal of the Royal African Society. Published quarterly. London, Macmillan.

Nada. Published annually. Salisbury, Southern Rhodesia.

Race Relations News. Published monthly. Johannesburg, South African Institute of Race Relations.

South African Outlook. Published monthly. Lovedale, Lovedale Press.

United Empire. Published monthly. London, Royal Empire Society.

West Africa. Published monthly. London, The West Africa Publishing Co.

Reports of International Anthropological Congresses:

Congrès international des sciences anthropologiques et ethnologiques. *1st, London, 1934.*

. . . Compte-rendu de la première session, Londres, 1934. Londres, Institut royal d'anthropologie, 1934. xxxii, 340 p. 24cm.

Congrès international des sciences anthropologiques et ethnologiques. *2d, Copenhagen, 1938.*

. . . Compte-rendu de la deuxième session, Copenhague, 1938. Copenhague, Munksgaard, 1939. 397 p. 26.5cm.

New works on Africa and its problems are frequently appearing. For instance, the Missionary Education Movement, 156 Fifth Avenue, New York, N. Y., has just received copies of *Five Points for Africa,* by Margaret Wrong (London, Edinburgh House Press, 1942).

Professor Frank J. Klingberg is about to publish, through the University of California Press, *The Rise of the Negro in Africa.*

List of Members of Committee

Dr. W. W. Alexander, Vice President of Julius Rosenwald Fund; former Director of Commission on Interracial Cooperation.

Mr. Claude A. Barnett, Director, Associated Negro Press.

Dr. Raymond Leslie Buell, Adviser on Foreign Affairs to *Fortune, Life,* and *Time;* former President, Foreign Policy Association. Author of *The Native Problem in Africa.*

*Dr. Ralph Johnson Bunche, Professor of Political Science, Howard University. Visitor to Africa on Social Science Research Fellowship.

Miss Mabel Carney, Professor of Rural Education, Teachers College, Columbia University. Visitor to Africa.

Dr. Charles W. Coulter, Head, Department of Sociology, University of New Hampshire. Carnegie Visiting Professor to Universities of South Africa 1929-30; Member of Commission to Study Poor White Problem in South Africa.

Miss Marion Cuthbert, Department of Study, Leadership Department, National Board of Y. W. C. A.

*Mr. Jackson Davis, Associate Director, General Education Board; President of New York State Colonization Society; President of Board of Trustees of Booker Washington Institute of Liberia. Carnegie Visitor to Africa in 1935.

*Mr. J. Merle Davis, Director of Social and Economic Research, International Missionary Council. Chairman of the Commission of Inquiry (1932); and Editor of Its Report (1933), *Modern Industry and the African.*

*Mr. Malcolm Davis, Associate Director of Division of Intercourse and Education of Carnegie Endowment for International Peace; formerly its representative in Paris and Geneva.

*Dr. Thomas S. Donohugh, Associate Secretary of Board of Missions and Church Extension Methodist Church. Visitor to Africa.

Professor W. E. B. DuBois, Professor of Sociology, Atlanta University. Author of *Black Folk: Then and Now.* Long a close student of African problems.

Mr. John Foster Dulles, Chairman of Committee to Study the Bases for a Just and Durable Peace, Federal Council of Churches.

*Miss Mabel E. Emerson, Secretary of American Board of Commissioners for Foreign Missions; Chairman of the Africa Committee of Foreign Missions Conference.

* An asterisk represents member of the Executive Committee.

Mr. Louis E. Frechtling, Expert on Africa of Foreign Policy Association.

Professor Benjamin Gerig, formerly attached to Mandates Section, League of Nations. Professor of Government, Haverford College.

Mr. Huntington Gilchrist, formerly Assistant Director Mandates Section, International Secretariat, League of Nations.

Dr. George E. Haynes, Executive Secretary, Department of Race Relations, Federal Council of Churches of Christ in America. Visitor to Africa.

*Dr. Charles S. Johnson, *First Vice Chairman.* Department of Sociology, Fisk University. Member of League of Nations Commission to Investigate Forced Labor in Liberia, 1930.

*Dr. Thomas Jesse Jones, Educational Director of the Phelps-Stokes Fund. Chairman of Phelps-Stokes Fund Education Commissions to Africa in 1920-21 and 1923-24.

Dr. Frederick P. Keppel, former President of Carnegie Corporation. Visitor to Africa in the interests of the Corporation.

*Father John LaFarge, Associate Editor of *America.* Authority on Negro Affairs.

Professor Rayford W. Logan, Professor of History, Howard University. Leader of group studying Status of Negro after present World War.

Father J. P. Lucey, C.S.Sp. Formerly missionary in East Africa, attached to Apostolic Delegation in Mombasa. Duquesne University.

Dean Robert Stewart McClenahan, Dean Emeritus, American University of Cairo.

Miss Sallie Lou MacKinnon, Secretary for Africa, Methodist Board of Missions, Woman's Division of Christian Service.

Rev. Henry C. McDowell, Missionary to Angola, American Board of Commissioners of Foreign Missions. Principal, Lincoln Academy, Kings Mountain, N. C.

Bishop Arthur J. Moore, President of the Board of Missions and Church Extension of the Methodist Church. Formerly in charge of Missions of the Methodist Episcopal Church South in the Belgian Congo.

Dr. Frederick Douglass Patterson, President of Tuskegee Institute.

Mr. John R. Reisner, Executive Secretary, Agricultural Missions, Inc. Visitor to Africa and authority on African agriculture.

*Dr. Emory Ross, *Second Vice Chairman.* General Secretary, Foreign Missions Conference of North America. Former Missionary to Belgian Congo.

Dr. George Schwab, former Missionary to Cameroun. Anthropologist. About to publish a Study of the Bassa Tribe, through Harvard University.

Dr. Homer LeRoy Shantz, U. S. Department of Agriculture, Washington, D. C. Member of Phelps-Stokes Education Commission to East and South Africa in 1923-24; Specialist on Agricultural possibilities of Africa with American Commission to Negotiate Peace, 1918-19.

*Dr. Anson Phelps Stokes, *Chairman*. President of Phelps-Stokes Fund, New York. Carnegie Visitor to Africa in 1932.

Dr. George K. Strode, Hygienist. Rockefeller Foundation (International Health Division). Member of American Society of Tropical Medicine.

Mr. Arthur Sweetser, formerly Director of Information Section, League of Nations.

*Dr. Channing H. Tobias, *Secretary*. Senior Secretary, Colored Work Department, National Council Y. M. C. A.

Dr. I. W. Underhill, Missionary of the Presbyterian Board U. S. A. in the Cameroun.

Mr. Walter White, Secretary National Association for the Advancement of Colored People.

Bishop R. R. Wright, Wilberforce University. Formerly Bishop of the A. M. E. Church in South Africa.

Although the late Charles T. Loram (1879-1940), Professor of Race Relations at Yale University, and previously Superintendent of Native Education in Natal, Union of South Africa, died before this Committee was organized, his spirit has been felt by its members—many of whom had long worked with him on similar problems—almost as much as though he had been present.

Index*

* This Index has been prepared by Miss Ellen C. Ahern.

ernment and welfare, 37-38; Egypt and Ethiopia under influence of, 39, 102; Civil Service policy, 41, 102-103; industrial policy in Northern Rhodesia and other colonies, 46; policy on compulsory native labor, 48; peace aim of Christian leaders of, 56, 65, 66, 68, 69, 70, 71; systematic national inspection plan by, favored, 73; groups in, interested in African problems, 87; health work in Africa, 89-90; colonial educational policy, 98-99; progressive social-welfare ideals adopted in colonies and protectorates of, 102-103; areas, populations, and governments in Africa under control of, 111, 112, 113; terms of agreement between Ethiopia and, 114; racial policy in Africa, 126-127, 128-129; terms of mandate agreement with, for East Africa, 133-137. See also separate African colonies, such as BRITISH SOMALILAND; CAMEROONS; etc.
GUGGISBERG, SIR GORDON, founder of Achimota College, 15.
GUMEDE, DR., an example of African potentiality, 123.

HAILÉ SELLASSIÉ, Agreement between Great Britain and, 114.
HAILEY, LORD, *An African Survey* by, recommended, xi; need for further research into African problems stressed by, 25-26; on British policy of self-government for Africa, 38; on housing conditions on the Rand, 54; on roots of African heritage, 58; on interpretation of word "trusteeship," 77; on representative government in Africa, 81; on Civil Service, 81-82; on the Bible in Africa, 100-101; on climate of Africa, 109-110; on population of Africa, 110*n*; on Arabian and Indian communities in Africa, 124-125; on European populations of Africa, 126; on Europeans in African government service, 127.
HARLECH, LORD, on true conception of trusteeship, 56.
HAWAII, Success of U. S. in, 19.
HEALTH CONDITIONS IN AFRICA, Better, needed, 11; better, an asset of European control, 16; work of Rockefeller Foundation for improved, 25; suggestion that U. S. aid in improving, 26; policy for bettering, developed at Le Zoute Conference, 64; improved, one of the social essentials of Africans, 88, 89-92; major needs in field of, 89-92; recommendations concerning, 106-107.
HILTON YOUNG COMMISSION, 129.
HINDEN, RITA, Quotations from book by, 129-130.
HITLER, ADOLF, Views on Negro inferiority, 24-25; plans for Africa, 113.
HOERNLÉ, PROF. R. F. ALFRED, Acknowledgement to, x.
HOFMEYR, JAN H., on government racial policy in Union of South Africa, ii, 34-35.
HOMES, Importance of African, 92.
HOTTENTOTS, 117.
HOUSE OF COMMONS, Debate in, on conscription for farm labor in Kenya, 3-4, 47-48.
HOUSING, Problem of, in Africa, 53-54.
HUSS, FATHER BERNARD, leader in agricultural education, 93-94.
HUXLEY, JULIAN S., consultant to Executive Committee, ix.

INDIA, Importance of Chiang-Kai-shek's recent appeals in regard to, 1-2; local industries and educational experiments in, an example for Africa, 49, 93, 98; government service statistics, 130.
"INDIRECT RULE," favored by Great Britain, 7, 113; in Nigeria, Uganda, Sierra Leone, and Tanganyika, 22-23; taxation under, 46-47; discussion of, 77-80; comparison of French and British attitudes toward, 82-83, 102; Free French Governor on, 83-84; recommendation concerning, 105.
INDUSTRIALIZATION, Evils of, a liability of European control of Africa, 16-17; close relationship between agriculture and, 49; training for, needed in Africa, 94-95.
INTERCOLONIAL DISCUSSIONS, in Africa recommended, 63-64.
INTERNATIONAL FORCED LABOR CONVENTION, 48.
INTERNATIONAL INSTITUTE OF AFRICAN LANGUAGES AND CULTURE, Acknowledgement to Sir Hanns Vischer, x; fine work of, 23, 87.
INTERNATIONAL LABOR ORGANIZATION (OFFICE), Suggestion that U. S. support efforts of, 26; recent conventions adopted at conferences of, 28; development of colonial section needed, 47, 53; experiences of, an aid to international peace, 62; exploitation reduced through efforts of, 104.
INTERNATIONAL MISSIONARY COUNCIL, Acknowledgement to Dr. Oldham of, x; educational films of, 98.
INTERNATIONAL ORGANIZATION, needed to carry out provisions of Atlantic Charter, 5, 31, 56; suggestion that U. S. help in developing, 26. See also LEAGUE OF NATIONS.
INTRODUCTION, 1-11.
ITALY, Discussion concerning African colonies, 35, 57; areas and populations in Africa under control of, 111, 112. See also ERITREA; ETHIOPIA; LIBYA.

JABAVU, DR., an example of African potentiality, 123.
JAPAN, not eligible as a Mandatory Power in Africa, 57; destruction of militarism of, necessary for peace, 71; trade of, with Africa, 117.
JEANES SCHOOLS, 94.
JOHANNESBURG, Recent housing improvements in, 53; wages in, 76.
JOHNSON, PROF. CHARLES S., member of Editorial Committee, ix.
JONES, CREECH, on need for coöperation between Great Britain and colonial peoples, 3.
JONES, SEN. RHEINALLT, Acknowledgement to, x; on land problem in Union of South Africa, 74-75.
JONES, DR. THOMAS JESSE, member of Editorial Committee, ix; on continent of Africa, 109.
JUSTICE, Higher standards of, an asset of European control of Africa, 16.

MILITARY SERVICE, Forced, for special groups unjustifiable, 46; compulsory imperialistic, opposed, 62, 76.
MINES; MINING. *See* RESOURCES.
MISSIONARIES, represented on Committee, viii; one reason for Europe's original interest
in Africa, 13, 15, 103; fine work of, in Africa, 15, 23, 119; interest of U. S. in African,
18; Americans urged to make larger expenditures for work in Africa, 26; conventions
regarding, negotiated at Paris Conference, 27-28; American Negro, excluded from Union
of South Africa, 60-61; rights of, in Africa to be guaranteed, 67; health work of, 90; in
relation to womanhood and the home, 92; leaders in agricultural education, 93-94; Ako
Adjei on need for new type of, 97-98; educational work of, 100-101, 103; figures on, in
Africa, 130-131; mandate provisions regarding, in East Africa, 136; list of American
organizations specifically interested in work in Africa, 138-142. *See also* LE ZOUTE CON-
FERENCE.
MISSIONS. *See* MISSIONARIES.
MOHAMMEDANISM, North Africa influenced by, 60; taught in some government schools,
100; importance of, in Africa, 119.
MONOPOLIES, disappearing in Mozambique, 53; mandate provisions regarding, in East
Africa, 135. *See also* FRANCHISES.
MOROCCO, Work of Marshal Lyautey in, 16; "indirect rule" in, 83-84.
MOSHESH, CHIEF, an example of African potentiality, 123.
MOZAMBIQUE, Large white population in, 9, 126; monopolies in, disappearing, 53.
MUKAMA OF THE BUNYORO, an example of African potentiality, 123.
MUMFORD, DR. W. B., consultant to Executive Committee, ix; quotation by, on impor-
tance to Africa of victory by United Nations, 24-25; on stages in securing self-government
for Africa, 38-39n; on potentiality of Africans, 122.

NATAL, Investigations in, by South African Institute of Race Relations, 86.
NATIONAL STUDY CONFERENCE, on racial potentialities, ii; on bases of durable
peace, ii; on racial discriminations in U. S., 20-21; guiding principles of, 66, 68, 69; on
international coöperation, 70; on armaments, 70-71.
NATIVE CULTURES, LANGUAGES, ETC., Great Britain committed to emphasis on,
7; fear of thoughtful African in regard to, 59; importance of study of, 101, 118; African
potentiality demonstrated by, 124.
NATIVES. *See* AFRICANS.
NAZISM, Solution of Africa's problems an opportunity for United Nations to show oppo-
sition to racial principles of, 6; Italy's adherence to, should preclude her ownership of
African colonies, 35; Gen. Smuts on, 55; destruction of, a major tenet of Atlantic
Charter, 58-60; destruction of, necessary for peace, 71; recommendation concerning racial
theories of, 105-106. *See also* HITLER, ADOLF.
NEGRO AMERICANS, one tenth of population of U. S., 4, 17, 102; wise settlement of
Africa's problems, important to, 6; need for, at Peace Conference, 10; one tenth of all
African people, 17; relationships between Africans and, 18; serious abuses in regard to,
20-21; statement of National Study Conference on discriminations against, 20-21; recent
favorable tendencies in U. S. in regard to, 21-22; Dr. Pickens on disastrous results to, of
Totalitarian victory, 24; exclusion policy in Union of South Africa toward, 60-61; edu-
cation of, an example for Africa, 97, 101, 120.
NEGROES. *See* AFRICANS; NEGRO AMERICANS.
NEHRU, Importance of Chiang-Kai-shek's visit to, 1.
NIELSEN, PETER, on potentiality of Africans, 121.
NIGERIA, Ibanga Udo Akpabio of, present at meeting of Executive Committee, ix; con-
ditions in, among best in Africa, 10; work of Lord Lugard in, 15; "indirect rule" in,
22-23, 77, 83, 113; elective representation in, 80; health work in, 90; large towns in
southern, 111; prominent Africans of, 123; European population, 126; civil service sta-
tistics, 130; area, 130. *See also* LAGOS.
NKRUMAH, FRANCIS, present at meeting of Executive Committee, ix.
NORTH AFRICA, Mohammedan influence in, 60. *See also* ALGERIA; EGYPT; LIBYA;
MOROCCO.
NORTHERN RHODESIA, Labor restrictions in, 45; industrial policy of British Govern-
ment in, 46; question of amalgamation of Nyasaland and, 113; East Indians in, 125;
European population, 126; racial problem in, 127, 129-130.
NOVA SCOTIA, Coöperative movement in, 98.
NYASALAND, Work of Dutch Reformed Church in, 15; example of well-governed pro-
tectorate, 113; East Indians in, 125; European population, 126.

OLDHAM, DR. J. H., Acknowledgement to, x.
ORDER, PUBLIC, one of the assets of European governmental control of Africa, 16.
ORGANIZATIONS, List of American, specifically interested in Africa, 138-143.

PASS LAWS, 76.
PASSFIELD, LORD, on racial policy of Great Britain, 129-130.
PEACE, Wise settlement of Africa's problems necessary to enduring, 6; National Study
Conference on social basis of durable, 20-21; comparison of various plans for, and application to Africa, 65-71; spiritual basis of, 66-67; individual and family rights to be
guaranteed by, 67-68; as related to economic welfare, 69; international coöperation and,
69-70; disarmament a necessary corollary of, 70-71; general conclusions concerning aims
of, 71.
PEACE CONFERENCE, Major objective of Committee to focus attention on just treatment of Africa by, viii, 4-5; need for study prior to, 4-5; suggested procedures at and
after, 10-12; no attempt should be made by, to deal with African problems in detail, 31;

EVENTS IN
AFRICAN HISTORY

Compiled by

EDWIN W. SMITH

A SUPPLEMENT TO

THE ATLANTIC CHARTER AND AFRICA

FROM AN AMERICAN STANDPOINT

Published for

THE COMMITTEE ON AFRICA, THE WAR, AND PEACE AIMS

NEW YORK, N. Y.

1942

Summary

The Committee on Africa, the War, and Peace Aims feels that it has been particularly fortunate in securing the services of the Reverend Edwin W. Smith, D.D., to prepare this Supplement on *Events in African History*. Dr. Smith is, at present, in the United States lecturing on Africa at the Kennedy School of Missions, Hartford Seminary Foundation. He has served as editor of the *Journal of the Royal African Society*, and as President of the Royal Anthropological Institute of Great Britain. Among his best known works are *The Ila-speaking Peoples of Northern Rhodesia, The Golden Stool, Aggrey of Africa,* and *The Mabilles of Basutoland.*

The Committee has also been fortunate in having the proof read by Mrs. Agnes C. L. Donohugh, Professor of Ethnology at the Kennedy School of Missions.

The Committee is indebted to Miss Ellen C. Ahern for preparing the Index. This is mainly a list of references to persons, places, and organizations. Entries have, however, been added to subjects such as the slave trade, exploration, Bible translation, "firsts," etc.

The references are in each case to dates, not pages. This will make it easier to secure the desired information quickly, and obviates the necessity of preparing an analytical index.

In the interest of uniformity the ancient term Ethiopia has been used throughout this publication instead of Abyssinia—the latter, according to *The Columbia Encyclopedia* (1935), being now considered as merely an "alternative name of the African Empire officially called Ethiopia."

Attention is called to the statement opposite the map near the back cover regarding the places where the Report of the Committee on *The Atlantic Charter and Africa from an American Standpoint* and this Supplement may be secured.

1. Ancient

B.C.

4241   First date in African chronology: Institution of the Calendar in Egypt.

3200   Menes unifies the kingdoms in Egypt.

1879   Pharaoh Sesostris iii sets up a stele 40 miles south of Wady Halfa forbidding 'Negroes' to pass down the Nile.

1700-1580   The Shepherd Kings (Hyksos) of Egypt.

1470   Queen Hatshepsut, of the xviiith Egyptian dynasty, sends a fleet to the land of Punt (northern Somaliland); trade with India follows.

1100   Phoenicians build the city of Utica on the coast of Tunisia.

945   An independent monarchy is founded in Nubia, with its centre at Napata.

813   Carthage is founded by Phoenicians from Tyre.

712-700   Shabaka, king of Nubia, sends armies under Tarhaka to assist King Hezekiah against Sennacherib of Assyria.

631   Greeks build the city of Cyrene.

610   Reputed circumnavigation of Africa by Phoenician mariners sent by Pharaoh Necho of Egypt.

525   Persian invasion of Egypt.

520 (or 470)   Hanno the Carthaginian rounds Cape Verde and reaches the vicinity of Sierra Leone.

448-445   Herodotus explores parts of Egypt and hears rumours of the River Niger.

332   Alexander the Great adds Egypt to his empire and builds the city of Alexandria.

B.C.

323   The Ptolemies begin to rule Egypt and extend their sway to Dongola and the verge of Ethiopia.

300c. The sovereignty of Nubia passes to Meroë.

285-247   Ptolemy ii, King of Egypt. The first portion of the Hebrew Scriptures—the 'Law'—is translated into Greek at Alexandria. Africa, the cradle of Biblical translation.

200c. The camel is introduced into North Africa.

168   The Romans establish a protectorate over Egypt.

146-145   The Romans destroy Carthage and found the province of 'Africa.'

43   The Romans rule over Cyrenaica.

23   The Romans march into Nubia and destroy Napata.

19   Egypt becomes an integral part of the Roman Empire.

A.D.

42   The Romans now rule North Africa and up the Nile to Wady Halfa.

66c. The Emperor Nero sends an expedition to discover the source of the White Nile; it reaches the land of naked Nilotic Negroes and is stopped by the 'sudd.'

80c. 'The Periplus of the Red Sea' tells of Graeco-Roman and Arabic enterprise in East Africa as far south as Dar-es-salaam, and of an active traffic in slaves.

100c. Christianity is by now established in Egypt and North Africa.

125-155   The geographer Ptolemy reports existence of 'The Mountains of the Moon' and of great lakes from which the Nile flows.

300   North Africa the first main home of Christian literature. Earliest Latin version of Scripture made there. Version in the Coptic language of Egypt also made about this time.

A.D.

300c. Foundation of the Sudanese kingdom of Ghana which endured till 1200.

326 Christianity introduced into Ethiopia; Frumentius, the first bishop consecrated. First translation of Scripture into Ethiopic.

350 The King of Axum (Ethiopia) destroys Meroë.

415 The Vandals invade North Africa and overthrow the Romans.

500c. The Nobadae of Nubia converted to Christianity by Julianus.

533-534 Roman rule re-established by Belisarius from Tripoli to Tangier.

566 Longinus commissioned Bishop of Nubia.

639-681 Muslims conquer Egypt and North Africa: the Christian Church is destroyed except in Egypt.

641 Arabs from Egypt invade Nubia.

700c. Arabs begin their colonization of the East African coastland: slave-trade with Arabia, Turkey, Persia, India and China.

700c. Rise of the Songhai power in western Sudan: 765, foundation of the city of Jenné.

711 The Muslims cross over into Spain.

850 Mamelukes seize power in Egypt.

1009 Songhai converted to Islam. Muslims introduce black slaves into Europe.

1020 Persian Muslims from Ormuz settle at Kilwa, Zanzibar, Sena and Sofala.

1148 Normans invade Tunisia from Sicily.

1150 Timbuktu is founded by Songhai merchants of Jenné and becomes centre of trade in western Sudan.

1169 Salah-ed-Din founds a Kurdish dynasty in Egypt.

1200 Christian bishoprics still exist in Nubia.

1219 Francis of Assisi in Egypt. Franciscans reach Morocco.

1260 Beybars usurps the throne of Egypt and organizes

the Mameluke system on an imperial basis; lays Nubia waste; Christianity almost disappears. Arabs push invasion of eastern Sudan.

1308-1331   The Mandingo empire of Melle reaches the height of its power under Mansa Musa; covers the whole of western Sudan; becomes a bulwark of Islam.

1336   Abu Zakariya, prince of Tunis, declares himself independent.

1401   Tripolitania reconquered by Tunisia.

2. Modern

A. 1415-1807: PERIOD OF UNRESTRICTED SLAVE-TRADE

    (1) 1415-1580: *Predominance of Portugal*

[Portugal, as a separate state, came into being during the long struggle against the Muslims in the Iberian peninsula after 1050. Alphonso i, who became Count of Portugal in 1128, and his successors, carried on the crusade until they drove the Muslims from Portugal. King John i transferred the war to Africa in 1451: with his three sons he took a fleet across to Ceuta (English men-at-arms took part in the expedition) and captured that fortress on the Moroccan coast. This was the beginning of the modern invasion and partition of Africa. The process began as a crusade.]

1415 The Portuguese establish a foothold in Africa by capturing Ceuta.

1418 Prince Henry, son of John i of Portugal, sends out his first exploring expedition with a view to outflanking the Muslims. Madeira discovered.

1434 Cape Bojador is rounded; 1440, Nuno Tristaõ doubles Cape Verde; 1444, the River Senegal is reached; 1455, Portuguese enter the Gambia River.

1441 The first 10 African slaves are landed in Portugal; they are presented to the Pope who confers on Portugal the sovereignty of all country to be discovered between Bojador and the Indies.

A.D.

1468   Mandingo Empire of Melle, overthrown by Omar Askia, King of Songhai.

1471   The Portuguese reach the Gold Coast.

1481   King John ii of Portugal takes up the enterprise started by his brother Henry.

1482   The Portuguese build the fort of Saõ Jorge da Mina on the Gold Coast. First regular modern European settlement in Africa.

1482-4   Diogo Caõ reaches the mouth of the Congo.

1483   French seamen at Cape Verde Islands.

1486-1493   Bengal is ruled by two African slave-soldiers.

1486   From this time gold imported by Portugal from West Africa becomes a factor in the economic life of Europe.

1488   Bartholomew Dias rounds the Cape of Good Hope.

1489   Pedro de Covilha reaches Ethiopia on embassy from Portugal.

1491   First Roman Catholic missionaries reach the Congo region: Saõ Salvador.

1492   Alliance of Portugal with the King of (lower) Congo.

1497-1498   Vasco da Gama sails round the Cape of Good Hope, calls at Mombasa and proceeds to India.

1502-1509   Portugal wrests control of Indian Ocean and East African coast from the Arabs.

1504   The Negroid Fung come into power on the Blue Nile and maintain it for 300 years. Their capital at Sennaar becomes a centre of African civilization.

1510   Ferdinand of Spain takes Tripolitania and gives it to the Knights of St. John.
First batch of African slaves landed in Haiti.

1517   Turks under Selim i conquer Egypt; occupy Massawa and Suakin.

1520   Portuguese begin occupation of Angola.

1531   Portuguese build a fort at Sena on Zambezi.

A.D.

1532 Portuguese send an army to Ethiopia to help resist Arab invasion.

1544 Portuguese build a station at Quilimane and trade in gold with the interior.

Portuguese slave-traders active on the coast of Angola.

1553 Turkish corsairs expel Knights of St. John from Tripolitania; these pirates become the scourge of the Mediterranean.

1560 Jesuits plant the first Christian mission in East Africa (Mozambique).

1561 Gonçalo da Silveira, Roman Catholic missionary and protomartyr, killed in Manicaland.

1562 Sir John Hawkins makes the first English venture in the slave-trade.

1572 Portuguese expedition to the Zambezi under Francisco Barreto. His successor reaches the Manica goldfield.

1573 Tunisia becomes a Turkish province.

1577 Dominican friars in Mozambique; 1586, at Sofala.

1578 Portuguese defeated heavily at Kasr-al-Kabir in Morocco; lose almost all possessions there.

1580 Portugal loses her independence to Spain; her power in West and East Africa declines.

(2) 1581-1807: *The Decline of Portugal; the Rise of Dutch, British, French and Arab Power; Beginning of Revulsion Against the Slave-Trade*

1581 Dutch throw off the yoke of Spain.

1588 First English chartered company: sends trading expeditions to West Africa.

1590 The Sultan of Morocco attacks the Songhai empire and takes Timbuktu.

1595 The Dutch appear on the Gold Coast and gain commercial supremacy.

A.D.

1602   Dutch East India Company formed.

1618   British merchants send ships to the Gambia; try to reach Timbuktu.

First African slaves introduced into Virginia.

1619   King James i of England grants a patent for exclusive right to trade with Guinea and Benin.

1621   Dutch West India Company formed.

Dutch take possession of the island of Goré off Cape Verde.

1622   Congregatio Sacra de Propaganda Fide established at Rome.

1626   Merchants of Rouen form a company to trade with Senegal and Gambia.

1631   Revival of Arab power in East Africa.

Charles i of England gives a new patent for exclusive trade between Cape Blanco and the Cape of Good Hope.

1637   Dutch capture Portuguese fort of Saõ Jorge on Gold Coast.

1640   Portugal recovers her independence.

1641   Dutch attack Angola in order to secure supply of slaves for Brazil: hold Loanda and Benguela till 1648.

1642   Portugal abandons to Dutch her possessions on Gold Coast in return for withdrawal of Dutch claims in Brazil.

Cardinal Richelieu creates a French company to colonize Madagascar.

1645-1651   Dutch occupy St. Helena.

1651   British build a fort on Gold Coast.

1652   First Dutch settlement under van Riebeeck at the Cape of Good Hope.

1662-1684   British hold Tangier as part of the dowry of

A.D.

Charles ii's Queen, Catherine of Braganza; abandon
it in 1684.

1662 Company of Royal Adventurers of England trading
into Africa is chartered by Charles ii to checkmate
the Dutch and supply slaves for West Indian and
American plantations.

1663 Portugal fully recovers power in Angola and monopoly of slave-trade with Brazil.

1664 British now established on the Gambia.

1665 War declared against Dutch by Britain: Cape Coast
Castle and other Dutch forts on Gold Coast taken
by British.

1672 New Royal African Company formed in England to
take place of the 1662 company; it is given the monopoly of trade for a thousand years from Morocco
to the Cape of Good Hope, but lasts only a few
years.

Danes build forts at Accra and elsewhere on Gold
Coast; hold them till 1850 when they sell out to
the British.

1677-1678 French displace Dutch on Senegambian coast.

1680-1786 2,130,000 slaves imported into British colonies
in West Indies and America.

1681-1720 Germans make a transient appearance in Africa.
Under the auspices of Frederick William, Great
Elector of Brandenburg, a trading company is
formed and carries on commerce between Prussia
and West Coast of Africa; outposts built on Gold
Coast and elsewhere.

1683 French Royal company develops settlements on
Senegal.

1689 French Huguenot immigrants land at Cape Town.

1693 Pennsylvania Quakers' 'Exhortation and Caution to
Friends concerning buying or keeping of Negroes.'

A.D.

1696 André de Brue begins to lay the foundation of French West Africa during 15 years in Senegambia.

1698 The Imam of Oman (in Arabia) sends fleet against Portuguese and captures Mombasa, Zanzibar and Kilwa, and lays siege to Mozambique. Portuguese sovereignty north of Cape Delgado ends in favour of Arabs. They retain their possessions south of that point.

1699 Society for Promoting Christian Knowledge is founded.

1700-1707 French build trading posts on Ivory Coast.

1701 Society for the Propagation of the Gospel in Foreign Parts is founded.

1737 First missionary station opened in Cape Colony: George Schmidt, Moravian, among Hottentots.

1737 Moravians begin a mission (not permanent) on Gold Coast; one of their converts makes a translation of a small part of Scripture in the Fanti: the first translation in a language of Negroes.

1738 From this year (John Wesley's "enlightenment") may be dated the Evangelical Movement which, under Wesley and Whitefield, swept over England and the American colonies.

1750 The English African Company of Merchants is constituted by Act of Parliament in place of the 1672 company; is given liberty to trade and form establishments on West Coast.

1751 Society for the Propagation of the Gospel (founded in 1701) sends Thomas Thompson to Gold Coast as chaplain to the African Company. One of his African converts, Philip Quaque, sent to England for training, returned to Gold Coast as an ordained Anglican clergyman: probably the first African in ministry of the Church of England.

A.D.

1759-1803 642,000 Negro slaves shipped from Angola to Brazil.

1760 Lower course of Orange River discovered; traced to mouth in 1779.

1764 French colonize island of Bourbon (Réunion).

1766-1775 James Bruce initiates modern exploration of Africa by his travels in Ethiopia and Eastern Sudan; discovers the source of the Blue Nile.

1772 Granville Sharp gets judicial decision by Lord Mansfield that as soon as any slave sets his foot on English soil he is free and cannot be taken back as a slave.

1774 American colonists, revolting against Britain, sign agreement not to purchase slaves imported after 1st December and not to have commerce with those concerned in slave-trade.

1787 Clarkson, Wilberforce and others form a society in England to secure the abolition of the slave-trade.

1787 Constitution of the United States, section 9:
"The migration or importation of such persons as any of the States now existing shall think proper to admit, shall not be prohibited by the Congress prior to the year one thousand eight hundred and eight, but a tax or duty may be imposed on such importation, not exceeding ten dollars for each person."
Rhode Island passes act to prevent importation of slaves into its territory and to encourage the abolition of slavery in the State.

1788 British Parliament passes a Bill to regulate the slave-trade.
New York State enacts that no slave shall be imported within its boundaries nor purchased within the State for export. Massachusetts prohibits the African

A.D.

slave-trade to its citizens. Pennsylvania prohibits the trade "to, from or between Europe, Asia, Africa or America, or any places or countries whatever."

1788 The African Association is founded in England to explore Africa and promote a legitimate commerce in order to supplant the slave-trade.

1789 Following a proposal made in 1786 to make a settlement for freed Negroes, 400 Africans are landed on the shore of St. George's Bay, Sierra Leone. This is the beginning of Freetown and the British colony.

1790 Congress by 29 votes to 25 resolves:
"That Congress have authority to restrain the citizens of the United States from carrying on the African trade for the purpose of supplying foreigners with slaves, and of providing by proper regulations for the humane treatment during their passage of slaves imported by the said citizens into the States admitting such importation." Further: "That Congress have authority to prohibit foreigners from fitting out vessels in any port of the United States for transporting persons from Africa to any foreign port." Congress adds that it has no authority to interfere in the emancipation of slaves.

1791 Control of the Freetown settlement is vested in the Sierra Leone Company, chartered, with Granville Sharp as president.

1792 The Baptist Missionary Society founded.

1794 First national act of United States against slave-trade. Congress prohibits carrying it on from the United States to any foreign country and the fitting out of slavers in the United States for a foreign country.
French revolutionary Convention abolishes slavery.

A.D.

1795   The African Association sends Mungo Park to investigate the course of the Niger: he reaches the Niger at Segou (by way of the Gambia) and follows it to Silla; is compelled to turn back.

The London Missionary Society is founded.

First British occupation of the Cape of Good Hope. This was done with the consent of the Prince of Orange (who was then in a similar position to the Queen of Holland in 1941) to save the strategically important Cape from falling into the hands of France which was at war with Britain and had driven the Prince into exile when it occupied Holland.

1796   U. S. A. begins to pay yearly tribute to the Pasha of Tripoli ($83,000) for the protection of its commerce from piracy.

1798   Francisco de Lacerda sets out to cross Africa from Tete on the Zambezi; dies at Cazembe's town near Lake Mweru.

Napoleon Bonaparte invades Egypt.

1799   The Church Missionary Society is founded in England.

1801   British compel surrender of French army in Egypt; they hand Egypt back to the Turks.

1801-1805   U. S. A. refuses to increase tribute to the ruler of Tripolitania. War follows; U. S. A. fleet blockades Tripoli and takes Derna.

1802   The geographer Arrowsmith presents to the African Association a map of Africa from which he has removed all hypothetical features. Morocco and Algeria fairly delineated; travels of Bruce and Park enable him to plot some regions with substantial accuracy; but for the rest, except in the extreme south and certain areas around Portuguese posses-

A.D.

sions, east and west, the interior is an unmitigated blank. Gentlemen, said Arrowsmith in effect, this is what we now know of Africa; get to work and fill up the map!

1803   Congress makes a law providing for forfeiture of any ship that should bring into any State, contrary to its laws, "any negro, mulatto or other person of color."

Following the Treaty of Amiens the British hand the Cape Colony to the Dutch Batavian republic.

1803-1805   Mungo Park returns to the Niger; traces its course to the Busa rapids and there perishes with his companions.

1804   The British and Foreign Bible Society is founded.

Fulani begin their conquest of the northern Nigerian region; Katsina and Kano are captured, 1805; Sokoto, the Fulani capital, is built in 1810, by which date their dominion is firmly established over all the Hausa states and others.

1804-1807   202 ships brought 39,075 slaves from Africa to Charleston, S. C. Consignees largely natives of Rhode Island.

1805   London Missionary Society sends two Dutch missionaries to Namaqualand, north of the Orange River.

1806   The American Bible Society is founded.

Following a renewal of the war with France and her satellites Britain sends a fleet to Cape Town and after a skirmish the city and colony capitulate. The inhabitants are guaranteed all their former rights and privileges.

1806   The Arab Said-bin-Sultan usurps the sovereignty of Muscat (Oman); later begins to extend his sway to East African coast and to revive trade in slaves and ivory in the interior.

A.D.

1806-1811   Two half-breeds (Portuguese) cross Africa from Angola to Tete on the Zambezi and back.

B. 1807-1918: *Period of* (1) *Struggle to Extirpate Slave-Trade and Slavery;* (2) *Exploration;* (3) *Partition;* (4) *Preliminary Economic Development;* (5) *Expansion of Christianity*

1807   Slave-trade "utterly abolished, prohibited and declared to be illegal" by Parliament for all British subjects.

Congress imposes heavy penalties on any one bringing into the United States, from any foreign country, any negro, mulatto, or person of color, with the intention of holding him or selling him as a slave.

These laws come into force 1st January, 1808.

British Government takes over the Freetown (Sierra Leone) settlement as a Crown Colony.

1807-1822   Muhammad Ali, an Albanian employed by the Sultan of Turkey, becomes Pasha of Egypt; invades the Sudan; sets up a reign of terror, with great extension of slave-trade.

1810   Rise of the Zulu power in South Africa under Chaka.

Foundation of the American Board of Commissioners for Foreign Missions.

1811   British Parliament makes slave-trading a felony.

1813   British Wesleyan Methodist Missionary Society founded; begins operations in South Africa, 1816.

1814-1815   Congress of Vienna at close of the Napoleonic wars.

Britain retains Cape Colony in consideration of £6,-000,000 paid on behalf of Holland.

At this time the position of foreign powers in Africa was briefly as follows:

Turkey alone had footing in North Africa; nominally suzerain of Egypt, Tunis and Tripolitania. [Algeria and Morocco independent.] No States laid claim to Saharan hinterland.

France: coastland from Cape Blanco to the Gambia; some extension inland (Senegal). Island of Bourbon (Réunion).

Portugal: Cape Verde Islands; patch on coast south of the Casamansa (Guinea); island of Principe; Angola (not so extensive as now); Delagoa Bay and coast to Cape Delgado; strip along Zambezi to Zumbo.

Spain: Fernando Po.

Britain: station on Gambia; patch in Sierra Leone; stations on Gold Coast, on Oil Rivers, in Cameroons and estuary of Congo; Cape Colony, then a relatively small area of 120,000 square miles; Mauritius.

Imam of Muscat held coast from Cape Delgado northwards.

Denmark and Holland still retained trading posts on west coast.

Madagascar practically independent. Ethiopia uncoveted and not yet cut off from the sea.

1815   U. S. A. sends a squadron to Tripoli and forces the Pasha to yield to her demands.

1816   The American Colonization Society founded for the repatriation to Africa of some of the 200,000 legally free colored persons in U. S. A.

1817   Britain bribes Spain to abolish the slave-trade.
France prohibits slave-trading.
Britain restores to France posts on the Senegal captured during the late war; France extends her influence inland.
Anglo-Portuguese Convention fixes north and south

A.D.

limits of Portuguese East Africa: Cape Delgado to Delagoa Bay.

1817 London Missionary Society sends Robert Moffat to South Africa.

1818 American Colonization Society sends Samuel J. Mills and Ebenezer Burgess to seek a site for a settlement in West Africa.

French establish a protectorate over the Sakalava in Madagascar.

British and Dutch fleets bombard Algiers in effort to put down piracy.

1818-1827 Réné Caille travels through Senegambia to Timbuktu and Morocco.

1819 Congress authorises President of U. S. A. to employ armed vessels to seize American slave-ships; and to appoint an agent to reside on the coast of Africa to receive and care for the Negroes when captured.

Piracy ceases in Tunisia after European Powers present a collective note.

1820 Arrival of 5,000 emigrants from Great Britain in South Africa: 'the 1820 settlers.'

Muhammad Ali orders the conquest of Eastern Sudan for Egypt. Congress makes a law providing death penalty for participating in the slave-trade. Congress requests President to negotiate with other governments on the means of effecting an entire and immediate abolition of the slave-trade.

Presbyterians of Scotland start mission in South Africa: Lovedale founded 1824.

American Colonization Society sends out 88 emigrants, with Samuel Bacon as Agent of U. S. A. and Samuel Crozer as Agent of A. C. S., to prepare for the reception of later comers. They locate on Island of

A.D.

Sherbro, off coast of Sierra Leone: and in a few weeks both Agents and over 20 emigrants are dead.

1820-1825 Captain Owen of the British navy surveys the African coast between Morocco and the Red Sea round the Cape.

1821 British Crown takes over trading settlements on Gold Coast.

British Wesleyans open mission on Gambia.

American Colonization Society sends out 52 Negro emigrants under leadership of Jehudi Ashmun; builds a settlement on Cape Montserado (Mesurado) which becomes Monrovia, capital of Liberia.

1821-22 British explorers, Oudney, Clapperton and Denham, cross Sahara from Tripoli, discover River Shari and Lake Chad.

1822 British make treaty with Sultan of Muscat by which he agrees to prohibit slave-trading by his subjects outside his dominions.

1824 Captain Owen, R.N., on his own initiative at the request of Arab rebels, hoists British flag at Mombasa; his action is disowned by the British Government.

British Parliament makes slave-trading a capital crime.

Sweden and Britain agree to a mutual right of search of slave-ships; U. S. A. declines to join in the agreement.

1825 Constitution of Liberian settlement approved by American Colonization Society.

Major Alexander Laing traverses the Sahara from Tripoli to Timbuktu; is assassinated by Tuareg on return journey.

1825-1827 Clapperton, on second journey, reaches the

A.D.

Lower Niger from Lagos on the coast and dies at Sokoto.

1827   British occupy Fernando Po temporarily (with permission of Spain) as base for operations of their navy against slave-trade.

Basel Mission opens on Gold Coast.

1827-1843   Administration of British trading posts on Gold Coast in the hands of committee of merchants: George Maclean governor.

1829   French Protestant Mission begun in South Africa.

1830   French begin conquest of Algeria (ends 1848) by taking Algiers.

Khartum becomes official capital of eastern Sudan under the oppressive Turco-Egyptian rule.

1830-1831   Richard Lander and his brother trace the Niger from Busa (where Mungo Park perished) to its outlet in the Gulf of Guinea.

1832   Macgregor Laird opens up trade on the Niger and Benue.

1833   Slavery abolished throughout British colonies at cost of £20,000,000 voted by Parliament as compensation to slave-holders.

The Great Trek of the Boers from Cape Colony begins.

Treaty of Britain with France to enforce suppression of slave-trade; agree to mutual right of search. They invite U. S. A. to join; but U. S. A. will not allow that an American slaver be treated as a pirate by any other authority than an American court.

Other Colonization Societies active in U. S. A. and Liberia: New York and Pennsylvania Societies start settlement at Bassa Cove; Mississippi Society at Greenville; Maryland Society at Cape Palmas.

A.B.C.F.M. sends John Leighton Wilson and Stephen

A.D.

Wyncoop with party of Maryland emigrants to explore; and in 1834 first station is planted at Cape Palmas.

1833   American Presbyterian Board sends missionaries to Liberia.

Methodist Episcopal Church does the same.

Protestant Episcopal Church follows suit in 1836.

French Protestant mission established in Basutoland.

Sultan of Muscat concludes commercial treaty with U. S. A.

1834   A.B.C.F.M. sends its first missionaries to South Africa —to Zulus and Matebele. Berlin Mission opened in South Africa. British Methodists on Gold Coast.

1835   A French merchant acquires a port (Ait) on the Red sea.

Tripolitania becomes integral part of Ottoman Empire.

1837   Church Missionary Society sends J. L. Krapf to Ethiopia.

Separate settlements in Liberia—except the Maryland settlement which stays out till 1857—come together in a central government, with Thomas Buchanan as governor.

1838   The Boers invade Zulu country (Natal)

1839   Britain annexes Aden on coast of Arabia.

Sultan of Muscat concludes commercial treaty with Britain.

1840   Seyyid Said moves the seat of his government from Muscat to Zanzibar, which becomes the principal port in East Africa and the biggest slave-market in the East.

U. S. A. becomes supreme in trade with Zanzibar.

Fowell Buxton issues "The African slave-trade and its remedy." Naval action alone seen to be insuf-

A.D.

ficient to stop the trade; legitimate commerce and territorial annexation advocated as a necessary means. New society founded for the extinction of the slave-trade and for the civilization of Africa. "The deliverance of Africa is to be effected by calling out her own resources."

1840-1843 France occupies Nossi-be, off coast of Madagascar, and Mayotta in Comoro Islands.

1841 To carry out Buxton's 'Positive Policy' British Government sends a civilizing expedition to the Niger under command of Captain Trotter, R.N. Two missionaries (one a Negro, Samuel Crowther, afterwards first African bishop of Anglican church) included. Sails "with the British conscience on board." Disaster befalls expedition on the Niger River; of 193 white men, 41 die. British public opinion receives a shock. "The British conscience too, it seemed, had been done to death in the mangroves and miasma of the Niger" (Coupland).

London Missionary Society sends David Livingstone to South Africa.

Jamaican Baptists start a mission on island of Fernando Po.

1841-1857 Captain Hamilton, British consul and political Agent at Zanzibar; succeeded by Captain Rigby in 1857.

1842 Ashburton Treaty between U. S. A. and Britain. U. S. A. to maintain an adequate naval squadron (with not less than 80 guns) on African coast to enforce suppression of slave-trade. Captain Foote in command.

French established on Gaboon River.

A.B.C.F.M. removes its mission from Liberia to the

A.D.

Gaboon where it continues until 1870 and then hands over to the Presbyterian Church.

1843 British annex Natal for the protection of the Zulus. They institute a formal protectorate on Gold Coast.

Legal status of slavery abolished in British India.

Fowell Buxton dissolves the African Civilization Society; dies broken-hearted in 1845.

Ethnological Society of London is founded.

1844 Missionary J. L. Krapf at Mombasa; joined by Rebmann in 1846 and by Erhardt in 1849. Krapf founds station at Rabai, first Protestant mission in East Africa.

1845 Britain resumes pressure on Sultan of Zanzibar and obtains a treaty which engages him to forbid all export of slaves from his African dominions. Slaves can still circulate between Zanzibar and the Arab coast-towns but they cannot henceforth be legally shipped to outside ports.

1846 United Presbyterian Church begins mission at Calabar as a result of a movement among the freed slaves of Jamaica.

1847 People of Liberia hold a convention and draw up a Declaration of Independence and a Constitution modelled on that of U. S. A. Motto: "The Love of Liberty Brought Us Here." Independence almost immediately recognised by Britain, followed by France. U. S. A. recognised Liberia in 1862.

David Livingstone builds at Kolobeng his third station in Bechuanaland.

1848 Persia agrees with Great Britain to prohibit importation of slaves by sea.

Dutch abolish slave-trade and slavery.

British sovereignty proclaimed between Orange and Vaal rivers in South Africa: abandoned in 1854.

A.D.

1848   Rebmann discovers snow-capped Kilimanjaro, over
        19,000 feet.

        Abbas i succeeds Muhammad Ali in Egypt. Railway
        begun from Alexandria under instigation of British.

1849   First British consulate in Gulf of Guinea. British
        influence in Nigeria begins to be established.

        J. L. Krapf discovers Mount Kenya near equator.

        David Livingstone begins his epoch-making explora-
        tions by discovering (with Oswell and Murray)
        Lake Ngami.

        *This year marks the beginning of the exploration of
        Central Africa.*

        Portuguese still shipping slaves from East Africa.

1850   British buy out Danes on Gold Coast.

        French 'Free Labour Emigration scheme' (camou-
        flaged slave-trade) between East Africa and Ré-
        union.

1850-1855   Heinrich Barth travels from Tripoli to Tim-
        buktu and explores wide area of western Sudan.

1851   Livingstone reaches the Zambezi from the south, and
        comes into contact with slave-trade: birth of his life
        purpose to rid Central Africa of 'the open sore of
        the world' by opening up the country to commerce
        and Christianity.

1852   Sand River Convention: Britain recognises independ-
        ence of the Transvaal republic.

1852-1856   Livingstone travels from Cape Town to Loanda
        by way of Barotseland; from Loanda to mouth of
        Zambezi, across Africa. "The greatest feat in Afri-
        can exploration."

1853-1856   Silva Porto crosses Africa from Benguela to
        mouth of Rovuma.

1854   Representative government set up in Cape Colony.

A.D.

1854-1865   General Faidherbe extends French power in western Sudan from Senegal.

1855   Erhardt, from information received at the coast, draws a map showing one huge lake in the interior, shaped like a monster slug.

By this date Arab caravans had reached the great lakes; Arab colonies established at Tabora and Ujiji; big traffic in slaves and ivory.

1856   Ferdinand Lesseps gets concession to construct Suez Canal.

Death of Said, Sultan of Zanzibar; succeeded by Majid (1856-1870).

1856-1859   Richard Burton and John Speke, sent by the Royal Geographical Society to investigate the lake reported by Erhardt and explore the traditional 'Mountains of the Moon,' reach Lake Tanganyika and explore its northern part. On the way back Speke sees and names Lake Victoria.

1857   Portuguese stop French 'Free Labour Emigration' from their East African territory.

Dec. 3. David Livingstone's historic address to the University of Cambridge. Great revival of interest in Africa: it suddenly becomes "the most interesting part of the globe" (Coupland). His revelation of the *internal* slave-trade strikes home.

Of 80 ships calling at Zanzibar this year, 35 were American. Great trade in 'merikani,' cotton cloth woven in Massachusetts.

1858   Baptist missionaries expelled from Spanish Fernando Po; found a settlement at Ambas Bay on coast of Cameroons.

1858-1863   With John Kirk and others, Livingstone returns to the Zambezi; discovers Lakes Shirwa and Nyasa

A.D.

and the colonizable highlands of Nyasaland; throws fresh light on extensive Arab slave trade.

1859   Albrecht Roscher travels with Arab caravan from Kilwa to eastern shore of Lake Nyasa, and is murdered.

Societé d'anthropologie de Paris is founded.

London Missionary Society sends abortive mission to Barotseland. Sends another party under Robert Moffat to Matebeleland: this settles successfully.

1860-1863   John H. Speke is commissioned with A. J. Grant by the Royal Geographical Society, with the support of the British Government, to investigate Lake Victoria more fully. They are the first Europeans to visit Uganda and to see the Nile issuing from the lake. They follow the Nile, more or less, down to the Mediterranean.

1861   Zanzibar separated from Muscat. By treaty with native ruler, Britain annexes island of Lagos (a nest of slavers) in course of fighting the slave-trade. British Universities' Mission to Nyasaland (under Livingstone's guidance). Bishop Mackenzie and others die.

Presbyterians of Scotland send James Stewart to reconnoitre in Nyasaland: does so in company with Livingstone.

1861-1862   Baron von der Decken ascends Juba River, surveys Mount Kilimanjaro; is killed.

1861-1865   Samuel Baker travels up the White Nile and discovers Lake Albert.

1862   Captain Nathaniel Gordon convicted in U. S. A. of slave-piracy and hanged.

1863   Universities' Mission transferred to Zanzibar from Nyasaland.

A.D.

1863-1879 Ismail, Khedive of Egypt: initiates reforms in
Sudan.

1864-1866; 1868-1871 Georg Schweinfurth, German explorer, reveals the geography of the south-western
basin of the Nile, the Bahr-al-Ghazal, and reaches
the upper waters of the Welle-Mubangi.

1866 A select committee of the House of Commons votes
that all extension of British territory is 'inexpedi-
ent' and recommends withdrawal from coastal trading stations.

John Kirk is appointed surgeon and vice-consul at
Zanzibar: later Consul.

1866-1873 David Livingstone's last expedition. Wanders
alone in Central Africa: discovers Lakes Mweru
and Bangweulu; reaches Congo at Nyangwe but
is prevented from following it.

1867 Momentous discovery of diamonds in South Africa.

1867-1868 British military expedition to Ethiopia to rescue
Europeans.

1868 Cardinal Lavigerie founds the White Fathers for
work in Africa.

Basutoland becomes a British protectorate, at request
of the Basuto to save them from the Boers.

1869 Sir Samuel Baker is appointed by Khedive of Egypt
"Governor-General of the Equatorial Nile Basin"
(the Sudan) with a commission to suppress the
slave-trade and open to navigation the great lakes
of the equator. In three years he achieves the closing of the upper Nile as the chief northward chan-
nel of the trade.

Opening of Suez Canal brings East Africa nearer by
2,000 miles to European ports; sets it on the map.

1870 Franco-German war: has profound effect upon history of Africa.

A.D.

Accession of Seyyid Barghash as Sultan of Zanzibar.

Italians purchase Assab Bay on Red Sea.

1871 H. M. Stanley sent by Gordon Bennett of *New York Herald* to find Livingstone; 'finds' him at Ujiji on Lake Tanganyika.

British annexation of Griqualand opens a new era in South African history: marks end of non-expansion policy.

Basutoland is now annexed to Cape Colony.

Royal Anthropological Institute of Great Britain and Ireland is founded.

1872 Responsible government in Cape Colony.

American Presbyterians start operations in Cameroons.

1873 David Livingstone dies (about) 1 May at Chitambo; on June 5 John Kirk signs with Sultan of Zanzibar a treaty which abolishes slave-trade in Sultan's dominions and closes the slave-markets. Culmination of Britain's long efforts to suppress the East African trade. Some smuggling still carried on after this legal abolition.

University of Cape of Good Hope incorporated as an examining body.

1873-1874 Britain at war with Ashanti. Sir Garnet Wolseley marches to Kumasi. Marks beginning of British penetration inland.

1873-1875 Commander Verney Lovett Cameron travels from Zanzibar, surveys Lake Tanganyika in part, reaches Nyangwe on the Congo, and proceeds to Benguela on coast of Angola. The first crossing by a European of Africa, east to west.

1874 Railway building begins in South Africa. First stages of future 'Cape to Cairo' route. Cape Town to Kimberley, 1885; to Vryburg, 1891; to Bulawayo,

1897; to Broken Hill, 1906; to border of Belgian Congo, 1909.

1874   Charles George Gordon succeeds Samuel Baker in Sudan; pursues campaign against slave-trade. Eduard Schnitzer ('Emin Pasha') joins him in 1875.

Khedive Ismail attempts annexation of parts of Ethiopia; is defeated in 1875 and retreats.

British settlements on Gold Coast and Sierra Leone created a colony.

1874-1877   H. M. Stanley's great journey of 999 days across Africa, commissioned by *New York Herald* and London *Daily Telegraph*. Circumnavigates Lakes Victoria and Tanganyika; follows the Congo from Nyangwe to its mouth. *This journey marks the end of the major exploration of Central Africa and the beginning of the era of partition.* Much detail of the map remains to be filled in.

1875   Lord Carnarvon proposes confederation of all South African states.

Egypt is bankrupt; international control of large part of the revenue.

Presbyterian Livingstonia mission founded in Nyasaland; steamer put on the lake, the first on any African lake.

Nov. 15. H. M. Stanley's letter in *Daily Telegraph* appealing for missionaries to be sent to Uganda finds immediate response: Church Missionary Society sends a party, survivors of which reach Uganda in 1877.

Count de Brazza exploring Ogowe district, opening the country for France.

1876   Conference of Brussels initiates partition of Africa. Summoned by Leopold, King of the Belgians, in a private capacity, to discuss the exploration and

A.D.

civilization of Africa and means of extinguishing slavery. Those who attended were not delegates of governments. It was agreed to form an International African Association to carry out the objects named. The Association soon ceased to be international; nations took their own course individually.

1877   Cathedral built in Zanzibar on site of slave-market.

London Missionary Society begins work on Lake Tanganyika.

British declare sovereignty over the Transvaal which is in chaotic state.

General Gordon Governor-General of Egyptian Sudan under Khedive. Slave-trade still flourishes there. He resigns 1879.

1877-1879   Portuguese explorer Serpa Pinto travels from Loanda to Natal.

1878   Germany, now a united country and empire, looks to expand abroad. German African Society formed and sends out Wissmann and other explorers.

France gets 'a free hand' in Tunisia.

The African Lakes Co. established in Nyasaland.

British Baptists begin mission in Congo region (Saõ Salvador).

François Coillard pioneers for the French Protestant Mission in Matebeleland and to Barotseland.

1879   H. M. Stanley, after trying in vain to induce British to take over the Congo basin, enters service of King Leopold, and returns to Congo (1879-1884) to make treaties and open roads. Meets a rival in Count de Brazza who is active on behalf of France.

Roman Catholic missionaries arrive in Uganda.

War between British and Zulus in South Africa.

A.D.

1879 General Council set up in French Senegal: 20 members elected by citizens of the four communes.

Ismail deposed from Khedivate by Sultan of Turkey: Tewfik succeeds as Khedive.

1879-1880 Keith Johnston and Joseph Thomson (the latter alone when K. J. dies) explore between Lakes Nyasa and Tanganyika.

1880 First Anglo-Boer war in South Africa: battle of Majuba.

French advance from Senegal to the Niger.

A.B.C.F.M. begins mission in Angola.

1881 Convention of Pretoria: independence of Transvaal recognised, subject to suzerainty of Britain.

French invade Tunisia and impose a protectorate.

Railway begun in French West Africa: Dakar-Niger.

Revolt against Turco-Egyptian rule in Sudan led by Mahdi, Muhammad Ahmed.

Universities' Mission restarts work on Lake Nyasa.

Joseph Thomson, as official geologist to Sultan of Zanzibar, seeks coal on the Rovuma.

1881-1885 F. S. Arnot, missionary of Plymouth Brethren, travels from Durban to Barotseland and through to Angola, then to Katanga in south Congoland. Opens way for Garenganze Mission of the Brethren.

1882 German Colonial Society formed with aim of annexing territory.

The Transvaal republic expands west into Bechwanaland: 'Stellaland' and 'Goshen.' Tries in vain to get footing in Matebeland, north of Limpopo River.

Chaos in Egypt. Britain intervenes when other Powers decline to do so. Arabi, the rebel, is crushed at Tel-el-Kebir.

1883 Basutoland, after the 'Gun War,' is surrendered by Cape Colony to the Imperial British authorities.

A.D.

1883 At this time some 15 German trading firms had among them about 60 outposts on the west coast of Africa; and two German missionary societies had many stations; but Germany possessed no territory in Africa.

Herr Luderitz sends an agent to the bay of Angra Pequeña and 'buys' from Africans 215 square miles of land, including 10 miles of coast; and the German flag is hoisted in Africa for the first time.

1883-1884 Joseph Thomson opens a trail between Mombasa and Lake Victoria through Masai country and the Kenya highlands.

1883-1891 Treaties of protection between French and Chiefs of the Gaboon.

1884 Following Herr Luderitz's action the German Government annexes the coast, and 20 miles inland, between the Orange River and the southern border of Angola; and so secures a hold on South-West Africa. Only Walvis Bay is left to be annexed by Britain.

Dr. Nachtigal goes in a warship and declares Togoland a German protectorate; then steams to the Cameroons and, forestalling the British whose protection has been requested by the Africans, hoists the German flag.

H. H. Johnston, sent by the Royal Geographical Society to study the fauna and flora of Kilimanjaro, privately acquires land in the Chaga highlands for colonization. His action is not countenanced by British Government.

Boers of Transvaal seize western Zululand and set up 'the New Republic.'

First important gold-field opened in Transvaal.

General Gordon is sent back to Sudan to evacuate the

A.D.

Egyptian garrisons. He is beleaguered in Khartum
by the Mahdists. Relief expedition under Sir Garnet Wolseley arrives too late. Khartum falls and
Gordon is killed, Jan., 1885. Sudan now abandoned to Mahdi.

1884 British protectorate over northern Somaliland.

Carl Peters (founder of Society for German Colonisa-
tion) and three companions enter East Africa sur-
reptitiously; he returns to coast after three weeks
with 12 'treaties' purporting to surrender to his
society 2,500 square miles in Usagara, etc., 200
miles inland from coast opposite Zanzibar—part of
the dominion of the Sultan of Zanzibar.

1884-1885 Berlin Conference is held especially to settle
question of the Congo basin. All European states,
except Switzerland, represented; H. M. Stanley at-
tends as expert adviser of U. S. A. plenipoten-
tiaries, Casson and Stanford. The General Act of
the Conference is signed by all except U. S. A.

a. confirms agreements recognising the independent
   Congo State. U. S. A. recognises it, 22 April,
   1884.

b. creates a free-trade Congo Basin, including the
   Congo State and what are now Kenya, Uganda,
   Nyasaland, and parts of Northern Rhodesia, of
   Portuguese East and West Africa.

c. pledges care for improvement of conditions of
   Natives' moral and material well-being; and help
   in suppressing slavery and slave-trade.

d. guarantees freedom of conscience and religious
   toleration.

e. defines conditions to be observed in occupying
   African territories.

A.D.

1885 Germany takes under imperial protection territory 'acquired' by Carl Peters. Sultan protests, Germany denies that Sultan's dominion extends to mainland, sends fleet "to bring the Sultan to a more correct bearing"; with guns trained on his palace, Sultan is forced to acknowledge the German protectorate.

British protectorate over north Bechwanaland; the south a Crown Colony, 'British Bechwanaland.'

Cape Colony annexes Transkei territories: Tembuland, Bomvanaland, Galekaland.

Britain proclaims 'Oil Rivers Protectorate': coastlands of Southern Nigeria.

Italy takes possession of Massawa on Red Sea.

Death of Mahdi; succeeded by Khalifa Abdullahi.

Belgian Parliament authorizes King Leopold to be sovereign of the Congo Free State.

1886 The Witwatersrand gold-fields opened in Transvaal; foundation of Johannesburg.

British Royal Niger Company founded under Sir George Goldie.

International Commission (Britain, France, Germany and Zanzibar) delimit the Sultan's dominions in East Africa. Sultan accepts findings. Strip of coast 600 miles long, 10 miles broad, with Zanzibar and Pemba, recognized as his.

British and German 'spheres of influence' marked out in East Africa.

1886-1889 Royal Niger Company extends British influence through commerce on the Niger and Benue rivers; and is active in suppressing slave-trade.

1887 Zululand annexed by British.

Italians and Ethiopians at war: Italian force almost annihilated at Dogali.

Mahdists invade Ethiopia.

A.D.

1887-1889 British merchants of African Lakes Corporation and missionaries conflict with Arab slave-traders in northern Nyasaland. F. D. Lugard makes his debut in African affairs.

H. M. Stanley heads an expedition for the relief of Emin Pasha; up Congo and Aruwimi rivers, to Lake Albert, and out to east coast.

Binger explores the country in the bend of the Niger.

1888 Imperial British East Africa Company formed, under Sir William Mackinnon, to acquire and administer territories within the British sphere of influence.

The De Beers Consolidated Mines Company formed with Cecil Rhodes its chief director.

John S. Moffat makes a treaty with Lobengula, king of Matebele, securing British supremacy.

Portuguese Mozambique Company formed.

1888-1892 France extends territories north and north-east of the Congo towards Lake Chad and Benue River.

1889 British South Africa Company, under Cecil Rhodes, obtains a charter.

British protectorate established in southern Nyasaland.

French explorer Crampel concludes treaties with tribes around Lake Chad.

Civil conflict in Uganda; Carl Peters appears on the scene.

Treaty of 'mutual protection' between Italy and Ethiopia.

Italy extends her rule into Somaliland.

Leopold bequeaths Congo Free State to Belgium in the event of his death.

1889-1890 Brussels Conference called by King Leopold on initiative of Britain to concert measures for the suppression of slave-trade "and the immediate closing of all the external markets which it still supplies." Conference declares that most effective means is progressive organization of the administrative, judicial, religious and military services in the territories taken over by the Powers; construction of roads and railways, establishment of steam-boats and telegraphic lines, restriction of importation of arms and ammunition. It also restricts traffic in spirituous liquors. U. S. A. subscribes to the General Act.

1889-1891   H. H. Johnston negotiates treaties with chiefs in Nyasa country.

1890   British South Africa Company occupies Mashonaland and secures concession from Lewanika in Barotseland, north of Zambezi.

British protectorate over Zanzibar and Pemba.

Anglo-German agreement draws boundaries in East Africa; recognizes British protectorate over Zanzibar and Pemba, and British priority in Uganda.

Anglo-French agreement delimits spheres in Chad region.

Jackson and Gedge sent to Uganda by I. B. E. A. Co.; British flag accepted by Mwanga, the king. Colonel Lugard follows and makes treaty with Mwanga for two years. Railway to Uganda projected.

1890-1891   Italian possessions on Red Sea constituted colony of Eritrea.

1890-1898   Building of railway from Matadi to Leopoldville, Belgian Congo.

1891   French explorer Monteil active on Lake Chad.

I. B. E. A. Co. announces that on financial grounds it must withdraw from Uganda. Mission supporters agitate for British government to step in.

Anglo-Portuguese convention defines spheres of influence of the two nations in East Africa.

A.D.

1891   Thomson and Sharpe set out separately to secure
       Mushidi's country (Katanga) for the B. S. A. Co.
       but are forestalled by the Belgians.

1892   French conquer Dahomey and annex Ivory Coast.
       Italians advance in Eritrea.
       Conflict between 'French' (Roman Catholic) and 'Eng-
       lish' (Protestant) parties in Uganda. Lugard restores
       peace and makes new treaty with King Mwanga for
       perpetual protection by Britain.

1893   Sir Gerald Portal sent by British Government to
       Uganda; makes fresh treaty with Mwanga; British
       flag hoisted.
       French occupy historic cities of Jenné and Timbuktu.
       War with Matebele: Lobengula defeated by British.
       Responsible government set up in Natal.
       American Board (A.B.C.F.M.) begins mission in South-
       ern Rhodesia on land given by Cecil Rhodes.

1894   Delimitation of British and Italian Somalilands.
       Italians defeat Mahdists and capture Kassala.
       B. S. A. Co. assumes administration of its sphere north
       of the Zambezi.
       British under H. H. Johnston attack slave-raiders in
       Nyasaland.
       Pondoland (last of the Transkeian territories) annexed
       by Cape Colony. Glen Grey Act sets up Native Dis-
       trict Councils and so initiates the Transkeian sys-
       tem of local government.
       Swaziland comes under control of Transvaal republic.
       Slave-traders in Belgian Congo finally quelled.
       Agreement between Britain and Congo Free State de-
       fining their boundaries.

1895   France establishes herself in Madagascar.
       Italians seriously defeated by Ethiopians at Adua.

A.D.

British government decides to retain Uganda; protectorate proclaimed. I. B. E. A. Co. ceases to operate.

1895 Cape Colony absorbs British Bechwanaland. The Bechwanaland Protectorate refused to the B. S. A. Co., but a strip is given along the border for the trunk railway to Bulawayo.

The Jameson raid into the Transvaal.

1895-1901 Railway built from Mombasa to Lake Victoria.

1896 French move into the Bahr-al-Ghazal region. Major Marchand is sent to extend French influence to the Nile.

Matebele rebellion in Southern Rhodesia.

British protectorate over tribes in hinterland of Sierra Leone.

Agitation begins against maltreatment of Africans in Congo Free State.

Native Affairs Commission established in Congo Free State (did not meet after 1901).

Railway begun in Sierra Leone.

British-Egyptian army under Sir Herbert Kitchener advances towards the Sudan to reconquer it from the Khalifa.

1897 Sir George Goldie attacks and deposes Sultan of Nupe, an obstinate slave-raider. Emir of Ilorin signs treaty agreeing to suppress slave-raiding.

The Methodist Episcopal Church begins its mission in Southern Rhodesia (old Umtali) on a site given by Cecil Rhodes.

1898 Paul Kruger elected President of Transvaal Republic for fourth time.

Legislative Council set up in Southern Rhodesia.

British-Egyptian army under Kitchener defeats Khalifa's forces at Atbara and Omdurman and enters Khartum.

A.D.

1898   Kitchener encounters Marchand at Fashoda. French
          withdraw.
          Railways begun in Nigeria and Gold Coast.

1899   Tension between French and British over Fashoda
          ends by French renunciation of claims to Nile
          Valley. France gets right to extend in Wadai, etc.
          Britain and Egypt agree to establish a separate and
          autonomous condominium in the Sudan. Import
          and export of slaves forbidden.
          Concession system established in French Equatorial
          Africa, the whole products of soil to belong to the
          concessionaires.

1899-1902   Anglo-Boer war in South Africa.

1900   Treaty between Britain and Uganda: the indigenous
          constitution to be continued and strengthened.
          Colonel F. D. Lugard goes to Northern Nigeria as
          High Commissioner. Organizes West Africa Fron-
          tier Force, and in three years establishes British
          authority over the Fulani rulers. He governs
          through them, thus initiating in Northern Nigeria
          the system of Indirect Rule.
          Military Territory of Chad organized by French.
          French definitely organize African troops for the pur-
          pose of acquiring and policing colonial empire.

1902   Treaty of Vereeniging (negotiated by Milner and
          Kitchener for British, by Botha and Smuts for
          Boers) closes the Anglo-Boer war.
          Gordon College, built in response to Kitchener's ap-
          peal for funds, opened in Khartum.

1903-1905   South Africa Native Affairs Commission.

1904   Temporary importation of Chinese labour in Trans-
          vaal.
          Agreement of the two Powers recognises the domi-

A.D.

nant position of France in Morocco and of Britain in Egypt.

1904   The general Council, 'Bunga,' established in Transkei.

Congo Reform Association founded by E. D. Morel. Similar societies in U. S. A., etc. President Theodore Roosevelt is asked by Southern Presbyterians to intervene for reform in Congo.

King Leopold appoints a Commission of Inquiry which suggests reforms in Congo.

French West Africa reorganized as a federation of Senegal, Guinea, Ivory Coast, Dahomey, Upper Senegal and Niger, and Mauritania, under a Governor-General.

1904-1905   Rebellion of Hereros in South-West Africa: Germans almost wipe them out.

1905   The German Kaiser visits Tangier as part of policy to provoke France.

1906   Responsible government granted by Britain to defeated Boers of Transvaal and Orange Free State. General Botha premier of Transvaal.

Zulu rebellion in Natal.

U. S. A. Senate advises President Roosevelt to cooperate with signatories of Berlin Act to secure reforms in Congo Free State. Reforms are carried out based on proposals of the 1904 Commission: native lands delimited; native chiefs to be recognised.

The Union Minière and other companies (one American) created by King Leopold to hold monopolies in Congo Free State.

Algeciras Conference summoned by Sultan of Morocco (at the instigation of Germany as part of its policy of provoking Britain and France) to consider the future of his country. Morocco recognised as independent; all nations to have economic equality

A.D.

there; direction of future reforms laid down. France is checked. President Roosevelt congratulates Kaiser on his "epoch-making success."

1906 Liberian Government negotiates a second loan in England.

1907 International Office of Public Hygiene founded.

Legislative Council in Kenya: 6 official, 2 nominated, members.

Lord Cromer retires, leaving Egypt in a state of unprecedented prosperity.

French occupy Casablanca on coast of Morocco.

1908 Congo Free State becomes part of Belgium. Great landholdings retained by companies (100,000 hectares by American Congo Company). Colonial Charter enacted; provides *inter alia* for a Commission for the Protection of Natives.

Railway reaches Congo border from south. Development of copper mines in Katanga and Northern Rhodesia.

1909 France and Germany reach a 'final' agreement on Morocco. By this time the country had fallen into anarchy.

U. S. A. sends commission to Liberia which reports that Liberia needs foreign assistance and proposes aid.

1909-1929 Railway building between Katanga and Lobito Bay.

1910 Four British self-governing colonies formed into the Union of South Africa. General Botha first premier.

French define principle of 'Association' distinct from 'Assimilation.'

New decree in Belgian Congo which is basis of native administration. Aim is to govern the people through native institutions. [Badly applied at first.]

A.D.

1910 Co-operative Societies (Sociétés de Prévoyances) established in French West Africa.

1911 North-East and North-West Rhodesia amalgamated
as Northern Rhodesia under administration of
B. S. A. Co.

France advances in Morocco: army marches to Fez to
relieve the Sultan from rebels. Germany intervenes
again: sends warship to Agadir. Spain starts on a
forward policy in Morocco. Tension in Europe:
threat of war. Lloyd-George's speech makes it clear
that Britain would stand with France. Germany demands a heavy price for allowing France a free hand
in Morocco: France gives her a slice of Cameroons.

Concessions (maximum of 2,900 sq. miles) granted to
Lever Bros. in Belgian Congo under lease at 25c a
hectare.

Mines and Works Act in South Africa authorizes Governor-General to regulate granting of competency
certificates to machinery workers: shiftsman in
charge of machine to be a white man.

1911-1912 Italy makes war on Turkey and takes Libya.

1912 France assumes protectorate over Morocco. General
Paul Lyautey (France's greatest colonial adminis-
trator) first Resident-General; effectively pacifies
Morocco; adopting system analogous to 'Indirect
Rule.'

France raises African army by conscription.

In South Africa Generals Botha and Hertzog disagree,
former advocating a 'One-stream' policy, latter a
'Two-stream' policy, keeping British and Dutch
apart. Hertzog forms the Nationalist Party.

African National Congress established in South Africa.

U. S. A. government did not accept all proposals of
the 1909 Commission that it should get financial con-

A.D.

trol in Liberia; now suggests that American and European bankers make a loan to Liberia. Agreement of banks with Liberia to lend $1,700,000; Liberia's finances to be reorganized.

1913 Natives Land Act in South Africa: divides territory into Native and non-Native areas, and establishes the principle that residence of Natives outside of reserved areas is justified only if in European employment or under a few other conditions.

1913-1916 Beaumont Commission in South Africa proposes so to divide land that 13.3% be for 5,000,000 Natives and rest for 1½ million Europeans.

1914 South African Native College founded at Fort Hare. Railway opened from coast to Lake Tanganyika.
The Harris Christian movement in French West Africa.
Libero-Spanish convention regulating import of labourers into Fernando Po.
Northern and Southern Nigeria amalgamated under Sir F. Lugard as Governor-General. Indirect Rule extended to the southern province.

1914-1918 First World War. General Smuts (1916) takes command of allied forces in Tanganyika Territory (German East Africa) against Germans. Belgians join in this campaign. Union forces under General Botha take South-West Africa from Germans. French and British troops drive Germans out of Cameroons and Togoland. So Germany loses all her African possessions.
French and British divide Cameroons provisionally.
Britain declares a protectorate over Egypt, and the nominal suzerainty of Turkey (which has sided with Germany) disappears. New Khedive, Hussein Kamil, installed.

A.D.

1917 U. S. A. government demands that Liberia enact reforms: "a radical change of policy"; or Liberia may lose its "friendly support."

U. S. A. enters the war; Liberia, at its request, follows suit.

Belgian Congo introduces compulsory cultivation of cotton and other crops.

Elected Advisory Council in Northern Rhodesia.

1918 School for native auxiliary doctors opened at Dakar.

University of Cape Town founds School of African Life and Languages.

Liberian government, having made some changes, appeals to U. S. A. for a loan of five million dollars and of "additional American agents." This is granted on condition of reforms.

President Wilson's last of 'Fourteen Points' states that after the war "A general association of nations must be formed." This in January. In March and July the Phillimore Committee reported to the British government on "a League of Nations." Colonel House, it is said, prepared a draft of a scheme after the Phillimore report reached President Wilson. In a modified form House's draft was taken by the President to Paris in December.

November 11, the Armistice.

In December General Smuts issues his plan. For 'backward peoples' he prescribes a mandatory system, with special emphasis on the ultimate authority of the League and its right to dismiss an unsatisfactory mandatory from its stewardship. Not all his suggestions are ultimately accepted.

1919 President Wilson lays his draft scheme for a League before the American Peace Commission in Paris; he adopts General Smuts' plan of Mandates.

A.D.

1919   May 7. Text of Versailles Treaty, including Covenant
        of League of Nations, is presented to the German
        plenipotentiaries; who sign it on June 28.
        Nov. 19. U. S. A. Senate fails to ratify the Treaty.

            C. 1919-1942: PERIOD OF TRUSTEESHIP
            [NOTE: It is not suggested that previous to 1919
            no European Power had a sense of its responsi-
            bility as a trustee for the well-being of Africans;
            nor that after 1919 all the Powers possessed it
            effectively. The sense of responsibility had
            been growing prior to 1919 and to some extent
            showed itself in action. The Covenant of the
            League accorded for the first time international
            sanction to the principle of trusteeship; it may
            rightly be taken as marking a re-orientation of
            policy. Henceforth it sets a standard to which
            all governing powers must aim to reach.]

1919   In drawing up the Treaty of Versailles the Allied and
        Associated Powers decide not to restore Germany's
        African possessions but to mandate them on condi-
        tions to be approved by, and under the supervision
        of, the League of Nations. The general principle
        is embodied in Article 22 of the Covenant of the
        League of Nations, which is part of the Treaty of
        Versailles.

        Mandates given to Britain for German East Africa
        (Tanganyika Territory) less Ruanda-Urundi which
        is mandated to Belgium; and for South West Africa,
        to be exercised by the Union of South Africa. The
        Powers place Cameroons and Togoland in the hands
        of Britain and France.

        A Commission composed of Lord Milner, with Lord
        Cecil as adviser, M. Simon (French colonial minis-

A.D.

ter), Chinda of Japan, Marconi of Italy, and Colonel House of U. S. A., prepare terms of mandates.

1919 Convention of Saint-Germain-en-Laye provides for the prohibition of the importation and sale of trade spirits.

Also at Saint-Germain the General Acts of the Conferences of Berlin and Brussels are revised to secure commercial equality to members of the League. The Signatory Powers agree to secure the complete suppression of slavery in all its forms; and to protect and favour religious and charitable institutions "which aim at leading the natives in the path of progress and civilization." They guarantee freedom of conscience and the free exercise of all forms of religion; and undertake to allow missionaries to enter into and to travel and reside in the territories.

Native subjects in French Africa made liable to conscription for three years.

Local advisory councils established in French Africa.

Increased local government in Kenya.

1920 Jan. 16. League of Nations formally inaugurated.

Convention of Negroes, New York: Marcus Garvey elected Provisional President of Africa.

First regular air-service in Africa: Leopoldville-Stanleyville.

Colonial Council set up for all Senegal; three-fourths of 44 members are African.

Native Affairs Act in South Africa: Councils established outside Transkei. Permanent Native Affairs Commission appointed.

Industrial and Commercial Union founded by Natives in South Africa.

1920-1921 Phelps-Stokes Education Commission under leadership of Dr. Thomas Jesse Jones tours West,

A.D.

South and East Africa. Its visit and recommendations have a wide-flung influence on educational
policy.

1921 Administrative officials in Belgian Congo now obliged
to inquire into tribal history and customs with a
view to recognition of African chiefs.

Election in South Africa: South African Party under
General Smuts gains a majority.

Construction begun of Brazzaville-Ocean railway in
French Equatorial Africa.

French regulate educational work of missions: "employment of native idioms is forbidden" in schools.

In France M. Delafosse follows M. Vignon in assailing
the principle of Assimilation.

Epidemic of relapsing fever sweeps across from French
West Africa: reaches Sudan in 1926.

Mulago school of medicine in Uganda.

Earl Buxton's commission proposes new constitution
for Southern Rhodesia, *i.e.* full responsible government save reservations for security of Africans.

1922 Referendum in Southern Rhodesia is against joining
the Union of South Africa.

Revolutionary strike of white miners in Transvaal.

Indirect Rule set up in Tanganyika Territory.

Devolution of powers to tribal authorities begins in
Anglo-Egyptian Sudan.

League of Nations confirms mandate to France for
part of Togoland and Cameroons; and to Britain
for Tanganyika and other part of Togoland and
Cameroons.

Britain brings to an end its protectorate over Egypt.

Egypt declared to be an independent, sovereign state,
with a few reservations in regard to defence and
foreign policy.

A.D.

1922-1925 Liberia makes efforts to reform.

1923 Harvey S. Firestone sends expert to investigate soil, etc., in Liberia.

Transvaal court decides that the 'Colour-bar' regulations on the mines are *ultra vires*.

Southern Rhodesia formally annexed to British Crown; new constitution, with Sir John Chancellor as governor, comes into operation. B. S. A. Co. retires but continues to hold 3,700,000 acres.

British imperial conference on education.

British Advisory Committee on Education appointed.

In the 'Devonshire White Paper' the British government defines Trusteeship: "the protection and advancement of the native races."

1924 Belgian government appoints commission to study labour problem on Congo: it makes important recommendations about the proportion of adult males that should be taken from the villages for work.

Albert Sarraut, French colonial minister, expresses himself favourable to preserving and adapting native institutions, and envisages French self-governing dominions.

Northern Rhodesia, hitherto ruled by B. S. A. Co., becomes a British Crown Colony (not a shot having been fired in its history), with Sir Herbert Stanley the first governor. Legislative council with minority of elected members. B. S. A. Co. retains mineral rights and much land.

First session of Legislative Assembly in Southern Rhodesia under responsible government: Sir Charles Coghlan, first premier.

High Leigh conference on education in Africa.

A.D.

1924 British East Africa Committee under Lord South-
borough.

Firestone requests concession from Liberia for establishment of rubber industry; and offers to improve
Monrovia harbor at cost of 300,000 dollars, to be
reimbursed by Liberia government plus 6%. Agreement reached: Firestone to choose a million acres
at 5c an acre for six years.

General Hertzog, supported by Labour Party, comes
into power in South Africa.

French more or less adopt scheme for Trans-Saharan
railway.

Britain cedes Jubaland to Italy.

1925 Fear of Liberians that French will invade their borders. President Barclay goes to U. S. A.

Italy and Egypt settle boundary questions.

Italians sign treaty of friendship with Ras Tafari,
regent of Ethiopia.

Labour decree in French West Africa limiting contracts to two years.

Completion of Senaar dam in Anglo-Egyptian Sudan;
the Gezira scheme of irrigation brings 500,000 acres
under cultivation (one-third cotton) by Sudanese.

Ruanda-Urundi, mandated to Belgium, is united with
Belgian Congo for purposes of administration.

First report of British Advisory Committee on Education lays down general lines of policy. Followed by
other reports in 1927, 1935, 1936, 1937.

Amani Institute constituted a centre of agricultural
research for Kenya, Uganda, Tanganyika and Zanzibar.

Liberian legislature approves agreements with Firestone; he inserts clause subsequently binding the
government to accept a loan of 5,000,000 dollars.

A.D.

Agreement signed with Finance Corporation of America for 7% loan of that amount.

1925 British Wesleyans open mission on Ivory Coast among the Harris Christians.

First Jeanes School in Africa started, with help of Carnegie Corporation, at Kabete in Kenya. Others at Mazabuka, N. Rhodesia; near Zomba, Nyasaland; Domboshawa, S. Rhodesia.

1926 Portuguese Government abolishes compulsory labour for private purposes.

League of Nations Slavery Convention. Signatories bind themselves to prevent and suppress slave-trade and bring about complete abolition of slavery in all its forms; regulates compulsory or forced labour.

Native courts given a legal basis in Belgian Congo.

Agricultural credit organized in French West Africa.

Legislative Council in Tanganyika with official majority. New Legislative Council in Gold Coast with 9 African members; and municipal councils with African majorities.

British Imperial Conference defines position of Dominions: "autonomous communities within the British Empire, equal in status . . . united by a common allegiance to the Crown."

Colour Bar legalised in South Africa. Premier Hertzog publishes text of four bills embodying his native policy.

International Institute of African Languages and Cultures founded.

Le Zoute Conference in Belgium on Christian Mission in Africa, attended by representative educators, government officials and missionaries; also by Native Africans. Fifteen nationalities represented.

A.D.

1926   Alan Cobham and two companions fly from England to Cape Town and back, in a single plane: 80 hours in air.

Hygiene Commission of League of Nations consider a report by Dr. Lucian Raynaud on African demography.

Liberian Government sets up Labour Bureau which is to supply Firestone plantations with 10,000 labourers a year.

1927   Agreements of Firestone with Liberian government go into operation; he has the right to lease a million acres, all produce to be exempt from taxation; and to construct harbor.

Belgian-Portuguese conference at Loanda: some exchange of territory; Belgium agrees to construct its part of the Lobito Bay railway.

Act for better control and management of Native Affairs in South Africa: Governor-General made Supreme Chief of Natives in Transvaal, Natal and Orange Free State.

New constitution in Kenya: 17 elected members of Council out of 37.

Churchill White Paper defines 'Dual Policy' in British Africa.

Agreement between India and South Africa regulating position of Indians in the Union.

Air-mail service between England and Uganda.

Two Frenchmen fly from France over Africa to Madagascar and back.

1928   Regent Ras Tafari crowned Negus of Ethiopia.

Treaty of friendship between Italy and Ethiopia: mutual pledge to do nothing for twenty years detrimental to the independence of either.

1929   The Senussi in Libya submit to Italy.

A.D.

1929 Prix Goncourt awarded to René Maran, a native of French Africa.

International Committee on Christian Literature set up by the International Missionary Council.

Hilton-Young Commission in British East Africa, *inter alia,* elaborates idea of the imperial government as arbiter between the ethnic groups, black and white and brown.

Development Fund of £1,000,000 a year voted by British Parliament. Up to 1938, grants of £4,259,000 are made for medical, agricultural, purposes: 55% to Africa.

1930 In their Memorandum on Native Policy in East Africa, the British Government again declare that they fully accept the principle that their relation to the native populations is one of trusteeship "which cannot be devolved and from which they cannot be relieved." Interests of Africans must be paramount. They define trusteeship in regard to social, political and economic questions. Native social and political institutions to be developed; until Africans can take their share in the governance of the territories. "Education, sanitation and a progressive raising of the economic standard of life should therefore go hand-in-hand."

Yaba medical school in Nigeria.

Achimota College in Gold Coast completed at an outlay of £617,000.

International Convention on Forced Labour.

Office of High Commissioner separated from that of Governor-General in South Africa. The Protectorates (Basutoland, Swaziland, Bechwanaland) remain outside the Union under the High Commissioner.

A.D.

1930-1932   Native Economic Commission in South Africa.

1931   Statute of Westminster defines position and mutual relations of the constituents of the British Commonwealth of Nations.

British Joint Committee on Closer Union in East Africa defines "paramountcy of native interests."

Co-operative societies in Gold Coast.

1932   Native Co-operative Union registered in Tanganyika.

Inter-university committee for African studies founded in South Africa.

1933   Bible published in the Afrikaans language of South Africa.

Political coalition of South African and Nationalist parties in South Africa.

British Government declares that the South African protectorates will not be transferred to the Union apart from debate in Parliament; and that the native populations will have full opportunity of expressing their views.

1934   French Equatorial Africa no longer a federation of Gaboon, Middle Congo, Ubangi-Shari, and Chad, but a unitary colony. Wadai a protectorate.

Reorganization of British colonial medical service.

Chair of Bantu Languages established at Cape Town University.

Also at Johannesburg.

1935   Italy invades and conquers Ethiopia.

Training of 'medical aids' begun at Fort Hare in South Africa.

Co-operative societies at work in Nigeria.

1936   Anglo-Egyptian treaty, provides *inter alia* for maintenance of a British military force in the Canal zone.

A.D.

1936   School for training native medical assistants at Leopoldville.

1937   Britain secures abolition of the Capitulations in Egypt
at Montreux Conference.

Egypt admitted member of League of Nations.

East African Education Commission recommends a
Higher College (an embryo university) for East
Africa; British Government intends to ask Parlia-
ment for £100,000 towards cost.

1938   British inter-territorial conference on education.

Publication of Lord Hailey's *An African Survey*, a
report of investigations set up by a British Research
Committee as a result of General Smuts' suggestion
in his Rhodes Memorial Lecture, 1929. The Carnegie Corporation granted funds.

1939   Sept. 3. Outbreak of the Second World War.

Egypt breaks off relations with Germany.

1940   Jan. Italy enacts that all persons of mixed blood in
her African territories will in future be classed as
natives. Italian parents forbidden by law to recog-
nise their mixed offspring.

General Hertzog moves in Union Parliament that
war with Germany should be ended forthwith. Defeated 81 to 59. He and Dr. Malan pronounce in
favour of republic in South Africa.

Jan. 18. Indians in South Africa offer to raise funds
and a force of 10,000 Indians born in Natal.

Feb. General Smuts speaks of the northern colonies
in Africa as "outposts of the Union" and promises
military aid, with no compulsory service.

Feb. 20. British Government announces legislation
providing £5,000,000 a year for ten years for the
development of, and welfare services in, the colonial empire; and up to £500,000 a year for research,

following the recommendation of the Hailey *Survey*. This 'Colonial Development and Welfare Act' declares again that H. M.'s Government are Trustees for the well-being of the peoples . . . to protect and advance their interests (and) provide their people with improved standards of life . . . and to promote prosperity and happiness.

1940 April. Troops from Southern Rhodesia arrive in Egypt; British and Egyptian troops take up emergency stations.

May. Kenya Defence Force called up, men 18 to 35.

June. Basutoland sends £10,000 as its first contribution towards war expenses.

South African troops operating on Ethiopian border.

Legislative Council of Northern Rhodesia passes compulsory service bill.

June 10. Italy declares war against Britain and France. "The hand that held the dagger has struck it into the back of its neighbour" (F. D. R.).

Egypt breaks off relations with Italy.

June 11. Italians invade British and French Somalilands.

South Africa declares war on Italy. General Hertzog appeals again that South Africa make a separate peace: "this dishonorable proposal," says General Smuts.

June 14. Gold Coast gives Britain £100,000 for purchase of air-craft.

International zone of Tangier occupied by Spanish Moroccan troops.

June 25. Franco-Italian armistice.

July 1. General Graziani takes command in Libya.

July 4. Nigeria gives £100,000 from reserve funds for

prosecution of the war. Sierra Leone contributes £100,000. Kabaka and people of Uganda send £10,000 as a gift for war purposes.

1940 July 17. Anglo-French agreement for abolition of Egyptian debt control, almost the last vestige of foreign control in Egypt.

July 25. Gold Coast regiment and native troops from Nigeria, and South African troops, arrive in Kenya.

Aug. 4. Italy pushes into British Somaliland and by the 19th has taken possession of it.

Aug. 7. Britain purchases the entire Egyptian cotton crop.

Aug. 13. Fourth war contribution of people of Gold Coast of £5,000.

Aug. 17. Mr. Hofmeyr, minister of Finance, says one of South Africa's war aims is "the forging of new links of co-operation with those countries to the north with which the Union is already co-operating."

Aug. 23. Italian airmen bomb and machine-gun American mission in Sudan: 2 of 4 missionaries killed and one wounded.

Aug. 29. French Equatorial Africa adheres to General de Gaulle to fight on the side of Britain. This will open up new transport routes across Africa to Sudan and Egypt.

General Hertzog again demands immediate peace, Britain being 'beaten.' Premier Smuts' policy approved, 83 votes to 65, in Union parliament.

Sept. The Grand Senussi, head of the Libyan tribes, issues call for holy war against Italy.

The people of Uganda have so far contributed £42,000 for air-craft.

A.D.

1940   Sept. 6. General Smuts says: "The destiny of Africa
       is being decided in this war."

       Sept. 13. Italians invade Egypt and occupy Sollum,
       etc., near the border.

       Sept. 17. Basutoland's war fund now reaches £20,000,
       one-half contributed by native Basuto.

       Sept. 23. Free French and British make faint attack on
       Dakar, thinking the inhabitants will side with them:
       they withdraw in face of opposition.

       Sept. 24. Kikuyu, Kamba and Meru tribes of Kenya
       send £10,000 from their reserve funds to purchase
       air-craft for Britain.

       Sept. 25. Legislative Council of Northern Rhodesia
       approve of loan of £200,000 from surplus balances
       free of interest to British Government. Fund for
       purchase of aircraft reaches £41,000.

       Oct. 19. Basuto Native Council, on proposal of Para-
       mount Chief, votes £100,000 (half their surplus
       funds) for air-craft.

       Dec. British advance against Italian armies in Libya.
       In eight weeks capture or destroy 150,000.

1941   Jan. 15. Emperor Haile Selassie returns to Ethiopia
       to direct patriot troops fighting with British to re-
       conquer the country from Italians.

       Jan. 22. Tobruk in Libya taken.

       Jan. 23. South African troops enter Ethiopia.

       Jan. 26. British invade Eritrea; have advanced 100
       miles.

       Jan. 31. British invading Italian Somaliland. Derna
       in Libya taken.

       Gold Coast fund for air-craft now reaches £55,000.

       Feb. 1. Agordat in Eritrea captured.

       Feb. 4. Secretary of State Eden announces that British
       government would welcome reappearance of an in-

dependent Ethiopian state and recognize the claim
of Emperor Haile Selassie to the throne. They re-
affirm that they themselves have no territorial ambi-
tions in Ethiopia.

1941   Feb. 6. Benghazi in Libya taken by British.

Feb. 7. Free French force from Chad captures Kufra.

Feb. 15. Kismayu in Italian Somaliland taken.

Feb. 18. Gold Coast brigade crosses Juba River into
Italian Somaliland; capture Italian general staff.

Feb. 23. Free French troops land at Red Sea port on
way to Eritrea.

March 1. Mogadishu in Italian Somaliland taken.
Operations rapidly ending a fortnight later.

March 7. General Hertzog elected leader of new Afri-
kaner party in South Africa, opposed on one hand
to General Smuts' policy and on the other hand
to extremist Dr. Malan.

March 16. British troops re-taking British Somaliland.
Berbera occupied.

March 24. West African column occupy Negelli in
Ethiopia. British Somaliland is now again in British hands.

March 25. British casualties in Africa up to Feb. 23
were 2,966 (604 killed). Italian losses over 200,000
(170,000 prisoners).

March 27. Tough fortress of Keren taken by British
and Indian troops. Harar captured in Ethiopia.

April 1. Asmara in Eritrea captured. British troops
advancing from Diredawa to Addis Ababa in
Ethiopia. British forces in Libya weakened through
sending troops to help Greece. Germans reinforce
Italians and take the offensive.

April 4. British evacuate Benghazi.

A.D.

1941   April 5. British troops from South, East and West Africa enter Addis Ababa, capital of Ethiopia.

April 8. Masawa in Eritrea taken, completing conquest of that country from Italy.

April 14. Germans take Sollum. The British, says Prime Minister Churchill, have suffered a "vexatious and damaging defeat" in Libya. Tobruk holds out.

May 5. Emperor Haile Selassie enters Addis Ababa on anniversary of Italian occupation in 1936.

Northern Rhodesia offers to present £296,000 towards cost of war; £50,000 being for air-craft.

May 14. Nyasaland celebrates 50th anniversary of Protectorate by making a gift of £39,150 towards cost of war: this brings her contributions to £117,-000 in the two years, 1939, 1940.

May 20. Surrender of Italian viceroy, Duke of Aosta, at Amba Alagi in Ethiopia, with 19,000 troops.

May 24. Soddu, keytown in Ethiopian lake area, captured. British Government agrees to purchase entire output of French Equatorial Africa.

Field-Marshal Smuts sending South African troops forward from Ethiopia to fight in Libya. America's membership in a post-war organization is, he says, "essential." "She holds the key. Let her use it and open the door through which the world can escape from chaos and suffering."

June 7. In S. W. Ethiopia African troops cross the Omo River and capture Abalti. Only two or three pockets of Italian troops now remain to be cleared up in Ethiopia.

June 17. Assab in Eritrea captured by Indian troops. British take offensive on Libyan frontier.

A.D.

Italians surrender at Soddu (Ethiopia). Italian prisoners now number 177,937; plus 66,000 native soldiers.

1941   July 3. Italians surrender at Debra Tabor. All Sidamo province of Ethiopia now cleared of enemy.

August. Agreement by which Pan-American Airways will ferry war-planes from U. S. A. to West Africa and thence to Egypt, etc.

Bureau of Missions and Colonial Planning established at Aberdeen by Sir John Orr and others.

August 14. The Atlantic Declaration by President Roosevelt and Prime Minister Churchill.

Emperor Haile Selassie begins re-construction in Ethiopia with British assistance.

August 21. Reported peace proposals of Germany to France. *Inter alia,* France to receive the British dependencies of Nigeria, Gold Coast and Sierra Leone to round off her African empire which she and Germany will then exploit conjointly.

Nov. 18. British take the offensive on Libyan frontier. Germans driven back.

Nov. 27. Italy's last stronghold at Gondar in Ethiopia surrendered; main share in fighting fell to East African native troops.

Dec. 7. Japan enters the war with a treacherous attack at Hawaii.

Dec. 9. South Africa declares war on Japan, Finland, Hungary and Rumania.

Dec. 17. Ethiopia formally at war with Japan. Germans in Libya under Rommel driven into Tripolitania.

1942   Jan. 6. Egypt breaks off relations with Vichy France.

Jan. 21. Germans advance again from Tripolitania.

A.D.

British retreat. Evacuate Benghazi on 28th. Subversive movement in South Africa disclosed.

1942   Jan. 23. Dr. Malan publishes draft constitution of a republic he proposes for South Africa; based on ascendancy of Dutch; English language to exist on sufferance.

Field-Marshal Smuts speaks of the cordial relations which have sprung up between South African (white) troops and West African (black) soldiers: sees in that mutual respect a good basis for future policy. "We want to take a holiday from old ideas which have brought nothing but bitterness and strife to our country and try to the best of our ability to fashion a variegated but harmonious race pattern in South Africa."

Jan. 31. Britain signs agreement with Emperor of Ethiopia, promising financial and other assistance. Emperor declares his intention to abolish slavery as soon as he can legislate.

Mar. 11. Field-Marshal Smuts declares in the Union Parliament that if the need were to arise, he would enlist every available man, white, colored, and native, for the defence of the country.

May 4. British forces take temporary possession of Madagascar to avert its use by the Japanese.

Index*

* The references are to dates, not pages. Where B.C. is not given it is understood that a date is A.D.

INFORMATION REGARDING THE PUBLICATIONS

of the

COMMITTEE ON AFRICA, THE WAR, AND PEACE AIMS

Agencies

U. S. and Canada—AFRICA BUREAU, 156 Fifth Avenue, New York, N. Y., or INTERRACIAL REVIEW, 20 Vesey Street, New York, N. Y.

Great Britain—EDINBURGH HOUSE, 2 Eaton Gate, London, S.W.1, England.

Union of South Africa—SOUTH AFRICAN INSTITUTE OF RACE RELATIONS, P.O. Box 97, Johannesburg.

Prices

(In U. S. and Canada—Postpaid)

Report—THE ATLANTIC CHARTER AND AFRICA FROM AN AMERICAN STANDPOINT

176 pages and Map of Africa in colors.........$0.75 each

(Ten or more copies to one address) .... 0.60 "

Supplement—EVENTS IN AFRICAN HISTORY

61 pages with Index .... 0.50 "

Report and *Supplement*—when ordered together 1.00

($0.90 a set when ten or more are ordered sent to one address for study groups.)

Outline of Study—A pamphlet outlining the use of the Report for international relations clubs, mission study classes, interracial, panel, forum, and other discussion groups, is being prepared for the Committee by Mrs. Agnes C. L. Donohugh, Professor of Ethnology at the Kennedy School of Missions, Hartford, Connecticut. This will be ready about September 20, 1942 ....$0.10 each

A limited number of this special edition, entitled *Africa*, in which the *Report* and *Supplement* are bound together in buckram may be obtained at $1.25 each by addressing the Committee on Africa, the War, and Peace Aims, care of the Phelps-Stokes Fund, 101 Park Avenue, New York, N. Y.